# CONSIGLIERI

'A fascinating account of the role of the leaders behind the leader – there are lessons here for every walk of life.'
    – Alastair Campbell, former Director of Communications and Strategy for Tony Blair

'Films and plays are littered with examples of the nefarious deputy, from Iago to Macbeth, Darth Vader and Scar in *The Lion King*. Richard Hytner rescues the deputy from the "disgruntled schemer" and instead celebrates their creative, supportive, positive impact in life, business, sport and even art.'
    – Rory Kinnear, actor

'As one who has never come first at anything, I love this elegantly written book.'
    – Lucy Kellaway, *Financial Times* columnist

'Any artist or any leading business person should know how to get the best out of those who help make them great. As I coach more and more stars and professional individuals in all walks of life, I'll be giving them *Consiglieri* to read as homework.'
    – Nicki Chapman, TV presenter and professional coach

'Hytner's original, much-needed contribution focuses on the unsung heroes – those who lead beyond the limelight. *Consiglieri* is a must-read.'
    – Lyn͏              ement Practice,
                   ͏ ͏ ͏ess School

**RICHARD HYTNER**, a law graduate from the University of Cambridge, joined Saatchi & Saatchi in 2003 as its CEO for Europe, Middle East and Africa. Today, as deputy chairman, he is responsible for global strategy and innovation and works with leaders and teams from many of Saatchi & Saatchi's worldwide clients. Richard is adjunct associate Professor of Marketing at the London Business School, where he graduated as a Sloan Fellow in 2003. He lives in London with his wife, Rosie, and has two children, Joe and Sophie. Beyond football and family, his loves are literature, theatre and film.

# CONSIGLIERI
## LEADING FROM THE SHADOWS

RICHARD HYTNER

PROFILE BOOKS

First published in Great Britain in 2014 by
PROFILE BOOKS LTD
3A Exmouth House
Pine Street
Exmouth Market
London EC1R OJH
*www.profilebooks.com*

A CIP catalogue record for this book is available from the British Library.

Hardback ISBN 978 1 78125 426 4
Paperback ISBN 978 1 78125 046 4
eISBN 978 1 84765 898 2

Typeset in Palatino by MacGuru Ltd
*info@macguru.org.uk*
Printed and bound in Britain by
Clays, Bungay, Suffolk

All reasonable efforts have been made to obtain copyright permissions where
required. Any omissions and errors of attribution are unintentional and will, if
notified in writing to the publisher, be corrected in future printings.

For Sophie

# CONTENTS

# ACKNOWLEDGEMENTS

I have listened to a collection of wonderful consiglieri in the process of writing this book and am deeply grateful to the following for their insights, ideas and occasional indiscretions.

William Alexander · Carlo Ancelotti · Angela Bailey · Gary Barlow · Fleur Bell · Amanda Blanc · Ken Blanc · Michael Bolingbroke · Nick Booth · Robert Bor · Ana Botín · Sir David Brailsford · Jonathan Brown · Alastair Campbell · Robert Care · Max Carruthers · Karim Chaiblaine · Nicki Chapman · Paul Clement · Bruno Demichelis · Philip Dilley · Ira Dubinsky · Grant Duncan · Vivienne Durham · Lou Ann Eckert-Lynch · Charles Falconer · Rocco Falconer · Jean-Pierre Farandou · Sean Fitzpatrick · Mike Forde · Alain Forget · Simon Fuller · Charles Garland · David Gill · Anna Gillingham · Nick Godwin · Lionel Goh · Mark Goyder · Nigel Griffiths · Joe Hytner · Gaytri Kachroo · Terry Kelly · Jane Kendall · Danny Lawrence · Ghizala Mahmood · Alain Marcetteau · Mohan Mohan · Peter Murray · Philip Norman · Jose María Nus · David Nussbaum · Jim O'Neill · Fernando Peire · Randall Peterson · Michael Phelan · Edward Philips · Ian Powell · Sara Rajeswaran · Matthew Reed · Kevin Roberts · Carlo Barel di Sant'Albano · Fabio Scappaticci · Louise Scott · John Shiels · Anthony Simonds-Gooding · Paul Skinner · The class of Sloan 2012/3 · Mike Smith · Phil Smith · Amanda Smithson

• Brian Sweeney • Annie Tansey • Robert Tansey • David Teece
• Phil Townsend • Jon Walker

I would like to thank Joshua Sutton, Edward Hughes and Alex Eisenthal, whose great minds helped with research, as well as Mark Lloyd Fox and Oli Winton for their generous introductions.

Over three years ago, on a train journey, I talked to Jeremy Franks and Mark de Rond about a book idea for No. 2s and they dared me to give it a go. My brilliant faculty colleagues at London Business School were encouraging, too, particularly Lynda Gratton, Nader Tavassoli and Dominic Houlder.

Friends and colleagues at work have been a source of inspiration. Many listened patiently and added graciously: the late Paul Jackson gave me his trademark three suggestions; the late Tony Hodges gave me an unrequested history supervision; Colin Burrows ripped through the final manuscript and made critical interventions; Roger Kennedy's creativity contributed greatly to the book cover design; Gerry Moira, Julian Borra, Peter Lovatt, Andrew Potter, Ampie Roberto and Matt Bamford all added insight. I have been blessed to work with some of the finest Cs and have only been able to highlight some of them in *Consiglieri*. Before I finished explaining the idea, Paul Edwards gave me new avenues to pursue and Adam Morgan, always in my corner, alerted me to cornermen. Jane Kendall, for six years, has been a case study in C-ship.

I have been blessed to work with some fine As, too, none more uplifting than Kevin Roberts, Saatchi & Saatchi's maverick chief executive. He was the first to see the consigliere in me and it has been a privilege to be his strategic sidekick.

I owe an enormous debt of gratitude to dinner companion Cecily Engle who directed me to Andrew Franklin. More

Oxford don than Mafia Don (though I never dared to mess with him), Andrew's thought leadership is unparalleled. As an A, he leads a team of superb professionals at Profile Books. Andrew gifted me Ned Pennant-Rea who edited and enhanced *Consiglieri* with tenacity, intellectual curiosity and wit. He proved to be a great collaborator. Fiona Screen and Paul Forty made the final touches count.

Many people showed me kindness during the writing of the book. I knew I could count on Philip Norman for his unmatched insight into the worlds of music and literature, but his mentorship on the process of writing was the epitome of generosity.

Home, as ever, has been the greatest source of strength: watching Joe build his business reminded me daily of the skill and sacrifice it takes to be a titanium A; Rosie, the least visible, most artful C I know, led from the shadows as she has throughout our life together; and my deepest gratitude goes to Sophie, researcher-in-chief, whose creative ideas, early edits and considered challenges liberated, enlightened, anchored and delivered. She has been the leading – and defining – C of *Consiglieri*.

# INTRODUCTION

*'First the worst, second the best, third the one with the hairy chest.'*

The aim of this book is to make sense of the central tenet of
the rule of the playground, invented and sung by people who
weren't quite first. It did not make the rounds at my primary
school. Had it done I would have worked less hard to come
first and made more effort to come second. (Without a hairy
chest, third would not have been an option.) You would think
that firsts, having left all others in their wake, would not give
the song a moment's thought. But many do remember it and
do so in earnest. Did they worry, even then, that seconds were
on to something?

I only found out that being first might be worst, or at
least second best, when I went back to school, aged 43. At
London Business School I discovered that life without the
CEO's armband, the PA and the car parking space felt like
unbridled liberation. Four years later, towards the end of my
tenure as CEO of Saatchi & Saatchi Europe, Middle East &
Africa, I reflected that I was rarely happy making the big, ugly
decisions, yet really happy influencing the cause. So I decided
to become a deputy instead of an all-singing, all-dancing,
always-deciding CEO. Being second became my first choice.
It proved the best one of my career.

I have wondered ever since why management books and

organisations focus solely on the firsts; why the role of the deputy, the adviser, the counsellor, the assistant, the 'anybody-but-the-No. 1', is not seen as worthwhile for an aspiring or talented leader; why those who fulfil these roles get such little recognition; and how best to create an alternative model of leadership that identifies, nurtures and celebrates these people and the profound influence they have on organisations.

While a Google of the word 'leadership' confirms a suspicion that leadership teaching is largely still confined to the creation and further advancement of the No. 1, most leadership commentators concur that no one person can fulfil all the duties expected of the boss. Even in organisations blessed with leaders of a humble, self-aware, emotionally wise disposition, it takes more than him or her to lead the organisation to greatness and keep it there. Leadership has always reached far beyond the boss's office.

Thankfully the top dog dressed as indomitable, all-conquering hero looks distinctly dated now. The latest business fashion magazines feature servant leaders, inward leaders, collegiate leaders and Zen leaders. In my work for some of the bluest-chip organisations across the world, I have seen those who truly believe that they are there to serve. Indeed, in parts of the world, particularly in the East, the self has long been subordinated to the higher purpose of family, community and enterprise. I have seen those, too, who hide behind their servant-leader clothes and carry on as autocratically as ever. But the point remains, the suit of the big bad boss has faded badly.

Yet in the world in which most of us operate, away from the business cat-walk, our relationship with hierarchy remains unhealthy and the code for the most part dispiritingly clear: you are a Number One or a Number Who, the supreme leader or a subordinate heeder. Even in the East, where one's position in the hierarchy is accepted gracefully to enable organisational cohesion and mutual respect, there is a growing awareness that we have allowed uncertain times to fuel a greater sense of superiority in the few, at the expense of the potential contribution of the many.

The belief that being No. 1 is all that matters opens up the majority to the debilitating effects of Second Syndrome. In some cultures, the Syndrome conditions people to accept, without question, limits to their roles and responsibilities; in others it punishes those reticent to join the race to be first, or those who cannot wait to retire from it. One suspects that Tom Stoppard was a Second Syndrome sufferer. Green room tittle-tattle has it that *The Real Inspector Hound*, Stoppard's satire about the profession of theatre critic, was originally conceived of as 'The Stand-ins'. Tired of being asked the whereabouts of the first-choice critic, Higgs, the stand-in critic, Moon, calls for rebellion:

> Sometimes I dream of revolution, a bloody coup d'état by the second rank – troupes of actors slaughtered by their understudies, magicians sawn in half by indefatigably smiling glamour girls, cricket teams wiped out by marauding bands of twelfth men – I dream of champions chopped down by rabbit-punching sparring partners while the eternal bridesmaids turn and rape the bridegrooms over the sausage rolls and parliamentary private secretaries plant bombs in the Minister's Humber – comedians die on provincial stages, robbed of their feeds by mutely triumphant stooges – and – march – an army of assistants and deputies, the seconds-in-command, the runners-up, the right-hand men – storming the palace gates wherein the second son has already mounted the throne

having committed regicide with a croquet mallet – stand-ins of the world stand up.

(Tom Stoppard, *The Real Inspector Hound*)

Stand up we must, for this is a profound problem throughout our institutions. Murmurings in the military mess rooms reveal that even some of our finest soldiers subscribe to the depressing idea that 'every career bar one ends in failure'.

Nothing triggers an outbreak of Second Syndrome like the sentiment 'He's a great No. 2'. Does a better example exist of damning with faint praise? In too many parts of the world 'He's a great No. 2' really means 'He'll never make a No. 1'. Numbering according to rank is demeaning to all except the No. 1. Even if the insult is unintended, Second Syndrome suits the self-preserving, myth-perpetuating leader: 'Whether I was born great, achieved greatness or had greatness thrust upon me, all others are destined to stand in my shadow.' That his No. 2s and 3s and 4s feel subordinate conveniently preserves No. 1's power base, keeping the queue of those tempted to plant a dagger in his back short and manageable.

We cannot entirely blame the No. 1s for Second Syndrome. Its symptoms are often avoidable and its wounds can be self-inflicted: 'I'm not cut out for the cut and thrust of leadership,' 'I'm a lousy decision-maker,' 'I prefer the security of keeping my head down,' 'I never captained a side,' 'I wasn't the lead singer in a band,' 'I've never been the guy to start something.' We have rationalised our second place in the world and come to accept it as a diminished one. In so doing we have unwittingly fed a damaging norm of numbering that inhibits people from taking roles – leadership roles – which might suit them and provide them with deep satisfaction.

Having acknowledged that not everything can or should

be decided by an all-powerful leader, why do we conspire to limit the sphere of influence of those beyond, beneath and alongside that leader? We treat with faint disdain those confident enough to declare that they do not have the inclination or the qualities to be **the** leader. We view those No. 1s who conclude that there might be more to life as lazy or burnt out; and we call those content with and committed to playing a supporting role to the leader unambitious. We must eliminate the numbers as a necessary first step for organisations wishing to apportion power more sensibly. (If there are concerns about losing the clarity of numbers, remember the Royal Navy's First Lieutenant, who is second-in-command yet called 'Number One'.)

At the same time as rejecting the cult of the No. 1, and liberating ourselves from our own self-imposed leadership limitations, we must stem another contributor to Second Syndrome, the flow of ever more ridiculous titles that confer chiefdom on people who are not chiefs. We understand why we need a Chief Executive, a Chief Financial Officer, and a Chief Operating Officer: one is the final decider, one keeps the decider out of trouble and the other makes the decider's decisions happen. But can anyone explain what the Chief Influence Officer does? Here we have not just a man of influence but an Officer of Influence and the Chief one at that. Actually he is an expensively re-branded Chief Information Officer who is, in turn, the Head of IT. With titles, as in life, it is better to under-promise and over-deliver. Better to make someone laugh than to say you are a comedian, and better as the top tech head to dish your boss the data, equip him or her to take the big decisions and move on to the next crucial thing we luddites need to know about. That will earn you more influence than a laughable description of what you do.

Chums of the Head of IT, without checking what they look like in the mirror, have all been fitted out at the same Chief department store: Heads of Credit, Risk, Compliance, Security, Design, Diversity, Customer Service, Communications, Innovation, Knowledge, Learning, Privacy – all now sport Chief and Officer clothing over their functional underwear. There is even a Chief Visionary Officer, a sponsorship opportunity screaming for Specsavers or other leading ophthalmologists. Must everyone be a Chief before they can feel proud enough to work hard? None of these vital roles deserves to be discredited with titular sleights of hand, which leave their occupants looking like genetically modified corporate chickens and their colleagues clueless as to what job they actually do.

Without numbering our leaders and without inflating everyone else with trumped-up titles, how can we clearly assign responsibility? This book is primarily about relationships between ultimate leaders and their many kinds of deputies. It is also about getting people into roles that are right for them, not squeezing them into roles they do not want and to which they are not best suited. We need a range of skills in leadership and we need people in the right leadership boxes at the right time, people happy to contribute to the work of the ultimate decision-taker and happy to collaborate with each other. The carnage that characterises some organisations can be caused by leadership's failure to acknowledge what the roles really are and how they relate to each other. This book does not offer up new titles for the multiplicity of roles that organisations have, although I do admire the dignified and descriptive Italian system: when you graduate in law, they call you the Lawyer, *Avvocato*; in engineering, *Ingegnere*; in business, *Dottore*. I am not suggesting that the ambitious leader should read Theology in an attempt to be called God, only that titles should describe the nature of a person's specific contribution. How much easier it would be when asked at a dinner party what one does to begin by saying 'I am the Decider, an Adviser or a Deliverer'?

My other brief answer to Second Syndrome's hierarchical numbers and trivial titles is to adopt the 'alpha' and 'beta' of wild baboons. In a recent study, some very clever field biologists concluded that alpha supremacy is not all it's cracked up to be, coming at some considerable cost to the creature on top. Baboon theory posits that beta males have a lot more fun, and enjoy a lot less stress, than their alpha counterparts. As a beta male, I agree. Our society has for too long been obsessed with the alphas. Their ambitions are unashamedly animal and their motivations, frankly, rather obvious. Now is the time to learn about the enigmatic betas, whose ambitions and motivations are little understood by the alphas, by the outside world, even by themselves. I thought of calling this book *Baboon Leadership* but substituting No. 1 and No. 2 for alpha and beta would only encourage the phrase, 'He's a brilliant beta'. No thank you. Nor is the remedy for power to be sliced and diced democratically. Other than in communist idylls and Hot Chocolate lyrics, not everyone can be a winner all of the time. My leadership philosophy remains rooted in the need for an out-and-out leader.

The answer lies in a way of assigning roles to leadership that preserves the primacy of the final decision-maker and acknowledges the importance of those around him or her; a way of identifying one's natural leadership bias while encouraging greater experimentation between leadership roles; a way of celebrating the different modes of leadership while side-stepping the naughtiness of numbers: 'consiglieri' are advisers to leaders of Italian mafia families, made famous by Mario Puzo's novel, *The Godfather*. In the book you are holding, which is my remedy to Second Syndrome, consiglieri operate in more legitimate fields. They are the deputies, assistants, and counsellors who support, inform and advise the final decision-makers of organisations. Consiglieri – or Cs – are leader-makers and leaders in their own right. While only a few go on to become ultimate A leaders, many more perform roles in which they make, shape, illuminate and enhance the success of the out-and-out A leader and the organisation.

My use of the letters A and C is inspired by a project management framework at Saatchi & Saatchi called RASCI. Many other organisations use RASCI or similar versions of the basic idea. Its aim is to create clarity for each person involved in a project. RASCI is non-hierarchical, and anybody, irrespective of age and experience, can play in any position. The specific letter to which you are assigned – R, A, S, C or I – gives you a discrete role and creates a relationship between you and the project's other players.

As a project management tool, it merits a book in its own right. In brief, the R is ultimately Responsible for driving and delivering the project; the A is there to review, coach, improve and Approve the R's output; the S members are the Supports, the worker bees who get the job done for the R. The Cs are the Consults whose wisdom, counsel and perspective are sought by the R. The Is are the people who need to be kept Informed about a project but not involved in it. There are organisations, not Saatchi & Saatchi, where an O is mischievously added to RASCI to designate those to be kept Out of the loop.

While project management benefits from the breaking down of responsibility into RASCI's five complementary categories, leadership demands greater simplicity. My theory of leadership conflates RASCI into just A and C. While the

A is ultimately Accountable for the enterprise, the Cs are the Consiglieri who counsel, support, and deliver for the A. The two leadership roles, A and C, demand different muscles and stimulate different experiences. The most rewarding place to be, in my view, is the C. No role has presented more challenge, required as much subtlety, or so demanded the leadership behaviour I most admire in others. How best to lead from the shadows is a question very seldom asked. William H. Seward led from the long shadow cast by Abraham Lincoln's top hat. This must have taken great humility. When they were rivals Seward had called Lincoln 'a little Illinois lawyer'. After he lost the presidential nomination to him, he became Lincoln's loyal Secretary of State and right-hand man.

*Consiglieri* is about the relationship between A and C leaders. It seeks to understand C leaders' particular, often peculiar, psychologies and pathologies. It identifies and dramatises some of the qualities, skills and behaviour that different types of C leader need to succeed. We will explore the kinds of C leadership exemplified by Chairmen and Chairwomen, Chief Operating Officers, Chief Financial Officers, Chiefs of Staff, Directors of Human Resources, Company Secretaries, Civil Servants, Department Heads, Project Managers, Team Leaders, Personal Assistants, Executive Assistants, Adjutants, First Lieutenants, First Violins and Vice Presidents.

When US Vice President Walter Mondale was running for President, one of his rivals for the Democratic nomination, Eugene McCarthy, was asked his opinion of Mondale. His reply – 'He has the soul of a vice president' – was one reason why Mondale never became President. Will *Consiglieri* succeed in rendering McCarthy's remark a compliment? By skipping the letter B and creating two leadership types, the ultimately accountable A and the many different types of C,

I hope to transform slurs like McCarthy's into high praise. *Consiglieri* represents the C Change in Leadership that I would like to see. The hope is to increase the numbers of consiglieri who make an active choice to lead from beyond the A, and to do so as contentedly and skilfully as possible.

There are three parts to *Consiglieri*.

**Part One** looks at the virtues that all leaders have in common, and begins to wonder if the A role deserves as many wide-eyed aspirants as it currently enjoys.

*Chapter 1* examines the qualities that the A and C share. It suggests that those with a talent for leadership should try both roles if possible, even if they feel predisposed to one.

*Chapter 2* explores the life of the A, celebrating those able and willing to live with aspects of leadership that many would find too ugly to contemplate.

**Part Two** is about the glories of the Cs, what gets them going, how they prove their worth, and the roles they play.

*Chapter 3* asks what motivates the C, which is altogether more mysterious than what motives the A. Great C leaders reveal the joy of a life spent learning, bringing other people on and making game-changing interventions.

*Chapter 4* examines the qualities of a C. To get the most out of everybody, Cs must be at ease, reliable in their actions, drivers of new ideas, and brave enough to tell the A what's what.

*Chapter 5* looks at some classic C types to show how the best Cs take pressure off their As, enlighten them with fresh thinking, help them remain true to themselves, and deliver favourable outcomes for them.

**Part Three** is about living with your leader. It seeks to help As and Cs make the most of each other.

*Chapter 6* offers advice for the A on choosing the right Cs, squashing dastardly C behaviour and coaxing the best out of them.

*Chapter 7* counsels the C on picking the right As, dealing with their inevitable narcissism, setting appropriate boundaries and leading them to glory.

A leaders are busy people and entitled to look for shortcuts. They should therefore feel free only to read the chapters that they conclude relate to them, while acknowledging that this cherry-picking will limit their understanding of those in positions to help them. It is, as ever, for them to decide. Inconveniently for the Cs, a quick flick through will not suffice. The A expects them to have done their homework. No matter, one of the defining qualities of the C is curiosity.

Providing role models to inspire, identifying the qualities of the C and giving practical guidance to As and Cs, *Consiglieri* was conceived to contribute to more effective leadership. The hope is that more As keep their jobs for longer; that more organisations enjoy a greater consistency, with dreams and direction that endure; that more people sign up for leadership roles which suit them and make them happy; and that more people, including proven As, are attracted to play the C.

The mafia kings have commissioned more than enough envy, admiration, articles and books. Now it's time to examine the consiglieri that make them tick. To put it in the words I want on my gravestone, this book *has the soul of a C.*

# PART ONE

# WHAT QUALITIES DO A AND C LEADERS SHARE?

*'Being a No. 1 is something he preferred to want rather than to be.'*

Tony Blair's view of Gordon Brown, quoted in the diaries of Alastair Campbell, misses the point. Entering the House of Commons at the same time, sharing an office and working together, Blair and Brown both learned how to be As and Cs. Much talk after New Labour's first election win was about the No. 2 from No. 11 desperate for the No. 1 job at No. 10. In fact, the noisy neighbour always had it in him as chancellor to be No. 1. Had Brown been a less formidable A, Blair might have had the courage to fire him when he felt undermined by him. Brown was a thwarted A, an A minus, we might conclude.

It is easy to want the top job; less easy to know whether being the ultimate decision-maker is right for you. *Consiglieri* will help inform that choice. Do you really wish to be an A, the main attraction and the ace of absolute accountability, or might you prefer to be a key C, on whom the A depends, the kind of person who leads, influences, counsels, guides, and helps the A deliver?

Some people are markedly predisposed to one type of leadership. Yet, like great sportspeople, musicians and politicians, great leaders are capable of mastering different positions on the field of play, of playing more than one instrument, of grasping a new brief. Great leaders can lead from the A or the C or from both. Some of the best midfielders in football were strikers at first. When they dropped back into midfield, they understood intuitively when to release the ball, and when to keep it.

Wearing both A and C hats is the best way to assess one's natural leadership inclinations. Most of the leaders we readily associate with out-and-out A leadership earned their remit by mastering the C role earlier in their careers. That experience encourages them to surround themselves with the best Cs when they take up the final decision-maker's mantle. Conversely, those who wear the C hat as chairman or chairwoman, after being CEOs themselves, can better understand the pressures their CEO is under, and coach with the conviction of previous successes and failures. Without direct experience of the cut and thrust of execution, the chairperson is no more useful than a clever consultant armed with a PowerPoint presentation and some predictable words, but no insight from the heat of battle. A consigliere clueless about running an organisation has limited value.

Many leaders now actively seek a life that involves being an A somewhere and a C somewhere else. The wisest leadership wannabes start looking for both opportunities early on in their careers. It is not always easy to find them. It pains me to look at photographs of my sister and I dressed as Batman and Robin. I still feel the injustice of it. Wanting to wear Batman's mask was probably the predominant driver of my ambition to one day be the main man. Perhaps if my sister had once, just once, given me the chance to be Batman, I might have concluded that Robin's role was at least as enjoyable as Batman's.

These days, the younger generation are better equipped to

make decisions about what kind of leader they wish to be. Untold millions around the world now have both A and C leadership role models to inspire them. Among others, we have J. K. Rowling to thank for this. Take Dumbledore, the all-powerful A of Hogwarts School of Witchcraft and Wizardry, yet at the same time a mentoring C to young Harry Potter. Dumbledore even ensures that Harry has other more accessible Cs to guide him, the knowledgeable Hermione Granger and the affable Ron Weasley. Dumbledore knows that As and Cs exist at all levels of organisations. Wherever there is a team there is an A and at least one C, giving aspirant leaders ample opportunity to learn both crafts on their leadership journey.

Before we go on to separate the A from the C to reveal their motivations, inclinations and respective roles, we must, in this chapter, look at the qualities that A-inclined and C-inclined leaders share. In my talks with A and C leaders of all shapes, sizes, sexes and seniority, there is one question that all have to answer every day and in every interaction: 'Can we trust them?' We need to know that our leaders will keep their word, will not abuse their authority and will ensure that fair play is done and seen to be done. We need to trust them to do the right thing. Trust in leadership has two main parts to it – credibility and confidence.

## TRUST

To be credible our leaders must be competent enough to participate in the action and to keep up, to stay contemporary. That does not mean they have to be tweeting about what they had for lunch in the boardroom. It means they cannot rely on having been competent in a bygone age. One upstart working for me had a healthy disrespect for seniority: 'You're only as good as your last game,' he said, when I was having an off day. To such unforgiving followers there is only ever one satisfactory response: raise your game and remain perfectly competent.

Competence yields credibility. Anthony Simonds-Gooding, former A at Whitbread Breweries, British Satellite Broadcasting and Macmillan Cancer Relief, recalls what the Navy taught him about credibility. As the A, being able to bring in the ship effectively was of disproportionate importance to his followers: 'Sailors on a ship were always ashamed if their captain brought the ship in badly. They had pride in their boss.' Leaders who lack credibility can be a source of embarrassment to those they lead. Like a Philippe Starck lemon squeezer, they may look the part but less good-looking versions get the job done better. Some superior capability in our leaders ought to be obvious, with expertise visibly rooted in hard or soft skills.

Michael Lewis' *Moneyball: The Art of Winning an Unfair Game* charts the turnaround of the Oakland Athletics, a basketball team with far fewer resources than their rich competitors. In the movie, general manager Billy Beane, played by Brad Pitt, stops listening to his head coach and starts taking counsel instead from Peter Brand, a statistics wizard in the team's backroom staff. Brand's expertise allows him to see things that the more seasoned scouts cannot, and Beane appoints him assistant general manager. Credibility borne of mastery of the stats gives Brand his influence (and Cs take note, it also gave Jonah Hill who played Brand an Oscar nomination for Best Supporting Actor).

Credibility fosters the second part of trust, confidence. In the sense that people can rely on you, confidence comes from successful outcomes delivered by appropriate judgements made, time after time. Professor Robert Bor is co-director of Dynamic Change Consultants, and a consultant clinical psychologist and executive coach. In helping leadership teams to substitute dynamism for dysfunction, Bor emphasises the importance of consistency: 'People like to know that they can trust you, and trust is predictable behaviour over time.'

Confidence demands, too, that we can trust our leader in conversation, that he or she can keep our confidences. This works for both A and C. Nicki Chapman began her career in the music industry as a Promotions Assistant at MCA Records, before starting her own company, Brilliant PR. As a C to artistes as diverse as Charlotte Church, Phil Collins, Billie Piper, David Bowie, Van Morrison and Amy Winehouse, Chapman has always observed total discretion. Gary Barlow is just one of Chapman's devoted clients and colleagues to trust her unconditionally: 'You get the true measure of someone's trust and honesty over a number of years. It's twenty-two years since we first started working together and I still haven't read a quote or headline about me that has come from Nicki. I'd imagine that will be true for the rest of my life!'

The need to allow people to talk to you in confidence is perhaps more acute if you are playing the C role, when you have the ear of your boss and unfettered access to him or her. Colleagues have to be able to trust you, to ask you the question they really want to ask. Safeguarding confidence is crucial for chiefs of staff too. Jonathan Brown reflected on his time as project management officer (in effect chief of staff) for John Manzoni, then the A at Talisman Energy in Canada:

I was at one stage thinking of turning my office into a confessional booth. I imagined myself pulling the little slot across to create a safe place for the confessor. 'Forgive me father for I have sinned.' 'Oh, really?' 'Yes, I've not delivered my project on time, what shall I do?' 'Say five Hail Marys and have it done by February.'

As a leader, A or C, do you engender sufficient trust for your office to feel like a confessional booth? Trust is driven by your interactions with people, the respect you show for them, the discretion you extend to their confidences.

As I have said, trust is about credibility and confidence: Your Trust Quotient is the sum of these two qualities. TQ = C+C. The sum is concerned with what your peers think of you. Now let's consider the reciprocal idea of how you make your peers feel.

## EMOTIONAL INTELLIGENCE

Professor Bor suggests that what makes the difference in a leader is how much he or she cares:

> We will sacrifice all sorts of things in our jobs where we think the leader is quite genuine, cares and has a master plan that makes sense. Some people will even leave the organisation nodding, not happy to lose their job but seeing it as necessary to make the place survive. Those leaders who are ruthless, who are doing it really just to demonstrate a bottom line, they may be effective in some aspects, they may even have succeeded in saving the organisation or managed a particular issue or problem, but if they have not demonstrated that they care, have they actually led?

Emotional intelligence is what drives distinctive leadership.

It is what Bruno Demichelis has looked for in all the As he has supported. Born in Venice, Demichelis is a black belt in karate, and was European champion and twice silver medallist at the World Championships before he became a leading instigator of sports science and psychology in football. Demichelis has a formidable, commanding presence which has earned him the nickname Big Bruno. Even now, years past his own sporting prime, you would not want to meet him in a martial arts arena, not just because of his physicality, but also because he's a maestro of the mind. Big Bruno was described as football coach Carlo Ancelotti's 'best piece of business' when he brought him with him to Chelsea from Milan in 2009 as first assistant coach, to oversee the human performance and medical side of team preparation. Here's what Bruno says about Carlo Ancelotti, one of the world's most admired football coaches: 'He's the manager, a natural leader, a social leader, he knows the way to let people love him and he has the key because he is not false. And this is what people buy with Carlo immediately. It's like trust, you know, he develops this empathy with people immediately because he has no mask.'

EQ may feel like a fad in the business world but it has been kicking around for a few centuries. Stoic philosophers in Ancient Greece held the same view of emotional thought as many Western A leaders today, namely that it must be overcome at all costs. By contrast, the artistic and scientific flowering of the Renaissance was all about the primacy of intuition, the merging of the categories 'rational' and 'emotional'. Enlightenment thinkers in the 17th and 18th centuries brought back the concrete Stoic categories of rational and emotional with a vengeance, before the Romantics breathed new life into intuition. Rooted in emotion, intuition was once more seen as a path to insight and wisdom.

While particular diets of EQ come and go, the most effective, in my view, has been cooked up by EQ commentators J.D. Mayer, & P. Salovey, with their four ingredients: perceiving, using, understanding and managing emotions. Learning how to understand and manage feelings in yourself and others, and to use those feelings as tools to facilitate thought and action, is guaranteed to give you substantial leadership weight gain, the best kind of corporate calories.

Fathom what you are feeling and why, and you will unearth those same feelings in other people, a distinct advantage to the leadership endeavour. Unleashing emotions liberates all kinds of activities, such as problem-solving, reasoning, decision-making and creativity. Recognising the often subtle relationships between different emotions will help you navigate complex interpersonal relationships. Learn to lead your own emotions and you will mastermind victories.

Over a cappuccino at the Bulgari Hotel in Milan, Big Bruno identified this leadership of self as the difference between being a leader and being a boss:

> I'll tell you what I really think is the main characteristic of a leader. A leader is someone who can lead his own thoughts and emotions. If you can't do that you are not a leader, not even a little bit. You can be the boss, you can be the head of something but leadership starts with being able to lead yourself, which means your thoughts and emotions. I have seen so few leaders being able to do that because a lot of leaders, they become the big boss and do things because they have the power. That can come from a sense of emptiness. They want to develop their being-ness through their having-ness and their doing-ness.

The leadership qualities shared by out-and-out leaders, the As, as well as by their more catalytic counterparts, the Cs, are founded on trust, determined by credibility and confidence. Where trust is the basic requirement, emotional intelligence is the differentiator.

Consider calculating your Leadership Quotient (LQ). First, work out your Trust Quotient (TQ), the sum of credibility and confidence, for which you can earn up to 5 points each. Then multiply your TQ by your EQ. Your EQ is marked out of 10 because it is a more potent driver of leadership distinction. In summary LQ = TQ(C+C) x EQ. The bigger the number, the more inspirational the leader. A TQ of 10 (5+5) multiplied by an EQ of 10 puts the maximum LQ score at 100.

The following questions are illustrative only. New ones should be invented by you. A great leader needs to be an expert self-questioner.

## TQ

*Credibility*

1. How well do you bring your metaphorical ship into harbour? Give yourself one point for a perfect manoeuvre and zero for the slightest scratch.
2. How proud are your people when you take to the stage or the screen? It is zero if their buttocks tighten in anticipation of an embarrassment, and one point if they know, beyond doubt, that you will cover the organisation in glory.
3. Do you have a special capability that is of value to your organisation, a signature strength with which you are identified? Can you point to a visible demonstration of it in the last week? If yes, give yourself a pat on the back and one point. If no, give yourself a zero and a nudge to develop such a signature strength fast.

4. Do you keep your commitments? Punish yourself with a zero if you cancel meetings or fail to follow through on agreed action. Reward yourself with one point if you have an unblemished reputation for keeping to your word.
5. When you last made a mistake did you concede that you might have had something to do with it? (one point) or did you ask your assistant to volunteer a suggestion for someone to blame? (zero).

*Confidence*
1. Can people predict how you are likely to behave? Having consistent judgement that people can rely on calms everyone's nerves – one point. Flying off the handle every time something displeases you is also predictable – but gets zero.
2. Is your office a safe haven for an exchange of sensitive information? One point if it feels as secure as a confessional booth, zero if suspicions point to you when unpleasant headlines appear in the press.
3. Have you shown recently that you care about your people? One point if this was a selfless act, without any hints of a photo opportunity, and zero if you know deep down that you are out for No. 1.
4. Are you a 'know it all' (zero) or a 'learn as much as you can' (one point)?
5. Do you give people your undivided attention when they need it, or will you peek at your device at the same time? If the former, you are in an ever-shrinking circle waging war on the disease of distraction (one point); if the latter, you lack courtesy (zero).

## EQ

A number of tests and quizzes have been developed to measure emotional intelligence. The following EQ test is a straightforward one:

Assuming you are not flying first class, what has the passenger next to you already concluded about your emotional intelligence? Did you know to leave him or her to a quiet night's sleep, or intuitively grasp that some form of human interaction, however fleeting, would be appreciated?

Have you remained broadly unruffled by the journey's inevitable stresses or have you already referred some pain to a member of the crew? How aware are you of the crew members' feelings? Do you have any empathy for them or would you just prefer them to flatten your bed and tuck you in?

Thinking about the meeting you have on arrival, are you feeling pessimistic because your self-esteem is running on empty or are you vulnerable to an onset of narcissism because your self-esteem has run away with itself? Neither is good.

EQ questions to invent and answer for yourself should probe mastery of your own feelings and those of others. You have a maximum of ten points to award yourself. A sure sign that you lack EQ is if you get a perfect ten.

## KNOW THY ROLE/S

Whether you play around with your own quiz or subscribe to more rigorous EQ examinations, understanding your EQ is essential for deciding which leadership role suits you best. One's ability to cast oneself in an appropriate role demands self-awareness. Happily, there is plenty of help at hand on the importance of Plato's invocation to 'Know thyself'.

Nigel Nicholson's *The I of Leadership*, with its strategies for seeing, being and doing, should be parked firmly at the top of that in-flight 'must read' folder. Yet there remains a vast gulf between a seemingly widespread understanding of the need for self-awareness and the practice of being self-aware. Pursuing self-awareness does not appear to come naturally to testosterone-fuelled Western leaders. If not dismissed as self-absorption, it is, like a dental appointment, dealt with as a rude interruption to the day's more important business.

When I met lawyer Gaytri Kachroo, fifth member of whistle-blower Harry Markopolos' 'Fox Hound' team that uncovered Bernie Madoff's Ponzi scheme, she proposed commitment to reflection throughout one's development, a 'constant exchange of self-reflection and external stimulation'. How else can you know if your leadership is working, for others as well as for you? Self-awareness cannot be consigned to a half-yearly away day of contemplation. That is not what Aristotle had in mind when he exhorted man to manage his own affairs, to lead himself, and command his own thoughts: 'He who knows things pertaining to himself, and is conversant with them, appears to be a prudent man.'

Far too many As and Cs are being imprudent, if economist Richard Layard's study of how people like to spend their time reflects the current state of play. 'With friends and family' comes first. 'With the boss' comes last, meaning people would prefer to be alone than to interact with their boss. Bosses lacking the essential awareness of self that might alert them to the effect they are having on colleagues should not simply take note, they should take action.

One of the great qualities of a C, as we shall witness throughout *Consiglieri*, is candour, the ability to speak the truth to one's leader and one's colleagues. This takes courage, no more so than when we apply the principle to ourselves. How can we become our own, most trusted critics? Echoing Plato, Alexander Pope has this to offer in his 'Essay on Criticism': 'Be sure yourself and your own reach to know ... With pleasure own your errors past, / And make each day a critique on the last.' We ought to know what works for us and what does not. Trial and error is only useful if we heed its verdict. Forming a reliable estimate of our ability and reach should be a regular item on our self-management menu.

By now you may have come to an unnerving question. If all leaders share the essentials of trust and the extraordinary power of emotional intelligence, how can I tell which of the A or C roles I should plump for? Is there a discernible difference? We will see many, but first we need to establish the core similarities. Such are those similarities that arguably anybody capable of being great at one is also capable of greatness at the other.

## TRY BOTH ROLES

If there can be more than one contender for the king's crown, and more than one for the king's counsellor, how best to cast the chief and his chair, Hamlet and Horatio, Macbeth and his Lady (okay that might be easier)? Can leadership life imitate art? If so, might leaders play the different lead roles in alternate performances, as Benedict Cumberbatch and Jonny Lee Miller did in Danny Boyle's production of *Frankenstein* at the National Theatre; Frankenstein one night, Creature the next?

Many As might not much like this idea. Have I not got the part of A because I am uniquely qualified to perform it? Was I not selected by a discerning electorate, an experienced panel who guaranteed that, as the cream, I rose to the top? What if the C opted out of the running for the A role by choice? What if he actually fancied playing Lear's Fool? What if he took one look at the script and decided the part gave him a surer shot at winning Best Supporting Actor than Best Actor? Some great actors and actresses have accepted that, in a long career, there is a time to play the lead and a time to play support, even a time to enjoy a cameo role. The greats do not let pride or vanity get in the way of their next appearance.

The art is in choosing which part – A or C – best suits you for the situation in which you wish to find yourself. In this way, everyone gets to play the A, the A of their own development programme. Nobody is better able to judge what is best at each stage of your development than you, or better qualified to be accountable for the decision. My strong conviction is that the more of us that try both A and C roles, and the more effortlessly we can switch between them, even wearing both hats at different times on the same day, the more successful we will be as leaders and the more successful will be our collective efforts. Cicero recognised the problem of gunning for one role at the beginning of one's career:

> We should determine in what condition we wish to be. In what
> kind of pursuits … a decision most difficult for all; for it is in
> early youth, when judgment is the weakest, that one chooses
> some mode of life with which one has become enamoured,
> and thus is involved in a fixed avocation and course before he
> is capable of judging what is best for him.

I was in a fixed avocation with the A role until I was 47, when I swapped the CEO's hat for a newly created C role as deputy chairman. Instead of commanding Saatchi & Saatchi's

52 Europe, Middle East and Africa operations and its 1,800 people, I now had no P&L accountability and not a single direct report. I was hauled in by our worldwide human resources director: 'If I were you, I wouldn't be overheard saying you don't ever want to be a chief executive again,' he said.

'Why not?'

'Because people might think you don't ever want to be a chief executive again.'

Peers were no less bemused, giving me hopeful looking thumbs-up, saying, 'Wow, that's courageous' and far too polite to say what they were thinking, 'You've lost your marbles'. If only I could claim it was anything to do with courage. It was a choice rooted in an appetite for a new experience and learning. There was an element of escape from the tensions at the top, too. Sticking with a role just because others think it suits us can be a lazy option born of anxiety. What is there to be anxious about if you're a good leader intent on a life of leading and learning?

Kevin Roberts enjoyed leadership stints at Gillette, Procter & Gamble, PepsiCo and brewery giant Lion Nathan before his sixteen years spent reinvigorating Saatchi & Saatchi after the departure of founding brothers Maurice and Charles. Roberts tells a story about turning down a C kind of role as chief marketing officer at PepsiCo, and opting instead for an even bigger A role, president and CEO of PepsiCo's Pepsi-Cola Canadian business:

> In hindsight, it was a big mistake. Roger Enrico, who would go on to become the chairman and CEO of PepsiCo from 1996 to 2001, said to me at the time, 'I understand why you turned it down, because you're a gung-ho ambitious leader and you want to get to the top, and that's the Pepsi way. Fantastic, but

you'll regret it.' And I said, 'Oh mate, no, no, you're wrong.' Enrico went over to be the CMO of Frito-Lay in Dallas. We all blinked in amazement. He was a type-A driving force. And he went to be a marketing guy for two, two and a half years. After that, he soon became the leader of leaders, the head of the Cola wars. So, he was right. He said the marketing job made him a better guy. I would have been stronger earlier if I'd have done a job without the ultimate accountability. If I had done it sooner I would have been better faster.

Too many Cs limit their development because of stereo-typical views of what being a real leader demands. Jonathan Brown is a man suited to out-and-out leadership. In 1998, for Shell UK's Exploration and Production arm, Brown took single point responsibility for the safety and welfare of 150 offshore personnel, managing their engineering, produc-tion and drilling activities for two of the Brent oil and gas field platforms, Alpha and Bravo. Seven years later he took command of two projects, both worth in excess of £200 million for British Gas in Trinidad and Tobago, delivering each on time and under budget. More recently, for Talisman, he ventured into the remote operating environment of Northern Iraq to take accountability for the delivery of safe and efficient well operations, eventually becoming general manager. Brown is an A through and through, so why doesn't the idea of a view from the top appeal to him? He explains:

I've honestly never really believed of myself as a CEO. I've always seen myself as a COO rather than a CEO because I shirk the limelight. I had this exact conversation with John Manzoni actually, a month or two before he left, and he said, 'Why would you say that? Why would you not aim for the top? I can't see any reason why you wouldn't be or couldn't be.'

I agree with Manzoni, having worked with Brown for a year on the Sloan leadership programme at London Business School, and having felt the esteem in which he was held by his fellow Sloans. Despite his natural bias as an operational C, Brown is also eminently capable of performing the A role.

David Attenborough was relentlessly heading towards the position of director-general of the BBC but took the unusual decision of refusing that post so that he could concentrate on wildlife programmes. He preferred communicating and edifying to making big decisions in the BBC boardroom. He called it the best decision of his life, and perhaps we can all agree. For many people there is a time to be an A and a time to be a C throughout their career. Paul Clements, for example, Carlo Ancelotti's current assistant at Real Madrid, a role he played for Ancelotti at both Chelsea and Paris St Germain, was an A for most of his career, then a C, and perhaps one day soon, an A again. Carlo Barel di Sant'Albano is the Turin-born executive chairman of the Agnelli family's Exor global property subsidiary, Cushman & Wakefield. He is also head of the firm's Europe, Middle East and Africa operations and, until recently, interim global chief executive. He can see a time when he might not be an A:

> Maybe you get to a point where you'd be happy to provide advice, and not have the weight of those decisions, and actually be very effective at it. Right now, say in the role of government, I'd rather be president of the United States than the president's right-hand man. But, in a few years' time, I'd be asking myself 'am I sure I want that aggravation much longer?'

We need the best leaders to go into both A and C roles because both are necessary, challenging and rewarding. Some people know in their heart which role, A or C, they most want. Sometimes clues emerge from one's past: if you never captained a side in sport, if you were never the lead singer in a band, if you were not the one to start a money-making scheme at school – you may not be the most natural fit for the A. But if it excites you, do not give up on the idea of becoming an A at some stage of your career. *20 Feet From Stardom,* the American documentary film directed by Morgan Neville, suggests that some of the most famously unknown backing singers have a burning ambition to succeed at the highest level. Darlene Love, called the 'world's most famous backup singer', craved a spot centre stage and landed it on Broadway and on screen – most notably as Trish Murtaugh in the *Lethal Weapon* films. Like Love, you could learn to be good at the A role, grow into it and flourish. You could create a team with your own advisers and backing singers to support and complement you. Start in some kind of adviser's role and watch like a hawk to see how the A role is done, and how it could be done better.

Conversely, can you be a C if you feel like a born A? If you could never quietly observe at school, or time your run from midfield, then a C role could well be a challenge for you. Can you train your mouth to disengage momentarily and let your ears have a go? Can you get better at chess if you practise? Can you coach other lead singers? Of course you can.

Such role reversals demand deliberate choice and practice. Do not wait too long. Dip your toe into a new experience where your learning curve is exponential. Robert Tansey is one person who rejected the linear leadership ladder in favour of a lateral one. Currently development director at Sky Sports,

Tansey has become used to swapping the A hat for the C hat, and now wears both.

I first met Tansey when I was leading the London office of Publicis, the French-owned advertising agency. He was a very good planner. After a brief stint as a senior planner at another advertising agency, Tansey was seduced by the media moguls at Sky to take up a role he describes as, 'The No. 2 to the then brand marketing director.' They had chosen him for his quality as a foot-on-the-ball thinker. He moved up through this function for six years, eventually reaching its ceiling. He describes the increasing intensity he experienced as he enjoyed greater responsibility:

> Every level you go up, you are immediately overwhelmed by the tsunami of extra work to do. I remember thinking probably 2½ years to 3 years in, 'gosh I don't know how people cope with this level of work. This is really stretching, and quite exhausting. How on earth does my boss cope, and how on earth does the chief executive above him cope?'

Tansey took on the A role for Sky Creative, the broadcaster's in-house creative function, before a promotion to development director at Sky Sports, reporting to Barney Francis, a new role rooted in the broadcaster's need to reduce its reliance on acquisition of sports rights and to find other ways to grow its business. It is a role which Tansey describes as 'show what needs to happen, and then make it happen'. He highlights the new leadership task:

> The challenges are different from what I've done before so I've got to make sure I've got some really good implementers alongside me, some drivers. Unlike the Sky Creative job,

which was to bring big improvement to what already existed, the Sky Sports position has been created to solve a problem which people were aware of, but perhaps had not fully accepted. So, how can I help my boss to communicate the urgency for change through the organisation?

The extent to which Robert Tansey can deliver as a C depends on the attitude, support and assessment of his A, Barney Francis. Will Tansey prove his worth in his newly created capacity? If he does, might he become a contender for the ultimate A job at Sky Sports? 'It's not beyond the realms of possibility... but it would signal a massive culture change, in the sense that people who are in these kinds of jobs have come from a production background, they've made programmes. So, to have someone in charge of the channel who hasn't made a single TV programme in their entire life, well it's unlikely.'

Much like the consigliere Tom Hagan, Irish outsider to the Corleone family and therefore not someone who will ever be in charge, Tansey is a consigliere without any production expertise and therefore unlikely to be seen as a threat by his current boss. Tansey is also unsure, having worn and still wearing both hats, whether the C hat is not better suited to him anyway: 'I'd be quite happy being a No. 2 as long as I deeply respected my boss, was inspired by them, saw them as a good leader, they trusted you, they valued the consigliere-type role, no problem whatsoever. It becomes frustrating only if you can almost certainly do a better job yourself.'

Tansey should be an inspiration for potential As and Cs. His career has been all the more successful because of his willingness to try both roles. If he had to plump for one or the other right now, he would conclude that the C hat fits him best, but if the circumstances dictated that he needed to take the out-and-out lead, he would, and he would do it well. His thought process may be worth applying to our own situations:

Could I do the job of No. 1? Probably. Would it get the best out of me? No. Would it be the best thing for Sky? No. So that's where you have to subsume your ego, and go, this is not right ... Life is not about a constant linear progression through functions, companies, departments. That is not the way to general happiness. Satisfaction is achieved by doing something that you're really interested in, knowing that you're contributing, and that may be as a No. 1, a No. 2 or something else altogether. So yes, I definitely think people should try both.

'You are your choices,' is Sartre's rejoinder. Make many.

## 2

# WHAT MAKES AN A?

We have established that great leaders can play both A and C roles. Now let's look at what it takes to be an A. This chapter is dedicated to the out-and-out leaders, people with the extraordinary capacity to lead from the front and rarely look back. What motivates them? What are their qualities? And what is it like to be one? Before answering let's raise a preliminary, philosophical question about the A role: Do you select it, or does it select you?

Peter Murray was special adviser to Dr Nigel Griffiths, business minister in Tony Blair's cabinet. Murray's grandfather was given a vote in the 1994 Labour Party leadership election, because he was a trade union member. He died that year so Murray chose to frame the voting slip, which now sits on his desk. There were three candidates, Tony Blair, John Prescott and Margaret Beckett. The slip has boxes for both the MPs and the union member to vote in. Under Beckett and Prescott there are two boxes, one for leader and one for deputy leader. Under Blair there is just the one box – leader. For Murray that was a revelation about leadership. Two were willing to compromise. One wasn't.

Yet A leadership is not confined to those who make it the only option. It has a knack of knocking on the doors of people who *will*, if necessary or if asked, fill a vacuum. Leaders sometimes find themselves in A roles, ushered there by circumstances beyond their control. The best people adapt to meet the needs of the group in which they belong. Some are transformed into strong As, even when the role is an unnatural fit.

Do you sometimes decide that you are uniquely qualified to lead your organisation's response to a particular challenge? Or has a team at work insisted that it is your drum to which they wish to march? Might there be a streak of A in you? Here is a test: You are sitting on an airport bus. You and all the other passengers have to catch a flight but the driver hasn't shown up. The keys are in the ignition. What do you do?

A) Stride to the front, install yourself in the driver's seat, start the ignition and crack on with the journey.
B) Note with reluctance that nobody is showing any sign of taking command, pause, pause some more and finally say, 'Well, someone needs to drive, so I will.'
C) Smile with relief as someone marches to the front and takes the wheel.

Answer A or B? Read on.

## MOTIVATIONS

What sets As on their surging path to the top? What are the future dreams that pull them forward and the past events that push them on? Amanda Blanc, a leading A at the global insurance giant AXA, disarms with her candour about the beginnings of her ambition. It all started at Sunday school in the Welsh valleys when she was four years old:

> We used to do this thing every year called Anniversary, which was like the Sunday school concert. I was the narrator. I was

the singer. I was the person that played the piano. I was the person that did all the recitations. And I loved being that person. I didn't want to be the person in the group. I wanted to be the person singing on their own. So if somebody suggested, God forbid, that we should do a song with a group of people, it was like, 'You've got to be joking, I want to do it on my own.'

The A is desperate to be in charge, to be able to look at the organisational chart and see her name at the top of it – 'Oh look, there's a team, I'll be the captain.' Some As want to emulate an admired family member. Others have faced tremendous adversity. Some were the eldest child and never wanted to let go of the reins of power. Others were rebels, refusing to accept that they would ever have a boss in life, even as they joined big global corporations on the lowest rung of the ladder.

The main motivation for many As can be phrased negatively. I asked Carlo Sant'Albano, long-time charismatic A in various roles at Exor, when he first realised he wished to be a No. 1: 'As soon as I realised that I didn't wish to be a No. 2.' The idea of playing any other role? 'You've got to be joking.' Ana Patricia Botín, the inspirational chief executive of Grupo Santander's UK bank, is also averse to playing any role other than the final decision-maker: 'In Spanish, there's a saying that it's better to be the head of a mouse than the tail of a lion.'

As well as being in charge, As need to have vast amounts of autonomy. If it feels like a lion's tail, the role is no longer tenable. The As need to make the big decisions, to shape the desired results, and then to build and grow a team capable of delivering them. On the way up the leadership ladder, As will look for situations that afford them independent commands, probably as far away from HQ as possible. New Zealand is a popular choice. The ideal, according to my A interviewees, is to run a department, a division or a regional operation with no more than two meetings per year with the powers that be – one to outline how you intend to develop the business in the next five years, the other to assess what happened in the previous year. Between those two fixed points the A wants to enjoy lashings of laissez faire, an opportunity to express a vision about how the business might develop, and how resources might be best used. Most of all, they want to be left alone to deliver the results – 'I'm an A. Leave me be.'

Oxygen for an A is having the final answer. Watch *Who Wants to be a Millionaire?* when the stakes are highest. Most people wince at Chris Tarrant's catchphrase question, while the A in the hot seat only smiles. The As love to make a difference and they think that giving the final answer and having the final say gives them the best chance to. They tend to realise that Cs make enormous contributions to successful outcomes, yet they also know that satisfaction in C positions depends on an A. Does your A value that contribution? Will they support your point of view? Will they act on it? Better to be the A and leave nothing to chance.

On their way to the top, the A will have had to help define another's leadership. However much they respected that A, at some point they wanted to get out of their shadow – and into the limelight. Before Peter Murray changed his mind, he wanted: ' … to be an MP. I wanted to be No. 1. I wanted to lead. And there's that big validation of standing on a stage – I don't know any other validation like it – and have your community, have 30,000 households say, "That's the man I want to represent us." That's hugely attractive.' In our increasingly always-on world, As must perform. If a stage or a platform is out of reach for a time, the natural A will feel withdrawal symptoms. Popularity is a popular motivation. Being adored and revered can be irresistible, intoxicating, though successful leaders know that congeniality rarely correlates with longevity.

What really gets the A going above all is power. The thirst for power explains the race to be captain of the team, top dog to the deputy, president to the vice president, the guy who carries the weight of the world on his shoulders and wants to carry some more, the final decision-maker with the final answer. The godfather.

Some or all of these temptations – being in charge, independent, on stage, in power – may appeal to you. But do you have what it takes?

## A QUALITIES

What makes As special? What are their distinguishing features? How do they endear themselves to their followers? A leaders have charisma, conviction and self-assurance. They are driven, single-minded, ruthless, competitive, risk-taking and fearless. They grasp situations quickly, cope with adversity calmly and get the best out of their Cs. Arriving at their new HQs, they set about bringing order to the headless chickens left running around by their dysfunctional predecessors. They are cool in a crisis and turned on by turnarounds.

Our A will be the last to arrive at the meeting and the first to leave, most at ease at the head of the table, agitating to feed their dizzying addiction for action. The Hopi Indian elders' exhortation is exclaimed to jolt the team into life: 'We are the ones we have been waiting for!' (The leader knows it did not end well for them, and we know that there is no evidence that the Obama-invoked phrase did in fact emanate from the elders, but the sentiment is right.) Direction needs to be set, resources aligned, energies marshalled, and the A wastes no time. The As love to set the unimaginable goal – a big, hairy audacious one, if they have read Collins & Porras' *Built to Last: Successful Habits of Visionary Companies*. They want to establish a culture, a way of doing things, to drive the team's performance to its peak.

Choices have to be made. Bold choices. Those worrying about any undesirable fall-out from such choices are told by the A, emphatically 'I will deal with that.' The A is ready to be ruthless and to keep being ruthless. George Bernard Shaw knew what was good for the A: 'All progress depends on the unreasonable man,' he wrote. The A's job is to agree which music to play: 'If I say it is Vivaldi, let me make one thing clear, we will play Vivaldi. There is no place for someone who insists on Mozart. My ego is strong, my self-belief boundless.'

The hallmark distinction of an A is courage, according to Jean-Pierre Farandou, a member of transport giant SNCF and executive chairman of its subsidiary Keolis, which employs over 50,000 people worldwide. When I asked Farandou to give me an example of an A who most embodied this quality, he offered up another Jean-Pierre, Jean-Pierre Rive, the French rugby icon whose bravery and long blond hair earned him the nickname Asterix. As Farandou observes about Rive: 'He was always so very brave, in the thick of it all, blood all over his face.'

David Teece is professor in global business and director of the Institute for Business Innovation at the University of California, Berkeley. Great leaders, he says, do not make decisions to be congenial. They make necessary ones that prove to be good most of the time. Professor Teece may be an academic but he is something of an A too, practising what he teaches.

Ten years ago, a fire broke out in the hills of San Francisco. The police came to Teece's home to evacuate the one hundred guests at his son's christening. Initially fifty stoics chose to ignore the police's advice to head for safety. As the fire approached, fifty became twenty, then ten, and, eventually, the house was manned by just Teece and his college buddy, Marny. Teece was feeling confident. He knew he had a hose and water. Marny was not so sure: 'I think we should leave now.'

'Why, Marny?'

'Because I think we're going to die.'

'We're not going to die, Marny.'

Teece concedes that he did doubt himself for 20 minutes and that Marny might have had a point, but he remained resolute and they stayed: 'It was stubborn, but it was not "stupid stubborn". I knew that Strategy B was always available to us, to run for our lives down the road.'

The As always have a Plan B. They are a competitive lot, with a rampant need to achieve. Not happy on the team, only happy as captains, not interested in being a prefect, scheming instead to be head of school. These aspirants to the A role share a perspective on primacy and a penchant for the pedestal: if not the leader, the loser; if not the first, the second; if not Hamlet or Lear then show me the exit.

Conductor, commander, matriarch, patriarch, chief executive, team leader, manager, minister – tough decisions await you. Are you willing to be finally accountable for making it all happen? The rest of us hope so. Responsibility means having a duty to deal with something, whereas accountability is more daunting, requiring you to justify decisions and outcomes. Once you have accepted that the buck stops with you, you must somehow persuade a group of selfish people to set aside their egos in pursuit of your grand vision, personifying, magnifying and amplifying that vision better than anyone else. The As' articulation of the direction they want us to take exemplifies their leadership.

They encourage us to air conflicting choices when they are not naturally emerging from debates, and then they make the final call. We sometimes label difficult decisions 'the tough calls', but they are not so for the As. What would you call the biggest decisions facing your team, department, organisation, country – tough or fun?

## A LIFE?

The A can take counsel, listen, reflect, mull, mitigate the risk of getting it wrong, make multiple bets, but ultimately the A must decide and, increasingly, decide fast. Small wonder that commentators describe the leader's job as a lonely one. In poker's early incarnation, when a player did not feel like dealing, he could pass the buck. But an A, particularly one in the judgemental glare of the media, has no such luxury.

The A is ready to take risks when few others would dare and to cope admirably when things go wrong. We might forgive them for seeming a little out of control at times. If only we knew how complete and well-disguised that feeling often is. An A must disguise, too, the sense of déjà vu they might feel towards final decision-making, whether to approve the pay rise, hire the unpopular candidate, sack the underperformer, fire the client, buy or sell the company.

They occupy the twilight zone of personal and professional trade-offs which we all have to visit occasionally – work or home; school play or client dinner; partner's birthday or boss's away day; annual health check or annual general meeting – but the A must reside there like a vampire. Once initiated, they must fly above the unrelenting threat of others who quietly pray for their failure from behind their office door. Perhaps it is only the PA who notices the silent relief of an A returning from a bout of illness, to find that nobody has yet occupied his office. Even towards the inevitable end, with the seeds of failure sown into their success, the A will remain fearless. The instinct for self-preservation overcoming their unpopularity, they will endure longer than anybody could have expected. Where there are heights, they understand, there must be precipices. AXA's Amanda Blanc can look over the cliff edge and remain vertigo free:

> I'm the person that gets sacked if something goes wrong, and I say this to my team regularly, 'You know, if something goes wrong here I go, not you, it's me.' The CEO is accountable and when you've got 1,700 people who are taking risks, however carefully and even with controls in place, there's still a huge element of having to trust those people that they're going to do the right thing. So, yes, the accountability is really tough.

Responsibility, we all have, for our bits of the action. But overall accountability for the whole belongs uniquely to the As. It seems that the top dog's life is in fact a dog's life. The average occupancy of the corner office with the three windows stretches now to no more than six years. Barely time to see the stock options mature, let alone the pot plant reach its potential. Take Roberto Mancini, the feted football coach who, in May 2013, was relieved of his leadership post at Manchester City a mere twelve months to the day after he had ended the club's forty-four year spell without a league title. Champion one year, chump the next, he was sacked because he missed the targets set, his team finishing second in the English league and runners-up in the domestic Cup competition.

Business is no less forgiving when its leaders fail to bring home the silverware. The roll call of rolling heads takes longer to read each year, as do the well-intentioned euphemisms for ritual sacrifice: 'We appreciate all that Alice has done for us. She has been with us for over four months now, so we understand her need for a fresh challenge.' 'Alan has decided he needs to spend more time with his family.' 'For some time we have been in discussions with Andrew about our future direction so we were saddened, but not surprised, by Andrew's decision to make today his last with us. He leaves a big void to fill. Please welcome Amy as our new leader.' From sports to politics to business, there are few second chances for firsts. Coming second constitutes failure and those at the helm must pay. 'You're fired!' is not just the stuff of entertaining television. Contestants exiting the show in business have included the bosses of Blackberry, Barclays, J C Penney, Procter & Gamble, Citigroup and Yahoo.

So As are not just ready to be accountable, but to live with consequences that might make the rest of us queasy. No readers can still be thinking that the A's life is a stroll in the park. For those of you who still feel as if they have the aptitude and the appetite for it, there are a couple of final demands to meet. First, an A has to endure relentless dissatisfaction. As an A, every single day you have to validate and justify your simply being there. Even when given recognition for doing a great job, most As are not happy with the job they are doing. They go out of their way to find things that are wrong in order to put them right. This romance with restlessness means that they can never, ever be happy. Cs can be and, as we shall see, need to be.

Second, As always have to be in the limelight. For some,

appearing centre stage for the good of the organisation is an insatiable pleasure, one that borders on the pathological – 'a particularly English disposition,' according to one of my southern European interviewees. Wellington jealously guarded his reputation as sole victor at Waterloo in the years after the battle. Nelson, too, like plenty of other British commanders, was happy to be assigned disproportionate credit for collective endeavour. Jonathan Miller has worked at the English National Opera for thirty-five years. He has had, deservedly, more credit than even his giant-sized polymath brain might be able to compute. Yet late into his illustrious career, he can still become extremely unhappy if he feels we have not clocked his brilliance. Programme notes for a recent production of *La Bohème* called it 'Jonathan Miller's production revived by Natascha Metherell'. This piqued the director. It was, Miller says, his production and he attended every rehearsal over a three-week period: 'Natascha was my assistant.'

Future generations may read of a different truth about the A's relative contribution in the Letters pages of the *Times* long after they have gone. Hopefully, history will be kind to those who shunned the limelight and reveal retrospectively their quiet contribution. For some As, the obligation to be seen really is unwelcome. But, even if you hire yourself a 'front man', as some less extrovert As wisely do, you will still come under increasingly public scrutiny. The A's job cannot be a private affair.

Applauding their performances, gasping in admiration, and following them on Twitter are minor inconveniences for the rest of us, given the slice of the organisation's stress the As willingly consume.

Encore. We need our As.

What about Cs?

# PART TWO

# 3

# WHAT MOTIVATES THE C?

The opening chapter of this book established that great leaders are prepared to share the burden and delights of responsibility for their enterprises, and that bi-leadership is the new black: A leaders, C leaders and A/C leaders. Talented leaders are agile enough to play more than one leadership role. Chapter 2 examined the makings of As and mused upon the appeal of their incomparably demanding and utterly indispensable role. Now we ask, what's in it for the Cs?

There are some people who choose the C role simply out of aversion to the awfulness of the A role. Chapter 2 will have given this minority pale faces and sweaty palms. Who needs the sleepless nights, the relentless scrutiny and the short tenure? Better surely to live on Easy Street, put the kids to bed, switch off the Blackberry and leave the mountain of email from the highly paid A, who is working on into the night?

Yet this chapter is intended for the majority of consiglieri, those who positively embrace their roles. They have not settled gloomily for C after having their love for A spurned. They have learnt the joys of influencing As they admire and respect. They wish to be close to power across their organisations and to have autonomy to get their jobs done. They are insatiable learners, accruing new experience like their life depends on it (which, as some consiglieri have discovered, it sometimes does). As we will see, my C leader interviewees have found their greatest and most consistent pleasure in helping others reach their full potential.

Christopher Seaman's book, *Inside Conducting*, starts with a story about a conductor who, at a moment in the score that was intended to be silent, signalled an emphatic downbeat bar to his orchestra. Ignoring their A's invitation, the players read their score correctly, keeping silent until a voice from the viola section piped up, 'He doesn't sound so good on his own, does he?' Other than for the fun of bringing attention to the A's flaws, what are the pleasures of a job as a C? How might someone who thinks he should chase the A slot be persuaded to take the C slot instead?

On a recent trip to work with colleagues in Asia, I shared the idea for *Consiglieri* with Lionel Goh, whose leadership perspective is shaped by his upbringing in a very traditional Asian family. 'Ah,' he said, 'you need to study Confucian historiographers on the eunuchs.' Eunuchs were kept by almost all Chinese emperors as trusted advisers. The motivations to be a eunuch were so abundant throughout the dynasties that many opted to pay the razor-sharp price for the post. Even eunuchs who served seemingly low domestic functions could earn the ruler's ear; the most powerful were put in charge of military and diplomatic affairs. They had unparalleled access to the ruler and could for that reason wield power. While castration was sometimes an involuntary procedure, the number of castrati who supplied themselves to courts by means of *self*-castration grew over the centuries to such an extent that during Ming rule the court had to take in thousands of eunuchs that it couldn't afford.

My interviewees had not gone so far as to offer themselves up to their As for castration but their commitment was no less striking. The interviews reveal some fascinating insights into what drives these extraordinary people, some of whom are well known for their contributions to celebrated leaders, others whose equally valuable support has thus far only been acknowledged by its immediate beneficiaries. The majority of my C leader interviewees chose the role because they found its variety to be of enduring appeal. Some have tried the A role and concluded that it is not for them, either because they didn't enjoy it, because it didn't bear comparison with the C role, or because they failed in their A assignment. Others have added a C role to their A role. A minority are yet to try A leadership either because of its horror associations, because they do not think it will play to their strengths, or because they are not quite ready for it.

From an early age, we look at the A and think that we, too, can be that A. My three-year-old nephew has examined the ultimate leader's life and feels sure he could breeze it. But Sam finds himself in the distinctly unfortunate position of being the second born. It is a raw deal. He finally tires of following his elder brother George, aged four, and screams in frustration: 'It's my turn to be leader!' Sam, my boy, I can cut this short for you. Your lust for leadership will be sated only when you're much older. In the meantime, take pity on George, it's a tough job he's got there. Take comfort, too, that the pupillage you are being forced to serve under George will make you a stronger A, when your time comes.

Sam and aspirant A leaders like him should test as many of the C archetypes in Chapter 4 as possible. It will make them more effective when they take complete command; or open their eyes to a C role, the merit of which they had not seen. Research and development should be their number one priority, in readiness for the leadership choices they will have to make. With any luck they can avoid the pain of underachievement felt, from time to time, by those with a natural skill for assisting and supporting, who leap from C to A with too much haste. Before we look at the range of C leader motivations, let us note the example of some famously brilliant Cs who made too hasty a leap.

## FROM 'C' TO 'A' AND BACK – THE WISER FOR IT

Peter Taylor spent nine years as Brian Clough's right-hand man at Hartlepool United, Derby County, Brighton & Hove Albion, and later at Nottingham Forest. There, in particular, the pair delivered enormous success. Clough once said of his colleague: 'I'm not equipped to manage successfully without Peter Taylor. I am the shop window and he is the goods in the back.' Taylor said of the partnership: 'We just gelled together, we filled in the gaps … My strength was buying and selecting the right player, then Brian's man management would shape the player.' When Taylor died, after a period in which the pair did not speak, Clough was distraught. He paid tribute to Taylor saying that he would like the 'Brian Clough Stand' to be renamed the 'Brian Clough and Peter Taylor Stand'. Taylor's success as an A simply never came close to the success he helped to deliver as a C. Beyond the partnership, both before it formed and after he went his own way, Taylor underachieved.

Sachin Tendulkar, while acknowledged as the best Test batsman of the modern era, was a truly poor Test captain. Objectively, he was bad because his team performed badly. He captained India in twenty-five test matches at the peak of his career. His team lost nine, drew twelve and won just four matches. Does it count that he was a reluctant A? 'You are the experienced one,' they told him, 'you should be the captain.' He could only ignore the siren calls to captaincy for so long, even though *he* knew he was happier not making the big decisions. Tendulkar continued to offer advice to Indian captains until his retirement in 2013, aged 40, but his major contribution to Indian cricket was as the most prolific Test batsman in history. Tendulkar, a loser wearing the Armband, was a leader from the Crease.

Brian Kidd was a European cup winner in a Manchester United team that featured George Best, Bobby Charlton and Nobby Stiles, whom Charlton told me without a beat was his best ever C on the pitch: 'I used to say to him, "just fetch me the ball, Nobby, then pass me the ball, Nobby, and I'll do the rest."' While Stiles went on to serve Charlton as his assistant when they both ventured, with little success, into management, Kidd went on to become one of Sir Alex Ferguson's assistants, enjoying sustained success in the great manager's slipstream. Together with Eric Harrison, Kidd had a hand in the development of 'Fergie's Class of '92' which included David Beckham, Gary and Phil Neville, Nicky Butt, Ryan Giggs, and Paul Scholes. During his time as Ferguson's assistant manager (1991–1998) Manchester United won the Football League Cup in '92, the Premier League title in '93, the double in '94 and '96, and the Premier League again in '97.

Weary in the wings, Kidd became the out-and-out manager of Blackburn Rovers in 1998. In less than a year, Blackburn Rovers were relegated and when Kidd was fired his team were perilously close to sinking into an even lower division. A superb C, a spectacularly poor A. Where is he now? Back in the wings supporting, as assistant, a rapidly revolving door of managers at Manchester City, a role to which he is infinitely better suited. His contribution as an assistant must have been sharpened by learning from defeat in the top job.

His motivations for a challenge, a new experience, a sterner test of his leadership, were not malign, nor even misplaced. Until he had a go, how could he know?

Jon Walker worked as a C to the dynamic Amanda Blanc. During Amanda's leadership of insurance giant Towergate, they built a powerful relationship. Amanda trusted Jon to do the right thing, and if he wasn't certain he was about to, he was very comfortable asking her for direction. Walker describes the reaction when Blanc left to join AXA in December 2010: 'That put the cat amongst the pigeons in Towergate; I think that's the first time Towergate lost a senior executive that it didn't want to lose. I was then asked to step into her role. It was an interesting moment for me: every instinct in my body was saying, 'Don't do it,' but I did it.' There were compelling reasons for Walker to turn down the A job on offer and to join Blanc at AXA instead:

> The timing was awful, the economy was up the creek, there was no organic growth in the business, there was no sign of any kind of rating increase for insurance, which would help drive the financial performance … I also knew that the share-holders of Towergate would continue to set budgets based on no foundation of growth, other than, well, we've got to be seen to be going forward. There was the slightly less rational thing, too, which was, 'Bloody hell, Amanda's a tough act to follow.'

Some of his Towergate colleagues echoed Walker's own misgivings, counselling him to follow Amanda, rather than step into her shoes. But the attraction of the A role at Towergate beat the logical choice of another C role at AXA. It took six months for Walker to conclude that he had made the wrong decision. He had the integrity and humility to hold his hands up to the mistake and resign. EQ in action. Walker is once more working for Blanc, more effective and stronger as a C leader for his brief stint as an A.

Taylor, Kidd, Tendulkar and Walker were preceded by Servius Sulpicius Galba, who was pronounced Rome's ruler after Nero's death in AD 68. He very swiftly failed to live up to the standard expected of an emperor. One wonders which he enjoyed less, his seven-month stint in charge or the severing of his head. He hadn't even asked for the job, so one has to feel somewhat sorry for him, though few did: he hadn't been a very likeable C. Other Cs through the centuries have 'done a Galba' – gone on to be As and not acquitted themselves as they, or we, might have hoped. Their fate stimulates one of our society's uglier appetites – for a spectacular loser. What the historian Tacitus had to say about Galba could easily have been a journalistic wisecrack about Gordon Brown: 'He was up to the job of emperor as long as he never became emperor.'

Why do we, in cases when the transition from behind the scenes to front of house ends badly, so enjoy the humiliation of the guy with the guts to have given it a go? Operational knowledge gained, a new experience, a greater understanding of the A's accountabilities, all these should make other Cs a little envious. Our sympathy levels seem to sink even lower and our schadenfreude rise higher when the loser is a chooser, not the reluctant A but the aspiring A. Yet the failures of those who depart the familiar for the dangers of the unknown should inspire us. They step up to the accountability of the A and give the shiny new leadership suit a try for size. It doesn't fit. They move on with some A scar tissue to become stronger Cs. Where is the shame in that?

## POSITIVE MOTIVATIONS

In an age where so much is played out in public, one of the most significant boons for Cs is the preservation of their privacy. Unless it is their functional job to perform, a life in the lens is not worth the flash of the bulb. Celebrated actor Ed Harris overcame shyness as a young man through his performing, but remains coy on his frequent trips up the red carpet. He once said: 'I made career decisions that came from the part of me that wanted to shun the limelight.' Like that of Harris, Charles Garland's career has not suffered from a distaste for paparazzi. Garland is the chief executive of SYCO, the global joint venture between Simon Cowell and Sony Music Entertainment. Through TV formats like *Pop Idol*, *Celebrity Idol* and *Britain's Got Talent* we have come to appreciate Cowell's relationship with the limelight. As he bathes in it, he positively bronzes. Cowell, the overall A, is smart enough to confer the status of CEO, and its commensurate responsibilities, on a relative unknown. Garland could not be more pleased that Cowell is the man out front, the visible manifestation of the company. It lets Garland get on with running the business. As he explains:

> It is not in my DNA to be in the limelight, which is perfect when you work for a colourful boss who loves all that, standing on stage ... mentoring 5,000 staff or talking to shareholders, analysts. Some people love that and they are very good at it. It's not something I really want to do ... I'm not interested in the intrusive nature of being too big a character, or being famous. It is a very potent drug, which I'm not really interested in getting hooked on. It has so many bad side-effects ...

Other Cs are keen to free their minds of the relentless burden of decision-making. The CEO's plight does not tend to garner much sympathy – with its golden handshakes, handcuffs and parachutes, stockpiles and country piles. But the Cs who have seen that leader up close may be more understanding. Unless we've done it ourselves, can we empathise with the leader who commits to deliver shareholders their demanding growth targets; to make an instant decision to land a plane full of passengers on the Hudson River when geese strike an engine; to set a new interest rate that will impact every householder in the country; to close down a factory; to approve an investment in a volatile emerging market; to give the go-ahead to acquire a new business knowing that it will upset many star performers in your existing business? Can we imagine what goes through the coach's mind as he weighs up whether to play or drop the out-of-form £50 million striker, bought by the owner himself?

Jose María Nus is executive director of Santander and responsible for the Risk Division. Previously he was chief risk officer at Banco Español de Crédito, S.A., where he was a member of the board and of the executive committee. Before that he held positions at Bankinter, S.A. and Argentaria-Corporación Bancaria de España, S.A., where he was managing director of risk. Why has Nus never been tempted to take the overall A role when he is clearly qualified to, and when he has held accountability for critically important functions during his illustrious career in global banking? 'I like a good lunch, but not a good lunch and a good dinner – ultimate leaders don't have a choice, they have to have both.'

To have 'more control over my life' is a familiar justification from Cs for the choice they have made. Nus believes he can make a more useful contribution to the leaders he serves if he has fewer distractions, some time to think, to experiment, to shape decisions and outcomes. While the A is fighting fires, batting today's questions and barking tomorrow's orders, the C can reflect on next week's – or next year's – agenda, separating the important from the urgent. Very few natural A leaders will be heard complaining about the long hours or the stress. They might concede that they are cursed by a melancholy that accompanies completion and achievement. Sir Alex Ferguson suffered this more than most because he won more than most. He has described the immediate anti-climax of winning trophies, the final whistle, a season's endeavour, all that stress, a triumphant march in front of the cheering fans, but a sense of deflation, and a mounting concern about how to do it all over again. Cs love to win, too, but they are freer to savour their triumphs than their ultra-accountable A counterparts.

The C can enjoy much of the A's pleasure without some of the pain, but to opt for a life as a C for pain or accountability avoidance alone would be like becoming a theatre director because you don't like wearing greasepaint, or an orchestra conductor because you don't fancy schlepping your cello on the bus. There are a plethora of positive motivations to plump for leading from the C, and the rest of this chapter is devoted to them.

I first had my eyes opened to the A/C leadership inclination by my son, Joe, who started directing plays at a young age. Shamefully, I concluded that he had inherited the leader's A gene and took great pride as he directed his way through almost every Pinter play. So what on earth did he think he was doing when he ditched the director's chair to become deputy stage manager? A self-inflicted demotion to deputy? What was wrong with the boy? At the very least, why not the stage manager in charge, rather than his stooge? Joe put me straight:

'As DSM you may not get the ultimate responsibility, but you do get a lot of power. You're out of the picture, but you get to call the show.' He was no longer the main man but he was in a seat of considerable influence and, not unimportantly, much happier. I followed his example when I swapped the A role for Saatchi & Saatchi's EMEA operations for a reinvented remit as deputy chairman. I have been much happier ever since.

For me it is not about being free from accountability. Cs like accountability but there are degrees of it. There are Cs – I am one of them – who make the wheels turn, who have decision-making accountability and who carry the stresses and the strains that go with that. There are also Cs who make things happen but who have far less accountability. They are still important but their ability to operate is different, as are their motivations.

Each C needs to know where they stand on this: are you a C with accountability for specific outcomes or are you a cigar-smoking C asked for your counsel with no need to defend your advice or decisions at all? Are you carrying the can or carrying the bags? In Chapter 5 we will meet some bag-carriers who take their leadership contribution so seriously that they become the competitive advantage for their A and, in some cases, become the A.

In his TED talk (www.ted.com/talks/derek_sivers_how_to_start_a_movement.html), Derek Sivers shows a clip of how to start a movement from start to finish. The talk lasts three minutes. Among his conclusions is that it takes a first follower, the first one to have the courage to follow, 'to transform a lone nut into a leader'. Subsequent followers in the movement follow the followers, not the original instigator, the leader. Not bad from an A best known for being the founder and former president of CD Baby, the online CD store for independent musicians. If you believe in your A, if you can influence how that leader perceives and deals with challenges, then the chance to be the first follower is a powerful motivating force. You encourage the rest to get behind the best.

When assessing the decision to accept Tony Blair's offer to become his press secretary, Alastair Campbell recalls stiff opposition from his partner Fiona, his parents, his friends and those inside the political bubble at the time, including Neil Kinnock who was 'violently against it'. Campbell told me how he justified his decision to himself:

> Although I was going to be helping someone who was 'the leader' I saw it very much as kind of a leadership thing … So even though I knew I was to some extent subsuming my ambition, at the same time I felt it was an act of leadership. And I felt instinctively that Tony was going to need a lot of support.

Campbell still took a month to think about Tony Blair's offer to join him. Why? 'I have quite a big ego, I don't mean in a bad way, but I do have quite a big ego and I had to ask myself, would I be able to subsume myself to somebody else?' Campbell was already well on his way to being a consistently high-achieving A in the media world before he was tempted away by New Labour. Although he did not think he could do Blair's job – well, not really – he knew perfectly well that other A jobs, including the political editor roles he had already performed at both the *Daily Mirror* and *Today*, were well within his capability. In the end Campbell only took the job when he heard Blair declare:

'I'm not hiring you as a press guy, I'm hiring you as part of the absolute core strategy team.' So, in addition to Blair, John Prescott, Gordon Brown, Robin Cook – they were seen as the

Big Four at the time – Tony said, 'Basically in my mind there is a Big Five and you're part of that team.'

All of them would be integral to Blair's leadership.

Bruno Demichelis spotted Fabio Capello's potential to make it as a coach and facilitated his sabbatical to learn problem-solving, decision-making, interpersonal communication and motivation. When I asked Big Bruno to describe the characteristics of his job supporting football coaches he chose the words 'visionary, pioneering, challenging, curious, resilient'. These all sound like textbook qualities of a leader, 'That's because I *am* a leader. A leader of thought and ideas,' explains Demichelis. The Brunos and the Campbells of this world do not take the C role and feel that a part of them has died, that they have ceded ambition, that they do not have what it takes to be an A. Their motivations are to influence, contribute and to share the leadership endeavour – to win.

The Mind Room at the Milanello is the training facility of Italian football club AC Milan, and the brainchild of Big Bruno. An equivalent was installed by Roman Abramovich when Bruno moved to Chelsea FC with Carlo Ancelotti in 2009. In the Mind Room Bruno trained his players to reach a meditative state, where they could watch replays of their mistakes with their heart rates remaining constant. The year before Bruno arrived, John Terry, when taking a penalty, had slipped on his backside on a rainy Moscow night to gift rivals Manchester United the Champions League crown. All such trauma had been overcome within a year of the Mind Room opening, with Chelsea lifting the Premier League trophy and the FA Cup.

For others like David Nussbaum, former chief executive of Transparency International and currently chief executive of World Wildlife Fund UK, it's about having a seat at the table:

If there is a table with the people around it making the decisions I want to be at it. I don't have to be at the head of the table but I want to be at the table, I don't want to be outside the room waiting to hear or be called into a presentation and then out again. I want to be part of the decision-making group at the point the decisions are being made.

Big Bruno does not want to be an A in football management because it is not where he would be most useful to the leadership endeavour. Given his breadth of knowledge, his years of experience and his close observations working with some of the great footballing coaches in Europe, has it *never* crossed his mind to become the A for a football team? 'I don't understand football. It's as simple as that ... I think that I attended 15,000 hours of training of the soccer players and maybe, I don't know, I watched about 2,000 games and I attended I don't know how many thousand technical meetings from all coaches, Sacchi, Capello, Ancelotti, and I still don't understand.'

Lateral leadership has much more appeal to Big Bruno than linear supremacy. The most important consideration for Bruno and Campbell was to be true to themselves and their principles. They didn't lack the ambition or courage to have a go at the leadership role. They made an active and positive choice. So should the rest of us, wherever the leadership and its shared activity is taking place within our organisation.

## Selfless power

The C role can give us autonomy and freedom to act, which good Cs crave just as much as their As. We dislike micro-managers. In Disney's version of *Peter Pan*, the Lost Boys follow their leader, John, and 'won't be home till morning because he told us so'. One wonders whether John asked for any advice before he issued his directive. Very few Cs I interviewed have a desire to subordinate themselves like a lost boy. Rather, they, too, have a grand vision and seek an A who will implement it. If that sounds like C to A leadership, it is. Some Cs have said that, as soon as your A is not ready to entertain or implement your will over time, you must call time on him.

Shocking though it may seem, power is not the exclusive preserve of the A, either. From Richelieu to Rasputin, Machiavelli to Mandelson, and Cromwell (Thomas) to Campbell (Alastair), there are many examples of Cs who have practised Joseph Nye's concept of soft power, the ability to influence the behaviour of others to get the outcomes you want – not always for the greater good. Nye, University Distinguished Service Professor at Harvard and former assistant secretary of defence under the Clinton administration, suggested that smart power was a combination of soft (co-option) and hard (coercion). I think there is another important combination within C power: selfless power and selfish power.

Soldiering, with hard power at one's disposal, is as selfless as it gets, literally putting one's life on the line for others. Of course, soldiers are skilled at exercising soft power too. Cs constantly testify to the enormous, usually private, pleasure of exercising soft power selflessly, facilitating others, helping them to find their voice, collaborate, problem-solve, and to produce their best performances. The C's ambition is housed in realising the potential of others: my achievement is your achievement. My success is your success. Here at your service are my abilities, influence and the authority I have earned. Of course, because your success and pleasure are also mine, there is a selfish strain to it; but the C's contribution to As and others, often made without recognition of any kind, is as selfless as it gets in leadership. Big Bruno puts it like this:

When I see that someone really achieves what he deep down wanted to achieve, and sometimes he didn't even know what he wanted to achieve – if I can help someone to get in touch with his deepest talent, his deepest motivation, his deepest ambition and help him realise it and fulfil it – and see someone happy because of that – then of course that makes me happy.

Some have compared Sir Dave Brailsford's coaching greatness to that of Sir Alex Ferguson and Vince Lombardi. Architect of the transformation of British cycling – now the most successful Olympic team ever – and mastermind behind the first British victories in the Tour de France, with Sir Bradley Wiggins and Chris Froome both wearers of the yellow jersey, Brailsford has no desire for recognition, or to be credited for others' excellence. He has used all the power he has accrued and, selflessly, put it on the line to get his cyclists to victory: 'My approach is as an orchestra conductor, with an absolute recognition that the most important people in our world are the people who win and they're the riders.'

Author Maya Angelou has worked with some exceptional political leaders from Martin Luther King, Jr and Malcolm X to Bill Clinton and Barack Obama. In a podcast on courage and creativity for the *Harvard Business Review* in 2013, she said of leadership: 'A leader sees greatness in other people. He nor she can be much of a leader if all she sees is herself.' I can agree with this, having worked for six years with Jane Kendall, worldwide director of strategy and innovation at Saatchi & Saatchi. She sees greatness in others. A more selfless C it would be difficult to find in any organisation. Kendall has the Henry Ford secret of success: the ability to get the other person's point of view and see things from that person's angle as well as from your own.

What first opened Jane Kendall's eyes to the value of walking in the shoes of others was a stint in the legal world of Washington D.C. She would, sometimes inconveniently, find herself developing more sympathy for the other party's point of view than the party she was representing. Her natural empathy for people with different perspectives was put to better use in the world of public health, where she signed up to work in rural refugee camps. She realised that in health, as in anything where the end goal is behaviour change, the ability to see the world through many people's eyes, to mediate situations and understand what drives people's behaviour, is at the heart of the process.

Kendall particularly loved to see her work have a multiplier effect, evidenced on her campaigns to promote the use of condoms in HIV/AIDS prevention:

How do you make the information you are presenting something that people want to hear instead of something depressing that they would rather ignore? When you get it right, as one person avoids illness or their child avoids illness, the net benefit for the family is massive. And if the family sees that it works, the likelihood is they'll pass it on to others. You feel the enormity of the multiplier effect and knowing that is as good as it gets.

Those who use power selflessly are energised by its impact on others. Through her personality, inclination and singular ability to coax reticent contributors to air an idea or raise a concern, Kendall has extraordinary power. I have only ever seen it used authentically and selflessly. She gets a particular pleasure from her C role:

Certainly I get pleasure from the positive outcome but it's also more that people feel that they have legitimately contributed to something and been able to have some influence over it. Too often it's the handful of the loudest and the brashest people that get to have the point of view that mattered. The pleasure is in helping many more know that their point of view actually mattered and that they had some kind of impact.

In the teaching work we do together, Kendall's talent is to encourage people to show courteous intolerance of those loudly declaring they have got the answer, to spot a better answer coming from the quietest person in the room, or from the team that has been struggling the most. It is often from these sources that the winning idea emerges. By advancing the learning, confidence and ambition of others, the C can use her power selflessly and to great effect. That is tougher to do as an A leader because the agenda of the organisation usually has the A putting her heart into the overall enterprise, ahead of the people that make it happen. The A cannot feel quite such a deep sense of satisfaction in seeing others succeed. When I met Big Bruno his first question to me was, 'How are you?' When I replied 'good' his second followed, 'So how can I make you better?' And he did, by challenging some of my assumptions, shaping my thinking and provoking new lines of inquiry.

That the pursuit and use of power is often known as selfish is in part attributable to its abuse. We will see in Chapter 6 that soft power, selfishly exercised, can produce snakes. Even at its most innocent the C's interest in power is not entirely pure in motive. Among other personal perks, Cs enjoy a status and influence within the organisation. PAs regularly get referred pain from their As, so they should be allowed to enjoy the aura of association. Selfish it may be, but they are entitled to any pleasure they can squeeze from their proximity to power. A PA may enjoy the buzz of being as close to the seat of power as you can get without being royalty – although my PA Annie McIsaac was known as Queen Anne for good reason. Most had rightly concluded that the Publicis UK throne room belonged to her.

Ira Dubinsky lent his talent to the late Jack Layton, at the time leader of the Democratic Party of Canada. Layton became leader in 2004 and Dubinsky joined his office in 2005, initially as a junior assistant and from 2007, for two years, as his executive assistant. Dubinsky ran Layton's office and was sometimes with him for twenty hours a day, often going over to his house to have breakfast with him and his family before shuttling along to the airport with his boss. Though the feeling would wear off, Dubinsky describes how it initially felt to be Layton's man:

> At first, I loved to tell people my title and I loved to tell people my job. Jack was obviously a very well-known personality. I loved being the guy who was with him when he got spotted at the airport. In Canada, the opposition leaders, ten years ago, didn't actually have any security, so once we had an election I was really the only guy looking after him. It felt like I was his Secret Service guy.

Even if the status is a guilty pleasure, the A needs his C to look important. How else will he be able to achieve all that he needs to in the A's service? When the leader declares to those assembled, 'I've brought my No. 2 with me,' the No. 2 looks just that little bit taller. It is not an illusion. Vicarious power is good for the posture, that extra inch disproportionately pleasing. Smart As throw their Cs a crumb of cachet, a soupçon of prestige. With proximity to power comes access routinely denied to others. You can circumvent the switch-board certainly. In a sense you can become the switchboard, as Alastair Campbell explains:

> I did have direct access, in that, if it was a Sunday and I phoned the switchboard and said, 'Can I speak to the Prime Minister?' they knew that they didn't have to ask him, they'd put me through. There weren't many people on that list. Jonathan [Powell] would have been on it, obviously, Anji [Hunter], Sally [Morgan], too. But I think even for most senior ministers, they weren't. They would have come through me.

Jonathan Powell served as the first Downing Street chief of staff, under Tony Blair throughout his premiership (1997–2007). What was his motivation? In *Blair: The Biography*, Anthony Seldon paints a picture of intense proximity to power:

> Powell became the person Blair saw first thing in the morning and with whom he could talk about work regularly through-out the day. He liaised closely with Kate Garvey, the diary secretary, and became the figure who decided which people and what paperwork Blair saw, monitoring closely the flow of information through the Prime Minister's boxes … Whitehall quickly learned that if they wanted Blair to see someone, or something, they should first contact Powell.

In his own account of wielding power as Blair's chief of staff, Powell says this:

I was a point of contact for ministers and civil servants and of course the staff of Number 10 when they needed a decision taken rapidly. I got to know when I could safely speak on the prime minister's behalf and when I needed to nobble him as he came out of the den [his private office] between meetings and get an instant decision from him, or when I should hold off for a proper discussion later.

Leo McGarry, President Bartlet's Chief of Staff in *The West Wing*, with an office adjacent to the Oval Office, and always with the president in the Situation Room, is often described as the man who 'runs the country'. Your name gets plenty of coverage when you develop this kind of power, when people realise that you are the one with the ear, the one who can make access possible.

With proximity to power also comes influence. Karim Chaiblaine, having worked in operational A positions for Thales Group, Faurecia and SNCF Group, was tapped on the shoulder by Jean-Pierre Farandou and asked to become his senior adviser for strategy & international development at Keolis, a C role Chaiblaine performed for over two years before returning to an A role to establish Keolis operations across the Middle East. Chaiblaine, from humble origins, describes himself as 'an Algerian in France and a Frenchman in Algiers'. He is a street fighter who helped form the Algerian ice hockey team and played for it until 2011. His approach to influencing Farandou was inspired by the maxim of his Canadian ice hockey hero, Wayne Gretzky: 'Skate to where the puck is going, not to where it was.' It was Chaiblaine's reading of how the game might play out that gave him influence with Farandou, who liked him for being clever, analytical and 'synthétique', for synthesising options from a sea of information:

You need people to classify information, to make it easier for you, so they have to do the analysis for you and to cover all the aspects of an issue – social, human, cultural, historical, economical … Then when the information is there, you can ask them what are the important things? What is the problem to be solved? And so on. So they help you in the process, gather information, classify information, help you to express the questions, even help you to reframe the problem.

Farandou stresses that a C's influence can stretch too far, however:

I want to keep my freedom and be independent in my decision-making so … if I can speak of some big guys I've seen, the danger is that there can be two or three people in the shadow around the CEO, or the chairman, and you see, wow, these guys have too much influence. For example you have a disagreement with your boss and ask yourself why. And you realise it's because he has been influenced by some people. You can't catch them. They're in the shadow. So you have this feeling, 'I tried to convince my boss and I can't succeed because his mind has been influenced by some people.'

Farandou cites Patrick Buisson, the man who guided former French president Nicolas Sarkozy to victory in 2007, and to defeat in 2012, as a man too much motivated by the need for influence. Buisson's nicknames have included 'The Shadow Strategist', 'Sarkozy's Oracle' and 'Sarkozy's Right Frontal Lobe'.

Chaiblaine simply wanted to have a positive influence on strategy and international development, never straying beyond the boundaries clearly defined by his A. He is used to playing as a natural centre on the ice and as an A in business but, he says, his two-year stint in a more defensive C role at Keolis – 'an offensive defence player' – allowed him to see and influence the business differently: 'You get a completely different view of the business and people have a completely different view of you, too.'

Proximity, access and influence all feed the C's ability to make a difference in the wider organisation. Carrying the bags for the chief executive and juggling their diary gives you the opportunity to meet almost every leader in the firm. Pick up the phone and you can make things happen. That kind of extensive, informal network and intensive, intimate contact with people across the organisation and beyond will open doors for you. You want to give one of your team some experience in South East Asia? Instead of negotiating with HR, call Mr Malaysia and make it happen. You can mix it with the big boys, not just the big boss.

The feeling of indispensability can be a bit of an addiction, a galvanising motivation for the C. It is also irrational. Bosses, organisations, electorates are fickle. We all know that we are fundamentally dispensable, yet we love to wonder, 'where would my leader be without me?' Cs have spent many a soothing hour fantasising about the creeks his A would be up, the paddles they would be missing, the lions' dens they'd be in, and the hells to which they would be rapidly descending. The C gets his kicks by being the person through whom every decision has to be made. When a crisis arises, the A rings him up. According to Alastair Campbell, Tony Blair occasionally dispensed the drug of indispensability: 'I remember him saying that if you and Anji left me I'd be in real shit ... We both did leave him eventually, although we never properly left, and he would still phone us up if there was an issue.' It's not always an entirely pleasant dependency and, as with most kicks, there are side effects, as Campbell reflects:

> The fact is, that feeling of indispensability, it did feel real. But it also felt like a real burden. I can remember once we were on holiday with the Kinnocks – this was when I was starting to get really fed up – and I said, 'I can't do this for much longer' and he said. 'Listen, you can't leave – you can't leave.' Bruce Grocott (later Lord Grocott, parliamentary private secretary to Tony Blair 1994–2001) used to say to me all the time, 'If you leave this place, it falls apart.' Now it's quite flattering on one level but I did feel it as a burden.

Still, in the words of Margaret Thatcher, describing her dependence on Lord Whitelaw, 'Everyone needs a Willie' and, for the most part, it feels good to be the Willie that's needed.

There are two more worthy and powerful incentives to lead from the C. First, the chance to develop an intimate relationship with an A that you have real affection for. Cs really do like to be close. Just how close should be explored between A and C (with the guidance of Chapters 6 and 7). An open and honest connection with your A, through which ideas may flow easily, will teach you invaluable lessons. The connection must be two-way. For the C to be an effective counsellor, for their advice to be heeded and acted upon, a degree of mutual affection is essential.

Second, and for some the most joyous C motivation of all, is the opportunity, indeed the requirement, for learning through new experience. Take Jonathan Brown, a trained oil well engineer and a natural A leader. Is accountability a burden to him? Does Brown worry that it falls to him to certify to the regulatory authorities that his organisation is doing all it should to operate safely? His is the judgement that allows projects to proceed with risk, both physical and financial, as progress demands. Brown loves it. He is a born A. What on earth, then, induced him to give up oil wells for oiling wheels in 2012, when he took on the role of executive project management officer, supporting the president of Canada's Talisman Energy Inc.? He certainly wasn't fooled by the title: 'PMO sounded good, but it was just a posh way to say I'd be carrying the bags.' John Manzoni, the charismatic president of Talisman, whose bags Brown would be carrying, apologised to Brown ahead of time, warning him that the job would be really stressful and that he might find him tough to work for. Brown was unconvinced:

> I said, 'Look, the worst that can happen to me in any given day is that you will be upset with me because I didn't dot the I's or cross the T's. No one is going to die as a consequence of anything I do in the next twelve months so, relative to my previous roles, it's a relaxed place to be for me.' It transpired that I had no accountability other than to make sure that the meetings started on time and that the muffins were fresh.

Even without the kind of accountability on which Brown thrives, he returned to the frontline a better A leader for the C experience, which he confessed often extended beyond muffins and meetings.

## Lifelong learning

One of the biggest challenges for leaders, even in small to medium-sized organisations whose operations are complex, is understanding how the organisation actually functions. As leaders advance in their careers they are often promoted within their existing specialist function or discipline, meaning they lack the broader understanding that comes from a firm-wide role. Brown's stint as a PMO gave him 'an invaluable map in my head of the way the firm really ticks over', an ability to place things in context, and an opportunity, as his CEO moved around the business, to develop a network within the organisation that would enhance his effectiveness in his next A role in the business. The learning from the C experience motivated even this hard-wired A.

Typically As have a lot less time to learn beyond the job than Cs. The Cs that I have met have been voracious readers, dedicated students, obsessive observers, all keen to stay alert, enhance their expertise, challenge their thinking, improve themselves. Becoming a C is an opportunity to learn new skills too: how to make things happen without any overt power; how to negotiate, among a diverse group of hotheads, a unified recommendation for the A; how to manage the fall-out from an unpopular decision, and smooth the way for its flawless execution.

Take just one of the many C roles potentially available, the chiefs of staff, or 'turtles' as they are known at BP. Lord Browne, then head of exploration and production at BP, instigated a career development initiative to fast-track bright young things. The chosen few acquired the sobriquet 'turtles' because the Teenage Mutant Ninja Turtles are all about making things happen. One wonders how much of their job at BP involved battling petty criminals, evil overlords and alien invaders. Jonathan Brown, our oil well engineer, saw Lord Browne's turtles in action when he was at BP:

> The downside, typically, is that you might only shadow, work for, and observe one chief executive, so you only get one data point … The upside is that being a Turtle demands that you

have access to the wider organisation which in turn means you learn to see the wider context, and then to see the world through the eyes of many less familiar to you.

If you want to be effective in a firm, and aspire to taking on more leadership responsibility, being a C is an opportunity to get your head around a complex organisation. Working next to the chief executive and seeing what they see deepens your appreciation of the whole, and demystifies some of the often self-imposed constraints on your modus operandi. On re-entry to a role with more accountability, you will be armed with a fresher perspective on the context in which your organisation operates, and equipped with a mental map to help you navigate it.

Cs need to continually challenge themselves if they are to be the best leaders they can be. New experiences are grist for the mill. When he is in Spain, José María Nus regularly meets three of his closest friends from the banking industry. During his twenties and thirties, his love of learning, insatiable appetite for analysis and enthusiasm for new experiences prompted his three amigos to nickname him 'El Professor'. Later they redubbed him 'Il Consigliere', though his love of learning and capacity for analysis has remained undimmed. Ana Botín, Santander UK's A, values Nus' appetite for complexity:

> I trust Jose María's judgement. He's honest and straightforward. Actually all of my team are. So he will say exactly what he is thinking. Also he has all the wisdom, so for certain key strategic things I think Jose María has huge experience. He understands very well how the business works, understands people and understands the difficulties and the complexities of the world. And then he sees the key things that we should be looking at.

David Gill, former chief executive of Manchester United and a voracious learner himself, explains why learning is particularly important to those supporting A leaders:

> It's a competitive world out there so if you're not improving your skills, doing qualifications, learning on the job, other people will be. I went out and got the skills to be the FD at Manchester United and when I was the FD, at the same time as doing a great FD job, I was looking to do other things to get the skills to be the CEO if it ever came up, and it did. You've got to have that desire to learn all the time.

If your boss is learning and you are not you are soon going to be left behind or out on your ear. Cs are dynamic learners, allergic to stasis of any kind. *The Economist* understood this perfectly when it ran the advertisement: 'If your assistant reads *The Economist*, don't play too much golf.' While the C may not want to take over from the A, she can grow with him and move on and up with him. Gill's secretary, Jackie, learned how to become a top-flight PA on his watch. Gill describes her as a 'good confidante; she was bright; she knew the mood of the staff; she always knew what was happening.' While Gill was growing in the CEO role, so was Jackie. Now that Gill has left Manchester United Jackie is working directly for David Moyes, the manager who succeeded Sir Alex Ferguson. Learning earned her that promotion.

I hope that the motivations that have magnetised most of my interviewees to their C suite will serve as a seductive force to many more. To attract, retain and galvanise C leaders we need to take a closer look at the qualities that make them.

# 4

# WHAT MAKES A C?

If you have made it this far the likelihood is you are seriously considering the consigliere role as a platform from which to stretch your leadership muscles. So, what makes a great C? In part, the answer is a great A. The strong C preying on the weak A for some mischievous advantage makes for good television but lousy leadership and, more often than not, an unhappy ending for both parties. Better in the real world for Cs to embrace the motivational forces explored in Chapter 3, to cast themselves alongside a strong A and work to strengthen that A.

Harry Hopkins had a unique position in the US government, responsible only to Franklin D. Roosevelt. A *Time* magazine piece on Hopkins in 1945 described him as 'a secretary, expediter, administrator, errand boy, good listener, executive, idea man, boon companion, and alter ego'. The article cited Raymond Clapper, one of the most influential reporters in Washington, and a keen observer of FDR:

> When government is fluid and dominated by the executive branch, [power] goes to the men who have the force to win it – the boldness, the resourcefulness and the sure judgment that command confidence ... Like his boss, Harry Hopkins has boldness and resourcefulness in high degree. His admirers think his judgment is not only uncannily swift, but uncannily sure to fit what the president is thinking.

In my time as an A – as a team leader and, later, as a CEO – I have been blessed with some bold, resourceful Cs, most of whom had been or went on to be great As: Anthony Simonds-Gooding provided wisdom on tap; Adam Morgan, founder of challenger brand company, eatbigfish, taught me how to think collaboratively and shared his ideas with an invitation to help improve them (usually impossible); Paul Edwards, my planning partner at Still Price Lintas and then at the Henley Centre (he later became its A), could go from problem to multiple solutions faster than a sports cars goes from 0–60; Gerry Moira, my creative partner at Publicis, used his wit and imagination to push, challenge and sharpen our competitive edge; Erika Darmstaedter, whose A role as CEO of Saatchi & Saatchi Switzerland I asked her to give up to become COO of Saatchi & Saatchi EMEA, had a capacity to grip operational problems and fix them dispassionately. Fixers can be reviled, Erika was revered. Jane Kendall, more philosopher than fixer, and C to me in my current job, has a thirst for learning that keeps her at the sharp edge of academic and cultural ideas.

In this shortlist of top Cs with whom I have collaborated, as well as in the many Cs I have interviewed, I have identified four things that the ideal C should be: content, constant, catalytic and courageous.

## CONTENT

Have you ever heard a leader say, 'Job done. Well done. I shall now put my feet up'? I have never heard that A. Not much more than a few centuries separate the ancient Aeneas from the modern A. While epic heroes are on teleological journeys towards ends decreed by the fates, today's A journeys are decreed by the market, the media and the masses.

Mythological heroes are driven by devotion to the gods and patriotism. We forgive Aeneas' sudden departure from his beloved Dido – 'No time to think, darling, I have a nation to establish.' In a similar vein the modern A has an organisation to champion, a destiny to fulfil, and little time to philosophise about what's best for him.

David McClelland, in *Power: the Inner Experience*, adapts Erik Erikson's Freud-inspired stages of ego-development to create four discrete power orientations. In Stage 1, 'It strengthens me', that is, power comes from someone else; in Stage 2, 'I strengthen myself'; in Stage 3, 'I have impact on others'; and in Stage 4, I am 'moved to do my duty', a stage in which 'the self drops out as a source of power and a person sees himself as an instrument of a higher authority which moves him to try to influence or serve others.' Contentment, I suggest, increases as one moves through the stages from 1 to 4. According to McClelland, even modern leaders are capable of reaching Stage 4, serving something beyond themselves, somehow the subject of power as well as its agent. The question becomes, then, which kind of leadership role is most likely to provide the Stage 4 opportunity, A or C?

Like Aeneas, the As begin their sprint without looking back. There is always somewhere else the A is heading: the next decision, the next promotion, The House of Lords. The constant need to justify why they are the supreme leader takes priority over temporary or lasting contentment. As we saw in Chapter 2, whether you are Sir Alex Ferguson or Arsène Wenger you are, like the Greek mortal Tantalus, destined to spend eternity in a pool of water with fruit branches overhead too high to be reached and bitten into. The A must live and thrive in a state of perpetual discontentment.

The C, on the other hand, needs to be content if they are to be a sympathetic promoter and guardian of the cause. To do their job contentedly, to be a source of power for others, the C must contemplate, cede and then contribute. Unfortunately for them only one of these activities can be accomplished with their feet up.

## Contemplate

What do I want at this point in my life? What am I aspiring to be? How might my work contribute to my personal goals? Am I prepared to reduce my expectations, and accept my limitations? Do I have limitations? Using myself as an example, I want my children to be more successful than I have been, so of course I accept that I have some limitations. Limitations compared to my peers? Ah, that's more difficult. Acknowledging that some things are beyond us can be quietly satisfying. Even Alastair Campbell's serial ambition had its boundaries:

> Ultimately the big calls were being made by Clinton and Tony and Chirac. I always felt that I had that sort of leadership instinct but I didn't conclude I could do it, other than regularly watching [David] Cameron, and occasionally watching Tony, very occasionally. Funnily enough, with Gordon I always thought, 'No I couldn't do it.' I always looked at Gordon's job when he was chancellor, and thought 'I couldn't do that, just couldn't do it.' I could sit down with him and absorb his strategy and find ways of explaining probably better than he was explaining, I could do all of that. But in terms of doing it, phew, couldn't do it.

Where do you stand when you contemplate what you can offer and what you want? Perhaps you do fancy a crack at the top job, in which case continue on that trajectory, embrace the mentoring, accelerate the learning, and bide your time until you are tapped on the shoulder. Or maybe the life of an A seems disagreeable. It's not about being averse to account-ability – you probably shoulder a lot at the moment – but you think that final accountability might be overwhelming. Perhaps, knowing how heavily decisions weigh on your mind, you prefer the currency of influence and a career as a consigliere makes most sense to you, professionally and personally. Professionally, I find it rewarding to help other people land their best ideas. Personally, I like my football, books and family. I choose the more knowable, less frantic C position.

If you have the qualities that we will explore in this chapter, then there is deep contentment to be felt, every day, in confi-dently and proficiently leading from the C. This contentment grows from a greater certainty, a kind of stillness that eludes most As.

## Cede

Stillness requires sacrifice. In some cases, like in Mario Puzo's *The Godfather*, the decision to give up the ambition to be the A is made for you. As Puzo writes: 'Being of Irish descent and knowing what other Sicilian families thought about that had taught Tom Hagan he could never hope to succeed the Don as the head of the Family business. But he was content. That had never been his goal. Such an ambition would have been a "disrespect" to his benefactor and his benefactor's blood family.'

To be a great C one must cede cash, status beyond a subtle association with the A, recognition, ultimate control and, at least temporarily, the ambition to be A. Carlo Sant'Albano is clear on the latter: 'I think the person who is a very good adviser to a very talented owner or boss knows deep down that he could almost certainly do that job. So mentally he has to make a decision to accept being a No. 2, knowing that he has ... the capabilities to be the No. 1.'

If you are a natural A revving up to test yourself in the toughest conditions then parking your ambition, even for a time of known duration, will represent a challenge. Look at the circle of Cs surrounding the Beatles, from Dick James to Derek Taylor, and from Brian Epstein to George Martin. Neil Aspinall, the roadie who safeguarded the band's legacy (and went on to run Apple Inc.) was happy, at that time, to do what was best for his A-list stars. Other people scarcely knew he existed.

I remember once visiting Saatchi & Saatchi's worldwide chairman, Bob Seelert. I wanted Bob's assessment of my time as the A of our EMEA operations and to explore the implications of my decision to take on the C role that Kevin Roberts and I had designed. Bob's book, *Start with the Answer*, draws on his years as a turnaround chief executive. He gave me his answer: 'You will earn less money.'

Fair enough. Cs are immensely valuable, but As deserve rewards commensurate with their greater accountability. Most Cs can't prove their creative worth anyway because they are in the business of making the best ideas the A's ideas. An idea only becomes indisputably theirs when things go badly wrong: 'No need for a DNA test to settle the parentage of that one, C: it was yours.'

Senior Cs do enjoy status either directly or by association, but begrudging the A his top billing is the madness of a malcontent, visible in Mohammed Hanif's novel *A Case of Exploding Mangoes*: 'The title of "second most powerful man in the land", which he had enjoyed in the beginning, had started to sound like an insult. How could you be the second most powerful when your boss was the **all**-powerful?'

Many residents of No. 11 Downing Street have been happy initially, only later to feel burning resentment towards their more powerful neighbour. You can give up on contentment if you prize power that much. Leave the glitzy kennel and shiny name tag to the top dog and cede your status gracefully. Ralph Waldo Emerson wrote, 'A great man is always willing to be little.' There is a difference between willing to be little and being little. Lisa Carver in the *New York Times* noticed another contender to the fifth Beatle crown who had the inner strength to stay small:

> It takes an enormous lack of ego to *not* put your imprint on everything you do, to *not* employ your learning and position. To stand back, to hold back, to keep your mouth shut. To yell with your silence, when you know you very well could make soothing and welcomed sounds at the drop of a hat. Yoko Ono could sing; she knows how. And being a Beatles wife could have been a magic charm – but she wasn't interested. It takes willpower to overpower the will to power.

It takes self-control to kick the craving for recognition. Even when kids at Disneyland show a preference for Pluto or Donald Duck, these characters know that there is only one Mickey on Main Street. It is the C's job to protect the conspiracy of exclusivity, to make the A look as good as possible. Tim Cook may be the A in Apple now but until the death of Steve Jobs he was a talented C. As Regis McKenna, a communications adviser to Apple in its early days, observed in the *Financial Times*: 'Tim made Steve look good, quite frankly, and he's happy with that. He doesn't have a huge ego that has to be in the forefront.' Jonathan Powell agrees: 'It helps for the chief of staff not to have a huge, or very obvious, ego – it gets in the way – nor to crave the limelight.'

Any C who consciously sucks oxygen away from their A is doing their organisation a disservice and may be heading for a beheading. The need for recognition is not a sin. A or C, we're all at it. We adore the appreciation and revel in the recognition. It is a variable but universal craving, one that the C needs to keep in check.

First, psychological studies, including those by Thomas Joiner Jr and Gerald Metalsky, demonstrated that goals tied to others' approval, such as fame, involve higher levels of stress than those concerned primarily with self-acceptance, suggesting that excessive reassurance-seeking is a risk factor in the development of depressive symptoms. Second, credit-craving reveals weakness. Sue Erikson Bloland, daughter of the renowned psychoanalyst Erik Erikson, wrote of her father in her memoirs, *In the Shadow of Fame*: 'His pursuit of reassurance was not simply the charming humility it was generally interpreted to be. It expressed a persistent and tormenting self-doubt.'

Third, your work as a C diminishes in value the more it is acknowledged. Saying 'I did that' damages your usefulness to those you did it for. This can be rather difficult to accept for people in the creative industries, where credit is more often hoovered than claimed – 'I told him to do that,' 'You should have seen what he was going to do before I got involved,' 'I gave him that idea two years ago' – every last speck of kudos is diligently sucked up.

Paul Scholes, one of Manchester United's greatest midfielders, was described by Zinedine Zidane, himself no slouch, as the 'complete footballer'. Despite some unforgettable

goals, Scholes the fiery Red is remembered for his complete-
ness: protecting his defence, providing ideas and cover for
his fellow midfielders, and producing opportunities for his
wingers and strikers. Even when, unnoticed, he did pop up
to score with a spectacular shot, he blushed profusely when
bathed in adulation for it. Recognition positively embarrassed
Scholes. He preferred quietly to contribute 90 minutes of
blood, sweat and opportunities for others. Harry S. Truman
had it right: 'It is amazing what you can accomplish if you do
not care who gets the credit.'

Truman never saw Scholes play for United, but he had
probably read his Shakespeare. King Lear was a man so
desperate for credit that he gave his realm away to the two
of his three daughters who flattered him best. Kent, a deputy
banished by Lear for giving sound advice, represents the
antithesis of a credit-seeker. Unwilling to break his oath of
service, Kent dresses up as a peasant and comes back from
exile to continue advising his master. When Cordelia, the
daughter who had refused to flatter Lear, is found by Kent
she expresses pain that his labours will go unrecognised and
unrewarded. Kent distances himself from the economies of
praise, recompense and recognition:

> To be acknowledged madam, is o'erpaid.
> All my reports go with the modest truth;
> Nor more nor clipped, but so.
>
> (William Shakespeare, *King Lear*, Act IV, Scene vii)

Kent is a career C with no inclination to step outside the
role of deputy and subject. When asked to take up the leadership of England by Albany, Kent insists on serving another
master, this time nature, and asks for permission to do so:

I have a journey, sir, shortly to go.

My master calls me, I must not say no.

(King Lear, Act V, Scene iii)

Bertrand Russell, philosopher, was another who would not have admired the unseemly goal celebrations of today's leaders: 'My whole religion is this: do every duty, and expect no reward for it, either here or hereafter.'

Absent the credit of others, you still can – and should – take the time to celebrate in private your significant contributions to the cause. To be able to know, choose and use the most appropriate outlet for your talent is something to feel good about. Raise a glass to Horace and let others answer his question, 'How does it happen ... that no one is content with that lot of which he has chosen ... but praises those who follow a different course?'

Contented consiglieri cede more than cash, status and recognition. They cede control, too. The As typically love to keep their hands on what they think are the wheels of control. Cs leave them to it or, better, gently remind them that complete control is an illusion. We will look in the next chapter at the playwright Molière's *raisonneur* characters, who demonstrate to their *imaginaire* protagonists that in a world where accurate prediction of outcomes or control of others is impossible, we have to be careful not to feel too in charge. This acceptance of external non-control is itself a form of control, of the self and of what academic Alex Eisenthal described to me as, 'the boundless capacity of imagination, vanity and delusion, the threefold follies of all Molière's comic protagonists.'

Knowing and deciding when to step in or to stay clear is crucial. If Cs cannot leave the ring, if their happiness is forever tied to controlling what they think is the right outcome, they will never find contentment. I used to take all seven hours of a transatlantic flight to Saatchi & Saatchi executive committee meetings to prepare my papers for the following day. I would walk in carrying folder upon folder, ready to fight tooth and nail for the interests of the EMEA region I represented. On the slightly shorter flight home I would stew over the few decisions that had not gone my way. Considered self-criticism can be constructive but a six-hour sulk is in no one's interests.

## Contribute

Contentment in all jobs correlates with contribution. You know when you are making a positive difference. Robert Care is a member of the Global Board of Arup Group and, until his latest appointment as principal at Arup Australasia, the chair of Arup Group's UK, Middle East and Africa region. His work, mainly as designer, project manager and leader, has had a lasting impact – he was the project manager of a team that developed the control, mitigation and recovery strategy for Railtrack (UK) following the Hatfield rail crash in October 2000. Yet Care's contribution will be felt as deeply through the wisdom he has shared as the engineering work he has masterminded. He devotes a large part of his time to teaching, coaching and mentoring 'members' (Arup's word for employees in its unique partnership structure). He feels his contribution is all the more satisfying – and effective – because from a seemingly unassailable position as an A superhero, Care came crashing down to earth:

> I unashamedly talk about the period I went through when I experienced significant depression which had consequences. I think that having an opportunity to share stuff with people creates possibilities in their minds ... This is probably not cor-

rect or fair but through the difficult period I felt I had a lot of patrons and sponsors but I'm not sure I had mentors.

Care has a passion for mentorship. His eyes light up when he talks about creating those possibilities in people's minds. It is not just what he shares and when he shares it, but how he shares it – with self-deprecating yet substantial wisdom – that makes his contribution to others so effective:

> I remember a few years ago with our annual group meeting, we had this session with the board up the front and we were answering questions. The question was asked, 'What have you done that you are most proud of in the last twelve months?' There was a bit of a silence and I spoke first. I said, 'Well, look, I am just very proud of taking on a coach.' And afterwards, one of the people in the audience came up to me and said, 'Thank you so much for sharing that because it has given me permission to seek a coach whereas up until now I've thought, well, you know, it's a sign of weakness.' So, they see some big, ugly Australian standing up the front there and he's saying, 'You know, I've just taken on a coach, elite athletes have coaches, why shouldn't elite business people have coaches?' and just the fact of saying it, sharing it, had an impact.

Charles Garland's contributions to the various companies he has worked for and the satisfaction he has derived from them have changed as his leadership roles have changed. As international managing director of Bartle, Bogle, Hegarty, Garland's pleasure was the thrill of business development, helping to spread the footprint of the famous UK advertising agency into Asia and the US. As chief operating officer of Simon Fuller's XIX Entertainment, Garland enjoyed attending to the nuts and bolts of the business, enabling Fuller, his A, to play to his strengths as a creative impresario and entrepreneur. With Simon Cowell at SYCO, Garland is a self-confessed 'workman-like CEO', because he recognises that in Cowell he has the leading character. Knowing what he has in his A has allowed Garland to shape and enjoy his contribution. What, though, is the real thrill?

> There are managers of change and there are managers of the continuum. It's Simon [Cowell's] show, he's the manager of the continuum entirely. I like dealing with dynamic businesses where you've got the challenge of growth and change and the problems that come with these. And we've got some very significant challenges here, but they're stimulating to deal with. We have the challenge that we've got two kinds of behemoth assets in *Got Talent* and *X Factor*. They aren't going to last forever, so you can write the future, which is about gentle decline, hopefully not rapid decline, gentle decline in a context of television that is in gentle decline. But on the other hand, these shows produce talent, so if we were closer to talent rather than just the television show, we could have our arms around the product of our shows as opposed to just passing it over the fence to management and Sony Records.

Garland scouts ahead of the wagon train, exploring new growth opportunities, and then makes things happen. What's new? What's the next thing? Answering these questions defines his contribution to those he serves as the C and as the CEO.

Fabio Scappaticci joined the Saatchi & Saatchi worldwide strategy team in 2011 after a year and a half with OXFAM Quebec in the Democratic Republic of Congo, where he developed and managed three water and sanitation projects. Before that he had been a Bombardier Aerospace engineer, managing air safety projects for the company's business aircraft division. These experiences and his competitive personality formed his contribution as a C to our team. He was, he declared, 'allergic to bullshit'. Before Fabio left us to pursue his passion for international development, I would often hear him quoting famous mafia lines to colleagues, with the specific objective of warning them not to give his team's A – me – any bullshit, 'or there might be consequences, serious consequences'. I am sure I failed to live up to the image he was creating – 'He is a killer, I'm warning you, a killer' – but he certainly streamlined other people's contributions.

Once you have done a Contentment cycle, contemplate some more. Aristotle described contemplation as the highest form of activity. Your A might not thank you for taking too much time away from the action but as their C you require some contentment and there are no shortcuts to it. There is even less chance of a shortcut to our next vital C state.

## CONSTANT

> There is nothing which is so becoming as to maintain
> consistency in all that we do and undertake.
>
> (Cicero, *On Duty*, Book I)

People who lead from the C have a strong sense of professional and personal purpose. They demonstrate commitment to their organisation's cause, their A, and their peers and subordinates. They embrace the cause as an expression of who they are, and that is at the root of the best kind of constancy. In my work for organisations around the world, to help leadership teams align their ambitions to the people on whom they depend to deliver them, a sense of purpose is the difference between winning causes and lost causes. What is the dream? Why do you bother to do what you do? What *is* the cause and why should your people give their discretionary effort to it?

While the A is most closely associated with dreaming up the 'vision thing', and can often be heard humming the company song, the C's active embrace imbues the vision with credibility. The C is a galvaniser more than a cheerleader. Through their deeds Cs create trust in the organisation's purpose and reduce friction in its ecosystem of relationships. One symbolic act by the C can establish integrity, foster confidence and promote a movement within and without the organisation.

Robert Tansey, development director at Sky Sports, was one of the originators of Sky's partnership with the British Cycling Federation. He describes his role as chairman of Team Sky as 'largely ceremonial' at the beginning. As the team grew in success so his position became more significant, as the bridge between his A, Team Sky performance director David Brailsford, his own organisation, Sky, and the other shareholders in the team. One incident in particular demonstrates Robert's personal and spontaneous devotion to the Team Sky cause.

In September 2012 Tyler Hamilton, American cyclist and one-time Olympic gold medal winner, released a book — *The Secret Race: Inside the Hidden World of the Tour de France: Doping, Cover-ups, and Winning at All Costs* – which detailed his doping practices and experiences in the world of cycling. Hamilton was a teammate of Lance Armstrong when Armstrong won the Tour de France in 1999, 2000 and 2001. The month after the book's publication, the American anti-doping agency,

USADA, released a report damning Armstrong and others: 'The evidence shows beyond any doubt that the US Postal Service Pro Cycling Team ran the most sophisticated, professionalized and successful doping program that sport has ever seen.'

From its inception Team Sky had been committed to riding clean. Nobody working on the team could have been a doper or been involved with doping. There could be no suspicion that any of the team's input might be tainted by malpractice. Nevertheless, Tyler Hamilton's book provoked some uncertainty. Might there be somebody, not necessarily a rider, but within the broader team, implicated in the scandal? USADA published its report on a Thursday morning, just as Robert Tansey was embarking on a long holiday weekend in Venice:

The flight left at half past seven. I was flicking through some of the media reports on the phone, thinking, 'This is probably worse than even we'd thought.' Annie [Tansey's wife] had actually said to me the night before as I'd started to fret about this, 'Do you think we should be going to Venice with this storm brewing?' I think out of a sense of duty, you know, work gets in the way too much anyway, I said, 'No, it's booked, it will be fine.' Essentially I was thinking, 'I don't want to upset Annie.'

Annie tells her side of the story:

So, we got up at five in the morning, and we got to Gatwick. In the two and a half hours that it took to fly to Venice everybody had been after him. He'd also read something on his phone during the flight that had made him realise that this was a really big deal, so he was on the phone from the moment he could turn it on. I could just tell by his demeanour that this was important. We got onto the little vaporetto, and he wasn't even looking at anything. We were in Venice and he wasn't looking at anything!

We've all been there, if not in Venice then somewhere else, when work feels closer than we'd like, when the guilt of being away begins to stir in the gut. What is our response at moments like these? 'To hell with work, they'll have to take care of it,' or 'I'm so sorry darling, you carry on to the hotel, I just have to fly back to the office to sort a few things out'? Tansey was, for the most part, a symbolic chairman for Team Sky, a C to director David Brailsford. The ultimate responsibility for driving an appropriate response to the crisis lay with Brailsford and with Sky boss, Jeremy Darroch. Annie relives the story:

> He's looking much more stressed than I've ever seen him about a work thing – I rarely see him looking stressed – and I say, 'Look, do you think we should be here?' I just thought, 'You know, this is going to be no fun for me, no fun for him, it's just going to be awful.' He had just phoned somebody to say, 'Look, I feel bad about being here,' and this guy had said, 'Oh, we'll get through, it'll be fine.'

Back to Robert: 'On the vaporetto to get into the town, all I'm doing is sitting there on my phone scrolling through a host of emails and messages, and Annie said, "You know, we shouldn't be here, should we?" I said, "Actually, do you know what? I don't think we should."'

That same Thursday night a celebration of Team Sky reaching its target of inspiring a million more Britons to cycle regularly was taking place. The celebration had been in the diary for a long time. Chris Hoy and Bradley Wiggins were attending. Jeremy Darroch, Sky's CEO, was going to be there. All the major stakeholders from the world of cycling would be there. The way the diaries had fallen, Robert Tansey would not. This was known and would not have mattered had the media frenzy not caught fire. 'But now I was thinking, you know, "It's going to look very odd if, at a time of crisis, the chairman of the team, and, day-to-day the most senior representative of the team in the organisation, isn't there." So I felt a responsibility to come back, and be there.'

As they waited for the vaporetto's return trip to the airport, Tansey called his PA, Shelley, another C in his circle of support, who got him back to London as soon as possible. C to many a CEO herself, Annie was even more strident than Robert on the importance of showing conspicuous commitment to the cause:

> It was a really good decision. We were back home by 5 o'clock, he was able to go to a meeting with David Brailsford and he was able to go on to the drinks do.

So, an element of personal sacrifice, a supportive partner and sound professional judgement led Tansey to demonstrate a commitment to the cause that touched all involved, but particularly Brailsford, who said:

> At the time, we were under severe scrutiny and real pressure from the media, and it was a tough, tough situation to find ourselves in. The entire team had come in for what was to be a celebratory weekend. It was just a piss up, basically, to celebrate the Tour de France, and it got completely hijacked by these events. This was when Rob was at his best: he's a struc-

tured thinker and he's quite logical, he's got some good perspective, he doesn't overreact or panic, and he's actually very
fair, so I feel, with Robert, you can talk to Robert, you know?
He's somebody that you can sit down with, 'you know what,
Rob? I've got a bit of a bloody problem here' or 'what do you
think about this? What do you think about that?' And, he's
very, very good at that. Rob's been useful in a whole range
of areas, but I think where I've been heavily reliant on Rob
has been when we've had some real crisis, and this was one
of them. We've had some tough times. He's been very, very
good then, you know, a real level head when there's a lot of
pressure.

Several other qualities define a C's constant attitude to his
A: devoted affection, a sense of duty, tough love and parental
protection. In *The History of England*, a six-volume work of
extraordinary scope, David Hume, the eighteenth-century
philosopher and historian, extolled the great Saxon virtues:

> The warriors of each tribe attached themselves to their leader
> with the most devoted affection and most unshaken constancy.
> They attended him as his ornament in peace, as his defence in
> war, as his council in the administration of justice. Their con-
> stant emulation in military renown dissolved not that inviola-
> ble friendship which they professed to their chieftain and to
> each other: to die for the honour of their band was their chief
> ambition: to survive its disgrace, or the death of their leader,
> was infamous.

For those of us unwilling to die for them, just how much
devoted affection should we have for our As? A complete
lack of warmth endangers constancy or makes it impossible.

You should not agree to work for an A for whom you feel no affection. How otherwise will you endure the unintentional ingratitude, the occasional selfishness, the narcissistic leanings and the inevitable lapses in judgement? If you find yourself working for a foul A, before concluding that you do not like the individual, listen to Abraham Lincoln and 'get to know him better'.

On that basis, Vogue's creative director Grace Coddington must have got to know Anna Wintour intimately. *September Issue*, the behind-the-scenes documentary movie, shows Coddington fighting with her tyrannical leader over every editorial decision that matters to her. Wintour's withering looks alone are worthy of an 18 certificate and Coddington could be forgiven for not liking her A. But her commitment to Vogue's artistic cause keeps her constancy undimmed. Chief of staff Jonathan Powell, aiming to challenge some of the more formal advice given to his prime minister, would also receive unwelcome responses from his A:

> My tuppenceworth was not always gratefully received and sometimes I must have been infuriating. I would put provocative points to Tony and he would roundly insult me in return but I couldn't help noticing that he was absorbing them anyway, and sometimes the suggestions would pop up later in speeches or in his conversations with ministers.

The constant C will endure the A's unpleasantness if there is evidence over time that the cause to which they are both committed will advance.

Constancy requires some genuine sympathy for the A's suffering. Anthony Simonds-Gooding had several high-profile A roles before he became a portfolio C. He continues to act as C to OMG plc, which develops, produces and sells imaging technology, and as a C to the Rose Theatre Kingston. He is a chairman who understands what an A faces. What is needed, he says:

> ... is someone with a large dose of empathy, who says the occasional 'well done' to the lonely CEO with a thousand bucks that have come to rest on his desk; someone who doesn't assume that the CEO is superhuman; someone who sees the leader dealing with a shitty meeting and congratulates him on navigating it; someone who thinks there's more to the story than, 'You're paid a bucketload of money so just get on with it.'

If constancy springs most naturally from devoted affection, it must also at times involve a sense of duty. Friedrich Nietzsche memorably condemned duty without a cause in *The Antichrist*: 'What destroys a man more quickly than to work, think, and feel without inner necessity, without any deep personal desire, without pleasure – as a mere automaton of duty?' Alastair Campbell describes his change from a dutiful Labour Party life to a life in which he exercises a personally defined sense of duty.

> I've gone from a life of 'should'; you should help the Labour party, you should help Tony Blair, you should help Gordon Brown, you should help the government – to a life of 'want'. I'm not saying I didn't want to do it, I did want to do it, but that was a driving thing, the sense of duty and service. I still exercise a sense of duty. I still help the Labour party. I still help charities but now I feel more, 'Do I want to do that?'

How does a life of 'should' manifest itself? The C should respect the A's distinguishing qualities, and the primacy of the A's authority and decisions. It is the C's duty to legitimise the A's decisions, even if that means energising a cause not entirely agreed with. On Margaret Thatcher's death Lord Cecil Parkinson paid tribute to the support of Willie Whitelaw, which transcended disagreement on policy:

> After her election victory, she asked Willie to be her deputy and he accepted the offer. Over the next 12 years, he supported her through thick and thin. He never really shared her economic views, but he felt that she had beaten him fairly and squarely in the leadership election and was therefore entitled to his support. I have always felt that the extent of his influence on her thinking was overstated, but it would be impossible to overstate the value of his support.

The same indispensability characterised William H. Seward, who overcame his disappointment at losing the Republican nomination to Abraham Lincoln, accepted Lincoln's invitation to become secretary of state and emerged as Lincoln's most prominent adviser, friend and right-hand man. In an echo of Lincoln's invitation, Barack Obama asked democratic nominee and acrimonious rival Hillary Clinton to become his secretary of state, a role she fulfilled for four years. Unlike Seward, Clinton still harbours a desire for a go at the top job and may yet decide to replace her current life of 'want' with a future life of 'should'.

While a C, Hillary Clinton showed support for her A through thick and thin. She accepted his position completely, despite friction with other Obama advisors, notably the president's fixer Valerie Jarrett, known by some as 'the third

Obama'. The C should protect the A's reputation from cynics within and beyond the organisation. In Clinton's case, this protection extended to Obama and the USA's reputation abroad. However she feels about the state of play, a great C will draw from her bank of contentedness to transmit positive energy throughout the organisation. At times when the organisation is experiencing stress and turbulence, and doubts are being expressed about the A's judgement, the C has a duty of care. The worst thing the C can do is sit around with the rest moaning about the terrible boss. The C has to watch out for everybody, irrespective of rank, and discourage the weather reporters.

When things are going badly, a C's affectionate duty must be expressed through tough love. Protection of the A and their organisational purpose has a parental quality to it: who else is going to shield the A from the dark forces out there? PAs, chiefs of staff, and assistants need to dish out tough love despite its not being appreciated in the moment. Nicki Chapman, publicist to some of the world's most famous artistes, is no pushover. When she left MCA to start her own company with lifelong collaborator Nick Goodwin, she was immediately engaged by Take That, Annie Lennox and the Spice Girls. She has worked with two of the titans in the world of entertainment, Simon Cowell and Simon Fuller, and is not afraid to give no-nonsense advice to anyone. Like all good parents Chapman teaches her As the basics in good manners. She insists that artists are prompt, courteous and focused. To help them shine she clears their dressing rooms of all distraction and fights to ensure the world sees how good they are. Simon Fuller respects Chapman's toughness: 'She is the person you would choose first to have by your side in any time of adversity. A number of times Nicki has stood up for me even against the most unpleasant and distasteful of characters and hasn't blinked.'

Fleur Bell offered me rock-solid protection as my executive assistant at Saatchi & Saatchi, as did Annie Tansey at Still Price Lintas and, later, at Publicis. Making sure I was well prepared was a key part of their job. An A's failure to respond in the appropriate time can leave them horribly exposed. The PA's job is to know when to intervene and with what intelligence. Fleur, now executive assistant to the chief executive of News International, never allows her boss to get caught on the hop: 'I've got lots of specific alerts set up on my phone, ready for news, and I check my phone like a mad woman, which I shouldn't do, probably, but I do.'

Like a protection officer, there is little that she has not anticipated. Once Tom Mockridge, the chief executive of Rupert Murdoch's press empire, moved on, Fleur inherited a new boss, Mike Darcey. He was a heavy-hitting leader, albeit one with no direct responsibility for programming or news in his previous roles for the company. Fleur told her new A that he should expect daily phone calls from *the* boss and advised Darcey what he would be expected to share:

> I told him that on his first day. I got all the information ready. I don't think he really believed that it was going to happen. At 2.30 the call came in from Mr Murdoch and Mike had all the information right there in front of him. When he put the phone down from that call I think he knew I was okay.

Protection, at times, demands provocation. Bosses have off days, they get complacent, they develop impatience and immunity to thinking that cuts across their intentions. Opinions, sometimes necessarily loud ones, can irritate the

A. Tongue lashings must not be taken personally. The C has a duty to protect the A especially when they are hell-bent on self-destruction. Nicki Chapman has a particular approach to artistic talent: 'I say, "You're paying me for my opinion. As long as I can give you that, I'm quite happy. It's down to you whether you want to take it. If you don't let me give you my opinion, I can't do a good job for you, so I will have to walk away."'

If Cs seem precious on occasion, it may be because they have a deep sense of protection over the causes to which they are committed and the As they have chosen to support. They greatly appreciate their expertise, opinion and ideas being sought. In all of this, duty, the life of 'should', can be a pleasure. If the C finds no personal meaning in supporting and protecting the A, they cannot be constant or successful.

A reputation for constancy may also see the C through the turbulence of a transition from one A to another. There is little that commends a C more to an A than proven constancy, especially when it extends to peers and others within the organisation. Respect, support, protection and tough love transcend hierarchy. Show those qualities to colleagues often enough and you will earn their unconditional trust.

Constancy dictates that you support your actors when they fluff their lines, forgive your musicians when they hit a wrong note, protect a project manager who overspends the budget and understand the politician who unintentionally gets their facts wrong when the microphones are thrust under their nose. The C should help colleagues out of a hole and protect them when they are attacked. The A must be driven above all else by performance and results, and must have an intolerance to mediocrity or anything in the way of their leading their cause to greatness. Their judgement often has to be binary – yes or no, in or out, black or white.

The C should share the same high standards, intolerance for underperformance and depth of commitment to the cause. However, depending on the nature of their remit, the Cs should spend time – that the A does not have – with colleagues or peers, lending a sympathetic ear and understanding their perspectives and pressures. A key responsibility of leadership is to support and protect its followers. Where better for that responsibility to reside in the leadership team than with the constant C?

## CATALYTIC

We have seen that contentment and constancy are active qualities that transmit positive energy to others. C leaders like to have a direct impact on those around them, to make things happen, to be catalytic. My C interviews suggest that a catalytic leader follows three steps. They consider, create and then complete. After taking the time to consider a situation, they stimulate game-changing ideas and create possible courses of action. Once the A has chosen a course of action, the C embraces it as if it were their own – which it often is. In so doing the C imbues the decision with legitimacy, persuades others of its merits, and leads them to make it happen.

### Consider

Let us consider Rabbit. During a round of Poohsticks, the game invented by Winnie-the-Pooh in which players drop sticks from the upstream side of a bridge and watch them 'race' to the downstream side, Pooh, Piglet, Rabbit and Roo look down from the bridge, awaiting the re-emergence of the winning stick. To their surprise, Eeyore appears instead, calm, dignified, but floating upside down in the river. The baffled Rabbit asks Eeyore what he is doing:

> 'I'll give you three guesses, Rabbit. Digging holes in the ground? Wrong. Leaping from branch to branch of a young oak-tree? Wrong. Waiting for somebody to help me out of the river? Right. Give Rabbit time, and he'll always get the answer.'
>
> (A. A. Milne, *The House at Pooh Corner*, Chapter VI)

Like Immanuel Kant, Rabbit knows truth to be a child of time. Eeyore, on this occasion, denies Rabbit that time. Cs take their time to think, which can drive the A crazy. 'I have to make a decision on the spot, and you need *how* much time to give me a point of view?' Kevin Roberts overcame his initial frustration that I couldn't shoot a hypothesis from the hip, and told my board colleagues, 'No use asking Richard for his point of view in the meeting, his best idea will come in 48 hours, so we'll give him a call then.' Action should be considered, not impulsive.

What should our foreign policy be on Iran? How will we launch our business in China or the US? What team formation and tactics should we use to beat Brazil? The C has to find the time and space to give diverse challenges due consideration, not with a towel around their head in solitary contemplation (though this may be part of it) but in a rigorous manner that addresses the complexity and interconnection of issues. Thinking is not a part-time activity. To arrive at plausible answers the C must be given the time to put their IQ, and the collective IQ of their team, to best use.

Daniel Kahneman, in his book *Thinking, Fast and Slow*, employs decades of cognitive research to demonstrate the two different modes in which we think. Mode 1 is fast, intuitive, associative, metaphorical, automatic and impressionistic. It is crucial to any engagement with the world, but is prone to a broad range of errors, such as the 'focusing illusion' which distorts the significance of what is on your mind: 'Nothing in life is as important as you think it is when you're thinking about it.' Mode 2 is slow, deliberative, methodical and logical. It allows us to escape many of the errors of Mode 1, but to use it requires time, focus and a lot of brain juice.

Lord Falconer was a C to Tony Blair and, as lord chancellor, a powerful A himself, presiding over a legal machine of 85,000 people. He worked with his fair share of advisers. One of them, Lord Hart, was his special adviser. Falconer most appreciated Hart for his careful analysis. He describes Hart's catalytic quality and Mode 2 thinking:

'It was clear that Garry Hart had a different way of looking at things, as if he were at a slightly different tilt to the world than the rest of us. He would think hard about a problem and come up with a solution that, in a way, only made sense because it was his.'

More than raw intellect and the ability to structure arguments, cases and proposals, the best Cs have superior contextual intelligence. The ability to discern situations and read patterns of play drives confidence in the A's final decisions.

## Create

Situational awareness and contextual intelligence will help Cs get intimate with their organisation's resources. Knowing how to put them to best use is an act of creativity, the next step for the catalytic C, as they manage talent to facilitate thinking. Knowing the people in your organisation, matching them to task, unleashing their capabilities, and making random connections between them, all help create fresh ideas and alternative options.

C leaders create multiple options. Even though he is famous for his naivety and simple-mindedness, Winnie-the-Pooh is a model for the consideration and creativity I am proposing. Head between his paws, brain juices flowing, Pooh thinks big thoughts, mulls matters over and eventually devises plans to clear all obstacles. In our first formal introduction to Christopher Robin's favourite bear, *Winnie-the-Pooh and some Bees*, Pooh faces a puzzle. After ambling for some time through the woods, he stumbles upon an oak tree and hears a buzzing sound above him. He pauses, and ponders. From where might the sound be coming? Bees. They're making honey – for him to eat, obviously. What's to be done?

Plan A: Pooh climbs up the tree, cracks a branch and tumbles back down again. 'Bump, bump, bump.'

Time for Plan B: Sourcing a balloon from Christopher Robin, Pooh covers himself in mud and drifts up the tree, hoping the bees will mistake him for a hovering black cloud. However, he senses they are suspicious.

Plan C: To combat the buzz of suspicion, Pooh asks Christopher Robin to get an umbrella, stand under the tree and voice concern about impending rain.

None of the plans achieve Pooh's desired outcome, but you have to hand it to him, there can be little carping about his creativity. He is not one to leap to assumptions. He pauses before drawing conclusions. He uses careful consideration and (endearingly flawed) logic to weigh up the possibilities. Once he has assessed the situational context, he creates options with which to approach the challenge. His mistake, or as Human Resources would put it, 'area of opportunity for growth and personal development,' was to act on his initial idea without first considering the alternatives. He should have weighed up all the options before rushing to climb the tree. His wise Cs – Rabbit, Piglet and Owl – might have done the analysis for him.

If you bring your A only one option, you back him into a corner. An A enjoys being presented with thinking that he has not requested. The pleasure is in the receiving not always in the agreeing. Leaders may only have time for one idea themselves, but they like to deal in the currency of many. Yet even multiple options can leave an A feeling cornered. Lord Falconer distinguishes between two of Blair's most prominent advisers during his years at No. 10. Both were eminently capable of identifying the three or four key issues as they saw them. For Falconer, though, Jeremy Hayward, who has served three prime ministers, was outstanding: 'There is a world of difference between Gus O'Donnell's "here are the three issues" and Jeremy Hayward's "here are the three issues and here are the three things I would do in your shoes right now".'

Catalysts need to be creative. They need to know how best to use people creatively, to imagine new processes, policies, and strategies, new ways to win. At London Business School, I run creativity courses for leaders from around the world. They all acknowledge the importance of creativity as a leadership function. Required reading for the course is Teresa Amabile's article 'How to Kill Creativity' for *Harvard Business Review*. The more senior they are, the more these leaders blush when they are forced to confess that they have had a hand in creating a working culture that inhibits their people's creativity.

The leaders recall on how many occasions they have said 'That's not the way we do things around here,' 'It's more important to get it right first time,' 'We tried that before and it didn't work then,' 'We have not got the time or the money to mess about.' Individually, they point a finger at their schooling, blaming the exam system for squeezing every ounce of creativity out of them. They have lost their creative confidence: 'I'm just not creative.' Maybe not in the artistic sense, but I defy anyone to say they cannot be creative in the catalytic sense – creating ideas, scenarios and alternatives. Engineers, doctors, auditors, charity workers, factory managers, military men – all soon rediscover that they do have a creative muscle after all. Here is a cycle for Cs to use to solve problems for their A creatively: **See, Scope, Surprise, Sell.**

A creative adviser anticipates a problem or a challenge well before their A has presented it to them for assessment and action. Part of the job of the chief of staff, according to Jonathan Powell, is 'to help the master out of scrapes and to think ahead'. The creative C, steeped in situational savvy and foresight, **sees** the problem coming. Jeremy Hayward-like, they summarise the issues and give the A 'The three things we (the team) would do in your shoes.' They **scope** the challenge for their diverse team of experts in a way that excites and stretches them. 'Here's a problem for you to fix, we have no time, no money and you're fired if you can't fix it' is not the kind of motivation we warm to, though some pressure and deadlines do spur creativity.

The C makes appropriate resources available to the team to ensure that they can collaborate creatively, while spotting the potential and flaws in their ideas. An enthusiastic practitioner of lateral thinking pin-up Edward de Bono's Six Thinking Hats, the C will have given the team ample opportunity to wear the Black hat to identify each idea's shortcomings, and they will have been encouraged to give equal emphasis and energy, wearing their Yellow hats, to identifying the good in their ideas. The C will have also been able to coach the team to adopt some of their preferred suite of problem-solving skills and techniques.

The C without a creative toolkit is about as useful as a bricklayer without a mortar board. To use that toolkit to build solutions that **surprise**, the C must avoid, as far as possible, *being* surprised. The C exists in the world of the predictive conditional, where a course of action depends upon some likely thing happening. 'If Mark is late, we will leave without him,' 'If Mark is on time, we will all leave together,' 'If the C fails to get my idea executed, I will fire him.' Philosophical and mathematical theories make use of this essential component of logic all the time. The C has to have courses of actions ready **if** certain situations arise in the future.

Philosopher, mathematician and midfield enigma Paul Scholes had the ability to make a quick short pass or, if the situation allowed it, to surprise with a 60-yarder that no player or awestruck spectator could have seen coming. Scholes would run through his problem-solving cycle in a matter of seconds: see, scope, surprise. Mike Forde, former director of football operations at Chelsea, is co-founder of Leaders in Performance, a network where experts in high performance share insights and ideas from different industries. Forde considers Frank Lampard's extraordinary ability to see opportunities before others: 'Foresight is not an accident. Lampard very rarely gets hit by a tackle. If you watch his head movement, he's moving his head more than anyone, well before he receives a ball. So he's already in a position where he looks like he's got more time than anyone else.'

Forde's analysis is challenging for all leaders, particularly those of us wishing to excel in the C position:

> Whereas you and I, as soon as we get the ball, then we look and then we get hit, right? Or if we are at the next level up, when the ball's coming to us, we might start to look then,

and feel pleased with our reading of the game. But the highly skilled leaders, like Lampard or Scholes, they are looking two passes ahead, so they're thinking about where they are, where others are and so, if they receive the ball within the next one or two passes, they have mastered everyone's location.

How good is your head movement? Do you know where everyone stands *if* the ball comes to you? Scholes and Lampard never look surprised when they receive the ball because they have already scoped several courses of action, and by the time they release it, several more. That is why they can surprise everyone with their service to their strikers – flicked-through passes, early crosses, deft one-twos. Whether you are a midfield magician or a catalytic C, pulling rabbits out of hats should not be beyond you.

In an organisational context, the C will need to **sell** his A, and others, the fruits of his team's collective creativity. If the A has little time for considered thought, he also has little time to receive it. Cs must organise their thinking carefully and share it succinctly. There are no marks for workings-out, just hand in the answers, please. Clear presentation lends an aura of authority and command of the subject. For a good idea to hit its mark it must be launched lucidly.

## Complete

Let us pretend that the (unusually polite) A is over the moon with the C's preferred recommendation: 'Thank you, C, it's approved.' The A will now assume (while teaching others never to assume anything) the immediate and immaculate implementation of 'their' idea. The message from their Nike-inspired view of the world is 'Just Do It.' Cs who keep a record of the emails they send to their As telling them what they are going to do may find they have wasted their time. As far as the A is concerned, once a course of action is promised, it gets delivered. No follow-up required.

The C has sold the idea to the A, and now must sell it to all those beyond the immediate circle who dreamed it up. How to do this? For 17th-century French philosopher Blaise Pascal, 'The art of persuasion consists in pleasing as much as in convincing' and is 'more difficult, more subtle, more useful, and more wonderful' than demonstrating. As they negotiate a minefield of competing agendas and preferences, Cs must use their charm to reach a settlement that the majority can live with.

Driving a decision towards completion is usually the hardest and longest stage in the catalytic cycle. To twist the maxim about vision, 'It's Not What The Decision Is, It's What The Decision Does.' Problems have to be solved, people have to produce and preferred outcomes have to be worked towards. Cs find deep satisfaction in making sure things are done properly. It's a simple, often private, pleasure. Outcomes are rarely perfect, but when they are better than expected the feeling is terrific.

When a C has successfully implemented an A idea, the catalyst has converted, taking the C full circle back to considering the world as it is and as it might be. The clairvoyant in them sees ahead, sensing, grappling with more hypothetical scenarios, contemplating, like Seneca, the dangers that lie ahead: 'By looking forward to whatever can happen as though it would happen, he will soften the attacks of all ills, which bring nothing strange to those who have been prepared beforehand and are expecting them.' Your A might even thank you for that, but only if you are brave enough to tell them.

## COURAGEOUS

The virtue most sought after in a C is courage, even though it is more readily associated with an A. The A suffers most of outrageous fortune's slings and arrows, facing up to ultimate accountability, the toughest decisions and the roughest sanctions. Yet to contribute properly to the leadership, Cs need courage, too – to look inside themselves, make sacrifices, cede control, show commitment to the cause and to exercise all their influence to get the job done.

While our society conforms to its 'winner takes all' cultural norm, the C has to rise above the negativity attached to their subordinate role. Other prejudices exist which Cs need backbone to withstand. Your delivery, less easily measured than that of colleagues working to clearer objectives, is called into question. You may have to dirty your hands with ruthless implementation, which will hardly endear you to your colleagues. Where is he getting his intelligence? Who belongs to his network of informers? Who is next on his hit list? Having the ear of your boss and unfettered access to them is a source of suspicion and fear, making you a lightning rod for resentment. Articles were written in newspapers about Rasputin's negative influence on the Tsar and Tsarina, deflecting anger that might otherwise have been directed at the royals themselves. Obama's favourite, Valerie Jarrett, has attracted deep envy, much of it attributable to the kind of access described in Richard Miniter's *Leading from Behind: The Reluctant President and the Advisers Who Decide for Him:*

> Jarrett's White House role is unprecedented. She meets privately with the president at least twice a day with no one else present. Her influence is enormous and wide-ranging. She wields informal power, like a first lady; scheduling power, like a

chief of staff; and power over policy, like a special envoy. She has the unusual freedom to put herself in any meeting she chooses and to set the priorities as she sees fit. When the *New York Times*'s Robert Draper asked Obama if he 'runs every decision past her,' the president answered immediately: 'Yep. Absolutely.'

In this hostile, fear-fuelled, envy-driven environment, a single slip can ruin your reputation, while your successes may perpetuate tall poppy syndrome: 'Even as you do your damnedest not to, we'll make sure you stand out so we can cut you down. Status is a relative value, so for you to rise in status, we must fall. Forget it, C.' The need for courage will diminish over time as your colleagues enjoy and benefit from your constant, catalytic qualities.

The C must be particularly courageous when he needs to dissent or disapprove. J. F. Kennedy was fascinated by courage and spent years gathering stories of statesmen who followed their hearts and principles to determine what they thought was best for the American people. Congress at the time, he wrote in *Profiles in Courage*, discouraged the use of political courage: '" The way to get along", I was told when I entered Congress, "is to go along."' He loathed this mentality, arguing instead that: 'Conformity is the jailer of freedom and the enemy of growth ... only the very courageous will be able to take the hard and unpopular decisions.'

Courageous Cs act in spite of personal consequences. They carry on regardless (even because) of disapproval from colleagues. Whatever their organisational context, they are aware of the damaging tendency to groupthink and are prepared to disrupt it with challenges that cannot be ignored. Courage demands the dispensation of sharp advice that cuts through crusty old opinion, something to jolt a group and its

A out of complacency. Aesop is easy on their ears: 'Please all, and you will please none.'

Consensus seeking must at times give way to conflict production. A field in which points of view and ideas compete for consideration must be cultivated. Good Cs fit snugly into the robes of the devil's advocate. In the interests of robust debate, Cs will sometimes serve up a deliberately naïve solution, and eat the resulting crow if they have to. The arguments of a C tend to be considered and reasonable but in the face of stiff internal resistance, a grand folly about to be perpetrated, the C may need to be unreasonably stubborn. When candour is called for, when the unspeakable needs to be spoken, the C stands up.

When Elizabeth I came to the throne in 1558, she immediately appointed William Cecil her principal secretary. 'This judgement I have of you,' she told him, 'that you will not be corrupted with any manner of gift, and that you will be faithful to the State, and that without respect of my private will you will give me that counsel that you think best.' Cecil's prodigious appetite for work and what Richard Cavendish in *History Today* describes as his 'vast, whale-like maw for detail', gave him the courage to be uncompromising in his candour.

Sometimes it may be in everybody's interest for the A to be sparing about the full picture: 'Gather round, men, the enemy has got twice as many men as we have, and a very favourable position at the top of the hill ...' is not so good for company morale. By contrast it can never be in the A's interest for the C to be anything other than candid when they are out of the public eye. The A needs the truth, no matter how dark it is, and should attach himself firmly to people who will tell it to him straight, rather than stroke his ego like King Lear's unctuous daughters.

Timing is important. The best coaches and counsellors have an instinct for when to impart advice. In his autobiography, Sir Alex Ferguson describes David Gill as, 'the best administrator or chief executive I ever dealt with... There were no complications with David. He might tell you something you didn't like, but he would not shirk from saying it. That was the only way to be.'

Gill gave me an example of telling something to Ferguson that he would not like:

> Alex would always go to the dressing room after the game. More often than not we won, but sometimes we lost and he'd be spitting blood about the referee in front of the players. I would say, 'calm down, we lost, you can't blame the referee for that'. It didn't always work, of course, but I had the authority ... authority's the wrong word ... I had the respect to do that with him.

There would be other times when Gill judged he should give his A unconditional support:

> After the Real Madrid loss (in March 2013) he was devastated, we were all devastated. Alex said, 'I won't speak to the press,' which I knew was, you know, not within the rules; but I said, 'I agree with you Alex, you can't speak to them after that'. But I said, 'we've got to put someone up', so we got Mike Phelan to go out. Even though we got a slap on the wrist from UEFA and a fine for going for it, it was the right thing to do.

Nicki Chapman chooses her moments with her artists carefully.

> When you're looking after artists it's a very delicate balance

because sometimes they say they want to hear the truth but in actual fact they don't, and sometimes the truth hurts, so I would much rather open a door and talk to them and let them come to their conclusions and be supportive, which might take a lot longer.

Sir David Brailsford, according to his first Tour de France winner, Sir Bradley Wiggins, also approaches truth-telling with courage and caution: 'Dave is not frightened to tell me what he thinks at times, but at the same time I'm kind of his asset so he wraps me in cotton wool a bit too much.' In Evelyn Waugh's novel *Scoop*, cotton wool is all that the fearsome Lord Copper of the *Daily Beast* receives from his obsequious foreign editor, Mr Salter. When asked if he agrees with a sound opinion, Mr Salter replies 'Definitely, Lord Copper.' When asked about a foolish one, the word 'No' always eludes him. Instead he croaks, 'Up to a point, Lord Copper.' Stalin came up with a way to deal with sycophants. After his speeches, which often lasted several hours, his Politburo puppets would clap and clap and clap – nobody daring to stop first. You can see on YouTube the mechanical device Stalin introduced to bring the toadying to a close (http://www.youtube.com/watch?v=wXGh_sbPUko).

One of Tony Blair's strengths as a leader, according to Alastair Campbell, was his desire to surround himself with straight talkers:

When we had our office meetings on a Monday morning, there wasn't a single 'yes person' in the room: there was me, Jonathan Powell, very irreverent, Sally Morgan, always challenging him, Bruce Grocott, Charlie Fordham, Derry Irving, Peter, of course, Pat McFadden, all the people he took advice from, nobody there was scared to say to him, 'Tony, that's bullshit.' Anji Hunter, she was always the one maybe closest to wanting to stroke him and make him feel good about himself, but she would challenge him as well.

How easily people can do candour has much to do with their leader. Don Quixote gives his C, Sancho Panza, an explicit instruction to tell it to him straight:

'You must tell me without adding anything to the good or taking anything away from the bad, for it is fitting that loyal vassals tell the exact and unvarnished truth to their lords, not swelling it because of adulation or allowing any other idle consideration to lessen it.'

Panza does not flinch from telling his A that, 'The common people think your grace is a great madman' and, worse, that the gentry think he has been ungentlemanly in giving himself knight-errant status and using the honorific title of Don without any right to it.

Campbell was able to speak freely with his A. He remembers Blair saying to him: '"You know the reason these guys – Bush, Clinton – why they really like being around us? It's because actually – Bush, in particular – they're fascinated by the way you talk to me." Bush couldn't quite believe it, he was really quite shocked, but he also rather admired it.' Sean Fitzpatrick, New Zealand All Black legend, courted candour from family and friends throughout his captaincy of rugby's serial winners:

> You need people that are going to challenge you, someone like my brother, he was the one, if he rang me up or sat me down and said 'you're being a dickhead' I'd say, 'right, yes, I am actually.' 'You didn't play well, because you didn't prepare properly last week' and I'd reply, 'you're right.' In that period

of '92 , Grant Fox and John Kirwan were two guys whom I trusted implicitly. I went to them after every training, every game, to ask them, 'what am I saying, am I saying too much, am I not saying enough?' Or they'd come up to me and say, 'Jesus mate, you didn't handle that very well. You can't speak to Inga Tuigamala like that, you know, he's a Polynesian and you can't yell at him.' 'Oh, really, can't I, okay', or 'you know you're not spending enough time with the young guys', 'aren't I, fuck, okay'. I trusted them because they wanted what was best for me and what was best for me was best for the team.

I once worked for an A who told me never to bring him bad news because it didn't inspire him. Indeed, it might spoil his day. His childish attitude was that it was up to me to prevent bad news from ever occurring. Inhibiting your C from giving you the truth is dangerous. Just imagine how Team Sky's response to the Lance Armstrong affair might have played out differently had people – Robert Tansey in particular – tiptoed around their team performance director, David Brailsford.

Anxiety was running high through Team Sky at that difficult time, especially through Brailsford who had formed close attachments with everybody in the team over the years. He was now forced to start having conversations with himself: 'Is zero tolerance really still possible given that doping was so widespread?' 'If so and so doped a little bit 12 years ago, and since they've been on the team they've been completely clean, can we relax the policy?'

Tansey, even en route to Venice, had gathered the extent of external pressure from the media for truth and reconciliation. It would have been less unpleasant for him to skirt around the bad news when he met to discuss Team Sky's position with Brailsford. It might have been less unpleasant for Brailsford, 'not to do bad news'. Yet, on candour, Cs do not flinch. Tansey was able to stiffen everyone's resolve and to influence a loud reaffirmation of the cause's founding principles from Brailsford and the whole team.

Conversations were had with all members of the team, some of whom had emotional links with people implicated in the doping. Team principle was reasserted in a tone more supportive than admonishing. Tansey, as chief counsellor to Brailsford, helped to ensure that Team Sky emerged from the crisis stronger. By taking action early, the protagonists avoided the lasting implications of scandals of phone-hacking proportions.

Tansey was fortunate to be supported by some strong-headed Cs who also deal in the currency of candour, including his wife, who has served a few bosses during moments of heavy stress, and Graham McWilliam, group director of corporate affairs, who sits on Robert's Team Sky Board:

> He knows the personalities involved, and he is very good at thinking through everything. Equally he is not someone you go to if you want your view reaffirming. He is not a comfort blanket. I would run through the conversations I'd been having with Dave, and then run through what to do next. In a sort of gentle way he kept me on my toes, and having talked it through with him, the path for me was very clear. Of course there had been moments when I had been tempted to go, 'Actually, do you know what, maybe we should rethink our position?' but then, very quickly, I knew that doing that would be the wrong thing to do.

Truth-telling should be at the top of any job spec the A has for his C. Kevin Roberts, A at Saatchi & Saatchi, put it to me characteristically straight:

I want advice that is truthful, not diluted. I can't stand people around me second guessing. When advisers mess up it's because they try and anticipate what I want. Because I don't know what I want, how can they know? If I knew what I wanted, I wouldn't waste my time asking them ... So if they spend time second guessing, 'what does the boss want?', that's just an exercise in futility.

Most employees close to the centre of power at Chelsea Football Club would struggle to give Roberts the undiluted advice he values, if Hugh McIlvanney's description in the *Sunday Times* is anything to go by:

The wildly impulsive autocracy Roman Abramovich established on his arrival as owner of Chelsea in 2003 has never seemed likely to be tempered by braking or balancing influences from the executives and so-called advisers he gathered around him. A zealous and indefatigable talent for agreeing with the master's wishes (or maybe, in moments of extravagant ambition, anticipating them) appears always to have been a main qualification for occupying such behind-the-scenes roles.

How best to do candour? Never ask your A, 'Can I be candid with you?' because there is nothing else any leader worth his pay packet would prefer you to be. Anthony Simonds-Gooding, my first ever chairman, was a stickler for full and frank exchanges, pulling people up short the second he detected the scent of deceit. 'To be quite honest with you', they would begin, before he pounced on them: 'There are no degrees of honesty, you either are honest or you are not, so I'm afraid "quite honest" just won't do it.'

Just as there are no degrees of honesty, there are no shortcuts to courage. As the C gains more influence, he will need more of it. In his biography of Cardinal Richelieu, Jean-Vincent Blanchard cites Spanish diplomat Diego de Saavedra Fajardo, who had this to say of Marie de Medici's favourite C, Concino Concini, a man shot dead outside the Louvre:

'Concini was close to Jupiter but also to its thunder.'

# 5

# TYPES OF C

When I first conceived *Consiglieri*, it ended with an 'e' not an 'i' – one person supporting one leader. The more I listened to As, the more I realised that the smartest among them don't bank on one, but sport several. Throughout throne rooms, green rooms, back rooms and boot rooms, there are complex networks of power with influential people fulfilling an array of functions to keep their leaders fed, watered, transported, coached, checked and cheerful. Whether PA, EA, PMO, NCO, COO, Chairwoman, Assistant, Adviser, Deputy, Turtle, Deputy Turtle, you should be able recognise yourself in this chapter. What type of C are you? Is there a different C role that might suit you better? Is this your first outing to the C store or are you after a sexy new leadership number to wear for the season?

The exact role the C plays will be determined by careful consideration and mutual agreement during the early stages of the relationship. Chapters 6 and 7 offer advice on this. *Consiglieri* is a celebration of the C's importance to the leadership endeavour as well as a reminder that the C exists for the A. What the A cares about is the main definer of the C's contribution. What is it that the A seeks from your leadership, discrete from other contributors to their cause? You may have all the hallmark motivations of the C and your strengths may reflect those we have observed in the best Cs. Now you need to be certain what kind of contribution you can make to the cause and its leader. What influence do you wish to have? What kind of interactions do you envisage? Given that your job is to be remembered barely at all, what will be your carefully concealed C legacy?

I have identified four overall C archetypes and their different influences on the A. Some of these roles sound unglamorously functional, occasionally menial, even peripheral to the A and their cause. You may do them a great service by carrying their bags, driving their car or keeping their spirits up, but these endeavours alone do not constitute leadership. They provide a platform from which to make a powerful contribution to the A. To demonstrate C leadership is to give the A not simply what they asked for, but what they never dreamed possible. To do this the C must first of all deal in the functional currency of the job spec, then in the emotional checks of the A's well-being, and finally in the treasure of game-changing counsel.

The C needs first to know the tasks that must be tackled and what metrics will be used to appraise their usefulness. Andrew Blick and George Jones' *At Power's Elbow* examines the utility of prime ministerial aides spanning three centuries. When we think of communication, we think of aides like Alastair Campbell for Tony Blair and Steve Hilton for David Cameron, providing round-the-clock media management. As early as 1723, Robert Walpole appointed Thomas Gordon as first commissioner of wine licences, 'something of a front for government publicity operations'. Edmund Gibson, nicknamed 'Walpole's Pope' was more useful as an adviser, convener and 'whipper-in' of men. Labour prime minister Harold Wilson had Trevor Lloyd-Hughes and then Joe Haines, his chief press secretary, helping him to communicate, George Wigg, nicknamed Wilson's 'Spymaster General', taking a keen interest in the intelligence and security agencies, and Marcia Williams providing more emotional support. Usefulness comes in many forms.

So ask not, in the first instance, what your A can do for you, but what you can do for your A. The emotional element can be kicked off with a simple question, 'How do you wish to feel and how can I help you to feel it?' There are four strong states of being that the As I have interviewed associate with their best performance: liberated, enlightened, authentic and decisive. Help the A feel any one or a mix of these and you are playing a lead role.

## Liberated

To liberate the A, the C must provide a loud enough drum beat, a constant signal to their lead singer that the support they need is right behind him. If left unsupported and unprotected, leaders carry the weight of the world on their shoulders. Cs who unburden As of their baggage leave them feeling lighter and free to do their job to the best of their abilities. Liberators do not send their A an email at the start of the day beginning 'I just thought I'd better let you know ...'. That would be the A's day killed. They know what the email means: 'I'm in deep trouble, and I'm sharing this with you, so you're now in deep trouble too.' No A wants that email.

## Enlightened

A leaders have little time to educate themselves. They have few opportunities to park the predictable, to get beyond the narrow confines of their own organisation and to challenge their own thinking. Cs who augment their A's experiential wisdom with intelligence, insight and inspiration, born from the C's continuous education, leave their A feeling enlightened.

## Authentic

A leaders do not set out in life to become inauthentic, narcissistic versions of themselves. It is fatigue at the top, the cut and thrust of decision-making and the uncertain, chaotic contexts in which they are forced to operate, that chip away at their principles, short-circuit their foundational beliefs, and short-change their colleagues. How can they possibly retain an accurate sense of self?

As pressures mount, the As feel less well understood and more isolated, with few to listen to them, fewer they can trust to tell all to and almost nobody to whom they can appear vulnerable. The sympathetic C who can deliver much-needed and much-deserved empathy, who has the courage to hold a mirror up to their A and who will remind them of their core values, can restore the A to their authentic self.

## Decisive

All As love to feel that they are fearless decision-makers, the font of all action. They may be admired in the moment for the decisions they take, but they are measured by the action and outcomes that flow from those decisions. By making things happen for the A, through individual action or by influencing others, the C fuels the A's intoxicating feeling that they have been decisive and that their legacy is secure. Reputation as an A is hard won and easily lost, the slightest slip being tweeted beyond the organisation before corporate affairs can muster a defence. The C can enhance the A's reputation by ensuring that the A's ideas are contextualised; the cause is well articulated and embraced; and business is conducted in the tone the A would like.

Feeling liberated, educated, authentic and decisive constitute the A's dream state. These four feelings shape my segmentation of C archetypes: **Lodestones** liberate; **Educators** educate; **Anchors** help the A feel authentic; **Deliverers** leave them feeling decisive. Because each of these feelings transcends hierarchy, seniority, length of tenure, discipline and gender, so too do the four C archetypes. No single archetype stands alone. The Cs whom I interviewed and studied, although rooted in one archetype, fostered feelings in their As of at least one other. It is up to the C and the A to discuss the A's dream scenario. This, in turn, should shape the responsibilities, influence and relationship that are imagined for the C.

## LODESTONE

Smart Cs are never too senior or too important to act as Lodestones to their As. The Lodestone takes jobs off the A's plate, frees them from the bland fodder of management and releases them from whatever ties them to the table of everyday leadership. When we think of the great organisational freedom fighters we think of our assistants – personal, executive and managerial.

You have just had an early morning meeting with your A. Over his double macchiato you tell him that you have taken three appointments out of his diary for which you judged his presence unnecessary; you've drafted the after-dinner speech he has to give in a fortnight, so he can think about it on his next train journey; you've informed him about the two key decisions you took on his behalf yesterday when his last meeting overran, and you hope they meet with his approval because action has already been taken; you have sensed recently a particular force field emerging in the corridors of power and have suggested that the A think about that as he walks the talk later; oh, and you have managed to reduce the costs of running his office, for which the bean counters have mumbled their grudging admiration. 'Finance happy?' he asks in disbelief, punching the air. Your A leaves the brisk fifteen-minute update with a spring in his step. Several victories have been notched up already in his day as master of the universe.

A lodestone means a 'leading stone' with a naturally magnetic quality to it. Sir Alex Ferguson surrounded himself with lodestones at all levels, from Lyn Laffin, his trusted PA, to David Gill, the quiet CEO behind the scenes, both magnets for unwanted items on Sir Alex's To Do list; Mike Phelan, Ferguson's assistant manager, told me that he happily stayed behind after Sir Alex left a room to pick up the glasses his boss would invariably forget. Phil Townsend, director of communications, described Sir Alex's mood and effectiveness both lifting when he had Lodestones around him:

> If you look at the times when Sir Alex has not been able to perform at the levels that he has at other times, quite often that's when he hasn't had a No. 2. He was much happier, for example, in my first season here in 2003–04 … it finished with us winning the cup, and he had brought Walter Smith in March, I think. He'd gone several months without his No. 2, and his mood seemed to change as soon as Walter came in because he was big mates with him. He was Scottish, he was the ex-Rangers manager. Sir Alex's mood seemed to change and he seemed to, you know, relax a little bit. Then Carlos Queiroz came back the following summer, and he went on an uninterrupted period of having these sounding boards, these people who took so much of the burden off his shoulders.

Lodestones can also keep the plane flying when it hits unexpected turbulence. When John Manzoni, Talisman Energy

Inc.'s chief executive, resigned unexpectedly, Jonathan Brown felt at his most effective as a C. Sudden switches from one CEO to another can create tremendous stress for an organisation. John Manzoni left the firm after a board meeting on a Saturday. Brown helped to keep the plane flying while a new captain eased himself into the cockpit:

> Everybody at Talisman went home on a Friday evening expecting to come to work on Monday and to be working for John. In fact, they came to work on Monday to discover that they were working for someone else. Everybody, the executive team included, was caught completely on the hop. There was already a lot going on without his departure to compound it. There were a lot of people asking, 'Well what do I do now?' including some of the more senior people. With the new CEO, I decided to act as a sort of sergeant major: 'May I move the men up to the frontline, Sir, and tell them to load their rifles? Would that be a good idea?'

Lodestones also take friction out of the system. People are understandably concerned to meet the expectations of their leader, particularly one who has a strong personality. Imagine that one such A asks a rhetorical question in a meeting. Someone eager to please or frightened about perceived lack of contribution decides to act on the question. Within days, an internal industry has been developed to try to answer the A's question; within a week, the project has grown a life of its own; after three months of late nights, heated debate and takeaway pizzas, an answer to the A's long-forgotten question lands with a thud on their desk. The A thumbs through the thick folder, calls in their C and, baffled at its origin, asks 'What on earth is this all about?' An answer from the C along the lines of, 'Well, you asked this question in a meeting three months ago,' wouldn't cut it. The A didn't mean for the machine to go into overdrive on their behalf and will be angry that you let that happen. People have suffered as a result of thinking too hard about what the big guy (or gal) wants. The intimidating A has got limited time. People are too nervous to stick their head around the door and ask, 'Hey, boss, that question you just raised in the meeting, do you want someone to take a look at it, or were you just thinking aloud?' A confident Lodestone may not even have to ask the question. They will have an instinct about what is important to the A based on the A's current agenda, which will enable the C to prevent friction, and months of wasted effort, by telling their colleagues, 'Don't bother with that one, the boss was just asking a question.'

When Paula Ickinger supported Steve Pateman, then head of Santander UK's Corporate and Commercial Banking Division, she had unfettered access to the machinery of power. I saw how she used it. The most subtle look from Steve Pateman signalled to her, 'Please Paula, just fix this for me and please don't make me ask you to in front of everyone else.' She knew what Pateman wanted her to do, and she did it without even being seen to accept the mission. Her motivation was the quiet pleasure of lifting weight off her A, his mind, not just his shoulders, unencumbered.

There are many lessons to be learnt from Lodestones who have played A-liberating roles with skill and grace, from roadies to caddies to circus undermen and boxing cornermen. The qualities that these roles require have certain overlaps. The archetypes are designed to inspire Cs, to encourage them to notice parallels with their own roles, and to emulate the best C attitudes. It is possible that fulfilling any one or more of them, including the least glamorous, could lead to an A role later on. Impresario David Geffen started life in the mailroom at the William Morris Agency. He later co-founded Dream-Works SKG with Steven Spielberg and Jeffrey Katzenberg. Sonny Corleone used his position as bodyguard for his father to learn the subtleties of being a Don.

## Caddie

A caddie packs a bag with fourteen clubs, an umbrella and some food, and carries the 20kg for four miles over five hours. Picking up and putting down the bag at least fifty times is only the half of it. A caddie has to clean his A's clubs and may even have to, indignity of all indignities, wash his balls. (Agents to today's top footballers perform caddie-like duties, keeping their charges out of nightclubs, drip-feeding them cash when they need it, doing whatever it takes to save them from bunkers of their own making.) Caddying is neither menial nor solely physical. As pro-golfer Luke Donald puts it: 'If I thought my guy was carrying my luggage, I wouldn't pay him nearly as much as I am. That says something right there.'

Often themselves outstanding golfers, caddies lighten the load by feeding their As information on how the course works, estimating the yardage of each hole, suggesting the club they might choose and advising on the direction and speed of the wind. More importantly, say the best golfers, a caddie imparts calm, confidence and focus. They contribute to the certainty of their A's decision-making. In some cases, the club lugger may prove to be the decisive factor, the difference between winner and runner-up. Tom Watson won all five of his British opens with Alfie Fyles as his caddie. When Jack Nicklaus and Watson fought for the Open title at Turnberry in 1977, Nicklaus was the seasoned professional and the bookmakers' favourite, with Watson only at the beginning of his legendary career. During the famous 'Duel in the Sun', when the two golfers reached the 18th hole Fyles proposed that Watson use a 7- rather than a 6-iron, judging that his adrenaline would make him hit the ball further. Fyles understood his player in context. Watson went on to win.

It doesn't always work out well for the caddie. Mike Doran was fired by Lee Westwood in 2005 despite finishing second in the Order of Merit that year. Doran said about the situation: 'If your player starts playing badly he is never going to blame himself – golf is far too much of a game of confidence and self-belief for a player to admit he is at fault. The first thing he will think about changing is either his caddie or his coach – usually in that order.'

To be a liberating Lodestone in the mould of a caddie, some questions to ask yourself include: Are you feeding your A all the information he needs? How extensively have you researched the course of action he is about to take? Do you know everything that the A needs to know and more than him? Can you detect hazards ahead? If not ball-washing, are you dealing with the grunt work with grace? Are you au fait with the A's work and the pressures he is under, so that you can credibly counsel him on his winning choice of 6- vs. 7-iron? Are you doing everything you possibly can to allow your A to simply take the shot?

## Roadie

As well as a caddie the Lodestone is a roadie, readying his A to take to the stage. Mal Evans succeeded Neil Aspinall as the Beatles' roadie when Aspinall took on a more significant role for the band. According to Beatles' biographer Philip Norman, Evans was: 'The big, nice, amiable chap who once lost Lennon's guitar. Mal was the one who carried the cases, he was a bit of Liverpool, some sanity that the Beatles could take with them on the road.' Evans' sanity was a support to the band but he was not a C leader.

Former Boston bartender Marvin Nicholson is the bit of sanity President Obama takes with him on the road. Nicolson organises the president's trips, carries his jacket and bags and, according to David Remnick's observations of Obama's close circle, is the guy who 'has the pens, the briefing books, the Nicorette, the Sharpies, the Advil, the throat lozenges, the iPad, the iPod, the protein bars, the bottle of Black Forest Berry Honest Tea.' Caddie for Senator John Kerry before becoming the president's Lodestone, Nicolson has also played over a hundred rounds of golf with Obama, giving him unique insight into how the president weighs up his decisions.

Neil Aspinall was a roadie to the Beatles and, like Nicholson, was valued for more than his companionship. He was intelligent, trustworthy and admired by each Beatle. He stood for the same kind of quality that the band members shared, and used his position as roadie tirelessly to give his As emotional support and hone his problem-solving skills, the kind that would eventually see him take over the lead of the Apple company. Perhaps it was his training as an accountant that enabled him to untangle so many of their business problems and to navigate through contractual mazes to compile the Beatles' archive footage that led to the *Beatles Anthology*. Aspinall was the man they trusted, even when the group stopped trusting each other. He was a C leader.

Whatever your C job title you need to decide where you sit on the spectrum from 'nice to have around' groupie, to 'essential to have at my side' roadie. Are you a lightweight or a Lodestone? It is easy to be likeable, much harder to be irreplaceable. The role of Turtle, Lord Browne's invention at

BP, was conceived as a Lodestone role, one that, says Jonathan Brown, swiftly became a fashion statement: 'As soon as the boss had a Turtle, everybody wanted a Turtle. It was a badge of rank, like "I've got a reserved parking space – oh, I've got a Turtle."' You could choose to be a lightweight Turtle, nice to have around, easy to shout at, retreating into one's shell when the going gets tough, or you could be a Lodestone Turtle, one that, according to cosmological myth, carries the world on its back. The challenge for the C is to use their proximity to power to lift the emotional baggage off the A's shoulders.

Further questions for the roadie-esque Lodestone include: Are you simply the A's sanity on the road or do you share the A's quality standards and enjoy their unconditional trust? How light have you made the A's day? Are you a badge of rank, the latest bling, or someone happy to take the weight of your star's world on your shoulders?

## Underman

One Lodestone who really knows what it means to carry weight is the circus underman. He lifts and supports the other members of an acrobatic team and is never happier than when they dazzle in the limelight. For him the limelight is the stuff of nightmare, glimpsed only when things have gone horribly wrong. Given the possibility that all eyes will be on him at the bottom of a collapsed heap, what on earth would induce a man to apply for the underman role? Probably not the dictionary definition: 'a man who is subordinate to, inferior to, or in some way disadvantageously placed with respect to others.' In Swedish 'ünderman' means wonder or miracle, so perhaps it is mainly Swedes who apply. Some of my A interviewees felt their Cs were something of a miracle.

After three years as campaign director of the NSPCC,

Nick Booth and his executive team felt that their campaign to protect children across the UK had reached a plateau. They decided to ask a heavyweight from the business world to join them. Booth explains that it was this leader's idea to insist on a C for Booth:

> This business leader said, 'I will do this on one condition. If I take this on you have to go and hire a number two because to shift the dynamic of the campaign, Nick, you're going to have to be able to shove some things off your plate onto someone else's. You need to be doing the front-facing stuff. So I need to hear from the trustees if they're going to use their budget to take on that aide-de-camp or a No. 2 for you, because having that person is going to free you up.'

Having the underman made all the difference to Booth and to the campaign. Miraculous as it may seem, this kind of load lifting can be shot through with pleasure. Fittingly, at the end of the seven-minute Banquine act in the Cirque du Soleil show 'Quidam', the underman who has been holding up a four-storey human pyramid takes a deeply deserved, if brief, bow.

You should take a bow as a Lodestone if you can answer these questions positively: Does your leader trust you to support them when they are flying high? Can they rely on your strength when the pressure is on and they are in the spotlight? Are you in constant training to ensure that, in the moment, you are the strongest link? If you were not there to act might there be no act at all?

## Cornerman

You are right for the Lodestone if, like the cornerman, you want to give direction but to stay firmly out of the ring. To the lazy C, the deal for the cornerman may look attractive: sit on a stool, hold a sponge and wait for your man to emerge at the end of the round for a minute's relaxation and a bit of a rub down. But beyond their functional duties, cornermen (a.k.a. cutmen, conditioners, and chief seconds), short of getting in the ring to take the punches themselves, are the most liberating of Lodestones. Muhammad Ali said that his cornerman, Angelo Dundee, may have had more faith in him than Ali had in himself. Dundee worked with fifteen world boxing champions and said of his job, 'When you're working with a fighter, you're a surgeon, an engineer and a psychologist.' Ronald Fried, in his book *Cornermen,* added to the list, 'father figures, babysitters, motivators and strategic advisers.'

These cornerman qualities are exemplified by Nicki Chapman. She is described by the artistes for whom she has worked, like Gary Barlow, or the As she has supported like Simon Fuller, as the person they most want to have in their corner. Nick Godwin, with whom she set up Brilliant PR, describes her as 'the rock I could depend on, never judging me'. Like Chapman the best Cs remain detached from their As, as well as devoted to their safety, well-being and talent. When it comes to the crunch, the cornerman must be lightening quick. Ray Arcel, whom former middleweight champion Jake La Motta described as 'the dean' of cornermen, said in an interview in 1953: 'They say "a second" only has 60 seconds to perform the functions of surgeon, nursemaid, general and comforting friend, but, when you subtract the time spent getting into and out of the ring, you actually have little more than 40 seconds.'

Perhaps we have alighted on a 'second' descriptor with a positive connotation. All Lodestones should have this cornerman quality, to get the job done when necessary in a ridiculously tight timeframe, much as the engineers do for their drivers in motorsports. One thing Angelo Dundee had no time for was cotton wool or sugar-coating when he saw his man Sugar Ray Leonard losing his fight with Tommy Hearn: 'You're blowin' it son, you're blowin' it!' was enough to change the course of the fight. If you want to take on the job of cornerman, to be Dundee to your prize fighter, try at all times to describe your contribution as modestly as he does: 'I just put the reflexes in the proper direction.'

To test your liberating qualities as a cornerman further, answer these questions: Are you like his magic sponge? How ready are you to make the critical intervention? Have you soaked up every ounce of learning during the bout to share with your A in double-quick time? Are you watching his back? How good are you at patching things up when your A returns from a bruising encounter in the ring? Does he find what you have to say sufficiently motivating to up his game? If 'You're blowin' it, son!' seems likely to produce the wrong response, what kind of language works with your A?

## EDUCATOR

If Lodestones liberate the A and leave him unencumbered, Educators enlighten him. Great Educators invert George Bernard Shaw's maxim: 'He who can, does. He who cannot, teaches.' As we shall see, the best doers are often the best teachers.

### Sherpa

Like the roadie and the caddie, the Sherpa porters heavy loads for his A. The A's life depends on his C's intimate knowledge of the mountains, his years of experience and his technical craft, not just his willingness to put the kettle on. Sherpas are as or more skilled than the mountaineers they serve. They know the way and they enjoy guiding people along it. They may be humble but the best of them can pass on the benefit of having been there and done it far more than their aspirant As. Apa Sherpa, a living legend among climbers around the world, only hung up his boots after he had climbed Everest twenty-one times. He was twelve when, despite his small frame, he began to carry loads greater than his own weight, with a wide smile that all Cs should carry.

Russian dancers say they learn roles 'legs to legs', from mentors who were once themselves stage dancers. Mountaineers who want to get to the top – and back again – may be wise to learn from their Sherpas, legs to legs. Eric Simonson, an American mountain guide who has conducted more than thirty expeditions to the Himalayas, said of the fixing team of Sherpas who run ahead to set up the ropes and ladder: 'It is the best of the best, the Sherpa A team. These are proud men. They see themselves as every bit as good as anyone out there.' They can do and they can teach. Smart As put authority for key decisions at the point of greatest knowledge. On the mountains, this can be the difference between life and death. Smart As also remember that Educators are often capable of doing their boss's job, but choose not to take that particular lead, as an act of humility. Of late that humility has been tested by nouveaux mountaineers on Everest and other must-bag peaks. Demanding tea in their tents, seeking luxury not learning, these novices are unworthy of the peerless porters at their disposal. Not unlike cocky young footballers who brashly overlook their coach's illustrious playing career once they've made it into the first team, these kind of As need an education, in courtesy as well as craft.

If you are an Educator with Sherpa qualities, you should be able to scale the following questions without crampons: Are you mountain-fit yourself? Do you know where the top is, and the best way to approach it? Have you the humility to pass on your wisdom to those who may at first appear undeserving? Will you schlepp your A's tent all the way to the summit and take a snap that makes it look (for the benefit of the A's entire address book) as though they conquered the impossible all by themselves? What risks are you prepared to take for your A as you run ahead to fix their climb?

## Philosopher

If As don't need their Educators on hand at all times (as a Sherpa is needed) a philosopher may be more to their liking. My first chairman, Anthony Simonds-Gooding, worked with me at a time in his life when, like Hector in *The History Boys*, he wanted to 'pass it on, boys, pass it on'. I used to look forward to the time of day when my philosopher's head would pop around my office door with an invitation, 'Mr Chief Executive, I wonder if you might have a minute?' This meant it was time for a fireside chat without the fire, some parental tutelage, unrequested at the time and unforgotten since. Simonds-Gooding's were laser-like interventions, counsel dispensed as or before situations arose or as the occasion demanded. He was clear from the outset that he would be the philosopher, which meant, he said, that I had to be the butcher willing to get blood on my hands when necessary. Every great organisation had one of each, he said, 'and I've had my turn at butchery.'

The philosopher needs to give an independent point of view that challenges. They are best when they have points of reference that lend authority to their counsel, when their interventions, if not always welcomed by the A and the executive team, are rooted in years of frontline experience. So, whether chairperson or non-executive director, the philosopher is there to impart wisdom and offer perspective. The interventions may be infrequent but they can be invaluable. If they are board-related, they must be independent, too. Many As have sturdy service to give after finishing their A tenure, so elevating them to a presidency, chairmanship or directorship, can be enlightening for the new A. Far better to promote the former A, pamper them and pump them for advice than to park them as far away as possible for fear of their continued influence. As many a former prime minister proves, they will have their say anyway. Time will tell how grateful David Moyes will be to have Sir Alex Ferguson, his managerial predecessor, in the boardroom at Manchester United and to be able to tap into his experience every week. Microsoft's newly appointed CEO Satya Nadella wasted no time inviting Bill Gates to become his consigliere, a shrewd use of the founder and former chairman's expertise in technology and experience spanning four decades as the A.

You can, of course, play the philosopher outside of the boardroom. I have been well educated in my time by Fleur Bell, my PA at Saatchi & Saatchi, who taught me the beauty of boundary definition, the art of identifying and dealing with passive aggressive behaviour, and much else. You can be an *éminence grise* without any grey hair. Like Sancho Panza, illiterate and obedient servant who becomes Don Quixote's sidekick, or Grigory Rasputin, semi-literate peasant from Pokrovskoye, you don't need formal education to be an Educator.

An organisation should be populated by philosophers and professors. Years of experience help but many are wise beyond their years. The question of a philosopher's usefulness may simply be, if they have half an hour with their A, how many enlightening ideas will they offer? The C who keeps telling their A things they already know is running out of intellectual steam, perhaps losing their own sense of enquiry, and ceasing to be useful.

Other questions for the philosopher to consider include: Why should the A submit themselves to your teaching? What wisdom do you wish to impart and how do you plan to impart it? Does the A want you as their sidekick or their sage, a Sancho or a Simonds-Gooding? How comfortable a chair is the A looking for? Are you better placed offering up thoughts for the day, or wisdom on tap as the occasion demands?

## Coach

More hands-on than the philosopher, the coach is a different kind of Educator. While working as a PE teacher in a secondary school in Sutton, Paul Clements began coaching ten- and eleven-year-olds in Chelsea FC's Centre of Excellence, in the evenings and at weekends. After five years he joined Fulham FC full-time, heading up education and welfare for its Academy. Seven years later he became coach of the Republic of Ireland under 21s. He moved back to Chelsea initially as coach for the under 16s, then for the under 18s, then the reserves, and eventually as the First Team Coach, from which position he won the double with Carlo Ancelotti. After a brief stint at Blackburn FC, Clements was reunited with Ancelotti at Paris Saint Germain where it took the pair just eighteen months to win the French league. Clements currently works with Ancelotti coaching Cristiano Ronaldo and other *galácti-cos* at Real Madrid. He now shares his Educator responsibilities with Madrid's other assistant coach, Zinedine Zidane.

We know that coaches are there to enhance performance, but the Educator coach's role has a strong social dimension to it, too. In his early days at Chelsea, when he looked after players aged nine to eighteen, Clements oversaw the older players' adherence to a government scheme which demanded they have twelve hours' education per week. He also ensured that their accommodation was taken care of, and was the point of liaison between club, school and family. This gave Clements insight into what professional footballers do before and after the three hours a day they spend being coached. He concluded that demotivation was rarely football related.

At a lunch to promote the work of the United Foundation a few months before he announced his retirement, Sir Alex Ferguson explained to me the importance of coaching:

> We take coaching very seriously at this club. Players do not choose what to do in training. At other clubs, left to their own choice, the players would choose to have a kick around. They can play six-a-side at Liverpool. Not at our place. We coach them, drill them and they practise ... We start skills coaching as early as six years old. Character coaching becomes critical between sixteen and eighteen. Players have to learn about failure. We cannot guarantee every Academy player makes the first team. Ninety-two current players in the league came out of our Academy. But remember, they can get injured; they can hit a run of bad form; they may never make it. For those who don't, at least we trained them in character.

How many As submit themselves to character coaching by their Cs? For the C, the more discrete the coaching context, the more complex it becomes. Taking drills and training teams is not the same as assigning yourself permanently to one aspiring winner. Nick Bollettieri is Andre Agassi's former coach, and the man behind, among others, Jim Courier,

Monica Seles, Mary Pierce, Maria Sharapova and Jelena Janković. Bollettieri founded the world's most famous Tennis Academy where the Williams sisters often prepare for their Grand Slams. He described the complexity of coaching, registering little surprise that there are very few great coaches out there: 'You have to understand your players' idiosyncrasies, know what makes them tick, know what makes them angry. You have to know how to handle the player. One of the things that players often forget is that coaches have their own lives to live as well.'

Roger Federer, winner of seventeen Grand Slams and regarded by many as the greatest player of all time, has worked with a number of coaches throughout his career. He has suggested that not one but several different voices over time can help a player develop: 'You go through different stages when you have different coaches early on. They always feed you a lot of information, they motivate you, they tell you how it used to be in the past maybe, they motivate you by telling you what you can achieve.'

The subtext is not too difficult to read: today's tennis coach to the star, tomorrow's hand-me-down to the over sixty-five mixed doubles pairings. In 2012 Andy Murray won the US Open to become the first British player since 1977 to win a Grand Slam singles tournament. In the following year he became the first British man to win Wimbledon since Fred Perry seventy-seven years before. Coaching voices that have been in Murray's head on his way up include Leon Smith, who coached him in his junior days; Pato Alvarez, his first coach on the ATP tour; Mark Petchey who lasted just ten months having quit as head of Training at the Lawn Tennis Association to take on the role; Brad Gilbert, a former coach of Andre Agassi and Andy Roddick; and Miles Maclagan. Yet the only coach most of us will end up associating with Murray's triumphs is his current stony-faced mentor, Ivan Lendl. Straight after the Wimbledon final Murray talked about Lendl's candour: 'I think he's always been very honest with me. He's always told me exactly what he thought. And in tennis it's not always that easy to do in a player-coach relationship. The player is sometimes the one in charge. I think sometimes coaches are not always that comfortable doing that.'

The player must always be considerably more in charge than the coach. Out there on the court the player powers the ball at another player, equally determined to be in charge; but great coaches, like Lendl, have the temerity to approach players off-court, to tell them what is wrong with their game in no uncertain terms, and suggest how they can put it right. Sir David Brailsford attributes a lot of the success that he and his team of coaches have had with British cyclists to their acceptance that ownership and ultimate accountability resides with the cyclists:

> The most important people in our world are the people who win, the riders, basically, not the coaching staff. Trying to get everybody to understand the relationship between a [coach's] supporting, giving and sometimes enforcing role and a [coach's] sometimes challenging role, as **against a dictatorial role**, was critical for us. I loathe guys in sports, in cycling or any other sport, when they talk about 'my' players, 'my' result, 'you let me down.'

For the educating coach, here are some questions to consider: Who was your favourite teacher and why? What is it about that teacher's educational approach that you wish to emulate? Are you prepared to coach your A in character and behaviour, as well as in skills? Can you be honest with your A without sounding like a dictator?

## ANCHOR

Those coaches who are prepared to give brutally candid advice, to 'speak truth unto power', as fearless Mandarins are charged to do by their ministers, act as Anchors to their As. The A's authenticity is under constant attack from others' sycophancy and the A's own vanity. Anchors both ward off and exorcise these demons. Here are some of the models for C leaders seeking to root their A in reality:

### Reasoner

Seventeenth-century playwright Molière invented the *raisonneur* character, the employer of reason, to moderate the excesses of the dreamer, the *imaginaire*, who, believing himself capable of changing the world around them, more often than not brings ridicule on both their heads. So, whether Chrysalde to Arnolphe in *The School for Wives*, Philinte to Alceste in *The Misanthrope*, or Cléante in *Tartuffe*, all Molière Cs attempt to anchor their As in reason. As the A, it is easy to drift, placing every question, issue or challenge into one's central belief system. The A feels no need to weigh up decisions according to the agonisingly delicate nuances of the individual situation. The Anchors around the A must not wed themselves to a particular dogma. To them falls the task of countering their A's fatally expansive view of the world with clarity, healthy scepticism, constant questioning and sense-making. This is the real work of leading as a C: leading as reading – carefully, clearly, slowly – the situation as it unfolds.

If Napoleon Bonaparte had paid attention to the reasoners

in his ranks, his army could well have been victorious in 1812. Napoleon took half a million men to engage with the Russian army in that year, but the Russians refused to play ball. Instead they spent three months retreating deep into their vast land and, to the horror of the French, burning villages, towns and crops as they went. After finally catching up with and engaging the Russians in a major battle, Napoleon and his men entered Moscow where there was enough winter wear to clothe every one of them. Napoleon needed to prevent his soldiers from looting, and get them instead to collect the six months' worth of provisions scattered around the city. In *War and Peace*, Leo Tolstoy tells us what happened next: 'Napoleon not merely did nothing of the kind, but on the contrary he used his power to select the most foolish and ruinous of all the courses open to him ... He remained in Moscow till October, letting the troops plunder the city; then, hesitating whether to leave a garrison behind him, he quitted Moscow.'

Napoleon's troops were not aided by the Muscovites, who started fires that eventually left three-quarters of their city in ashes. Nevertheless, Napoleon's odd decision to leave Moscow left his troops at the mercy of the Russian winter, lacking food and appropriate clothing. In the bitter days that followed, 380,000 Frenchmen succumbed to starvation or hypothermia. Tolstoy goes on:

> Napoleon, the man of genius, did this! But to say that he destroyed his army because he wished to, or because he was very stupid, would be as unjust as to say that he had brought his troops to Moscow because he wished to and because he was very clever and a genius. In both cases his personal activity, having no more force than the personal activity of any soldier, merely coincided with the laws that guided the event.

In *War and Peace* Tolstoy draws into question, and finally rejects as an illusion, the notion of free will. No matter how good a reasoner you are, unless you work in a philosophy department your A will not want you to lecture him on free will: whether it's illusory or not, As feed off the feeling that they run the show. Nevertheless, there are useful lessons for both As and C reasoners to be found in Tolstoy's great novel. We rely too heavily on A leaders when we analyse organisations. The character and decision-making ability of As does, of course, have an impact on the organisations that they lead. Tolstoy's key insight is instead about cause and effect. We are quick to see the A leader as the cause of outcomes, yet slow to stop and think how far he may be an effect: the tip of a floating iceberg, itself moved along by currents that flowed before, and will flow after, its existence.

Don't worry if your A switches off at this point in your relation of the fate of Napoleon's army in 1812. The reasoner is not a storyteller as much as a dispassionate observer of events and evaluator of courses of action. However short your A's attention span, or expansive his ambitions, can you reason with him straight?

## Confidant

In the work of the other great seventeenth-century French dramatist, Racine, we see the need for C sense-making even more, because the plight of the A is starker. If the *imaginaire* in a Molière play requires his *raisonneur* to stop him from getting lost in a mess largely of his own making, the protagonists in Racine plays are empty vessels wracked by passions they can't control. The confidant to whom the Racinian A unburdens himself is the only person standing between him and total isolation. In his work *On Racine*, Roland Barthes calls the Racinian protagonist 'a man confined, a man who cannot *get out* without dying'. The Racinian confidant helps the A mediate between the internal world of his dreams and passions, and the external world of his responsibilities and obligations. The two are ultimately irreconcilable.

Cs should study the Anchors in Racine, to avoid their own unhappy ending. His play *Andromache* illustrates the C's dilemma. After Andromache, the Trojan queen, is brought back to the Greek state of Epirus as a captive following the Trojan War, she faces an impossible choice: either she marries Pyrrhus, King of Epirus and son of Achilles – nemesis of her dead husband Hector – or she refuses and her son Astyanax pays for it with his life. In a situation in which she might otherwise fall into complete despair, Andromache can talk to her lady-in-waiting and confidante, Cephise. She comes close to accepting advice from Cephise that would secure the best possible outcome for her. Yet in the end the queen chides Cephise for not knowing her enough inwardly:

> Dearest Cephise
> Between my heart and yours I keep no secret,
> In my misfortunes you've been staunch and true,
> But in my turn I thought you better knew
> Me.
>
> (*Andromache*, Act IV, Scene I)

Cs might well wince when they recognise their own A in the petulant emphasis on the 'Me'. Andromache might insist that her Anchor exactly identify with her internal thoughts but, surely, in order to fulfil her role as an Anchor, the confidante is right to bring her leader into a more realistic relationship with the world? In Racine, the C's efforts inevitably end in failure because their sagacious advice is valued less than their complete agreement with the A. Barthes suggests that the confidant and the protagonist never speak the same language. The protagonists depart from their confidant's help with tragic consequences. The As drop their Anchors at their peril. What both Racine and Molière imply for those confidants or *raisonneurs* wishing to anchor their As is the need to be resourceful in their strategic revelations of the truth. Any A who is unable to look at the reality of a situation straight on needs to be shown it in profile.

To avert Racinian tragedy, questions the C must address include: Can you assess each situation facing the A on its own merits? How well do you know your A? How healthy is your scepticism and how persistent your questioning? Do you know how to speak the same language as your A? Can you speak truth in a way that makes the A embrace it?

## Joker

Mike Phelan, Sir Alex Ferguson's last assistant manager, said that one of his greatest contributions to the Ferguson leadership was to make his boss laugh. In my interviews, the same comedic quality was attributed to another of Ferguson's coaches, Steve McClaren, to both John Prescott and Alastair Campbell for Tony Blair, and Nicki Chapman for her many artistes. Funny Cs can break down the structure of A opinion, and put it back together somehow modified, all in a pleasurable whirl.

Jokes alone do not qualify a gagster for a C leadership gong. Vehicles for comic relief, like Shakespeare's Falstaff, Bottom the weaver, or Dogberry the constable, cannot have much impact as Cs. Anchors are fools with substance, and the truths they dispense, though clothed in comedy, take precedence over amusing antics. They are professional fools, intelligent fools that know exactly what they are doing. Discerning and wise, these fools coax, cajole, instruct and criticise their leaders, transforming their mindsets, anchoring and initiating changes in their behaviour, without fear of retribution. Shakespeare's 'professional fools', from Feste to Touchstone, are cruel to be kind, courageous to be compassionate.

When the Fool enters in *King Lear*, he offers the king his coxcomb to show him how foolish his abdication was. In a pithy poem, the Fool declares that the king has traded places with him. 'Do you call me a fool, boy?' Lear asks. 'All thy other titles thou hast given away; that thou wast born with,' replies the Fool. Lear is hostage to many of the A weaknesses that we will witness in Chapter 6. He falls out with his daughter Cordelia because she refuses to inflate his oversized ego; he then falls out with Kent, his closest adviser, when Kent calls his decision into question. When another of his daughters, Goneril, who later betrays her father, breaks in upon Lear and the Fool's first exchange, the Fool interjects with a song that likens Goneril to a killer-cuckoo, focusing Lear's attention on her attitude instead of her words. Only the Fool can speak others' censored thoughts without repercussions, often intensifying Lear's misery in order to lead his master to the severest truths. Such, though, is the Fool's compassion for Lear that he will not leave his side once the King's madness spirals. When Lear is sent out into the storm because of his daughter's selfishness, his devoted Anchor attends him.

How much better might David Cameron have weathered his political storms had he been able to cast Boris Johnson, and not Nick Clegg, as his Fool? Serious questions for the C inspired by jokers include: Can you make your A laugh out loud? Is there method in your merriment? Just how cruel can you get away with being? Do you know how to use your A's dizzied state of hilarity to slip in a new way to look at an issue?

## Friend

In keeping their As true to their authentic selves, good friends can make effective Anchors. Friends in high places are understandably treated with suspicion, particularly when they are appointed without the kind of qualifications or life experiences we would expect. Packing a cabinet with cronies, we assume, is just a ruse to insulate the A from contrarian thinking. Occasionally we are proved right, but we should try to distinguish between inappropriate cronyism and effective friendship. Great friends are in a unique position to know which decisions their A can live with or not. While her official role is as assistant to the US president for public engagement and international affairs, Valerie Jarrett is Barack (and Michelle) Obama's first friend, a Chicagoan known to the couple before Barack's foray into politics. A former White House aide, quoted in the *International Herald Tribune*, said Jarrett was there 'to promote what she understands to be what the President wants'. In this vein it may be right for the business to close down a nice-to-have in-house function in favour of outsourcing, but the A loves the people in it, they bring a smile to his face and he'll hate himself for turfing them out on the street, all for some minor incremental cost saving – so the friend tells him not to do it. Friendly Cs raise a red flag when they see their chum veering off-piste behaviour-wise, and hold a mirror up to any sign of madness. While others in Obama's circle of Cs – such as Rahm Emanuel, Robert Gibbs, David Plouffe and David Axelrod – have come and gone, Jarrett remains.

The fact that a friend is ever present with their A is more important than the specific function or issues for which they are made responsible. In his book, *The Hopkins Touch*, David Roll describes Franklin D. Roosevelt's friend Harry Hopkins as 'the perfect confidant'. Roosevelt 'needed a little touch of frivolity and sparkling, occasionally aimless, conversation in his life,' wrote James Roosevelt of his father, and Hopkins had just that touch. He was great fun to be around. Hopkins' ability to anchor was more about humanising the president than humouring him. Roosevelt respected Hopkins' judgement and admired his understanding of human nature. Like FDR himself, Hopkins was shrewd in sizing up people and their motives. He understood power, how it motivates and corrupts. Making use of that faculty, 'Harry could disarm you,' recalled Franklin Roosevelt Jr, 'He could make you his friend in the first five minutes of the conversation.' Hopkins had a marvellous ability to draw people out, and his judgements, passed along to the president, were valued. Roll identifies other people who could have acted as Roosevelt's first among Cs: his wife Eleanor; his sons and daughter; Louis Howe, his political mentor; Tommy Corcoran, once his good friend, on his way out of the administration; and Missy LeHand, who some regarded as the second wife. She, too, would soon depart. This, in effect, left Hopkins as Roosevelt's remaining friend, but he was one who was ready to take the fight to Roosevelt, as well as to 'throw sand in the gears' of any potential competitive counsellor influence over FDR, according to future Supreme Court Judge William O. Douglas.

When Roosevelt invited Hopkins to live with him in the White House, Wendell Wilkie, Republican presidential contender, asked him why he would choose to keep Hopkins so close. Wilkie intensely disliked Hopkins, believing him not worthy of the president's trust. Roosevelt's retort did not flatter Hopkins but it reveals just how much FDR needed him:

> I can understand that you wonder why I need that half man around me. But – someday you may well be sitting here where I am now as President of the United States. And when you are, you'll be looking at that door over there and knowing that practically everybody who walks through it wants something out of you. You'll learn what a lonely job this is, and you'll discover the need for somebody like Harry Hopkins, who asks for nothing except to serve you.

Anchors can expect more from their Cs than simply the honour of serving them, but great friends find giving help even more enjoyable than receiving it. Simon Fuller, the man behind global entertainment company XIX, describes Nicki Chapman as someone on whom he still relies for advice, guidance and insights about people:

> Nicki has great intuition and her warnings to me several times about certain people have proved to be incredibly helpful over the years. There was one person in particular that she warned me about being 'a ruthless, immoral individual who would stop at nothing to get what they wanted' and those words stayed in my mind and allowed me to pre-empt something that could have caused me a great problem had I not been prepared.

Sir David Brailsford hired Fran Millar, sister of rider David Millar, whom Brailsford considered 'family':

> Fran had her own business but when I started Team Sky, I thought, I need somebody to come and help get stuff done

here. Fran came and that's what her role was to start with, but she would give me very honest feedback, and I think maybe because I knew the family, it wasn't just a straightforward relationship. She would be quite happy to go, 'you know you pissed everybody off today'.

As an Anchor, could your friendship be used to this kind of effect? A friendly Anchor has particular sacrifices to make. You may be dismissed by others as a crony with a capital C. Where do you stand on intimacy, because your professional and personal lives are likely to be inseparable? Have you got the Hopkins touch of sparkling conversation and frivolity? Can you beat his ability to make someone your friend in less than five minutes? Other than to serve, what do you ask of your A? Do you want your A to know your family and does he want to know yours? Would you, like Ira Dubinsky, be happy to show up and have breakfast with the children of Jack Layton? Do you really want to see your PM in his superman pyjamas? Or the Queen in hers? If yes, you will still need to stay a couple of paces behind her on official duties as consort, and, if you are a duke and hail from Edinburgh, be careful not to offend when telling your jokes. We may not be amused.

## Seeker

In his book *How to Get Out of this World Alive*, Alain Forget offers us a four-step process by which we can anchor ourselves. Distancing lets us witness our self; discernment reveals what lies beneath our dysfunction; disidentification comes from letting go; and discrimination takes us to places where our ego might not wish to wander. The more the A can be their own anchor or, to use Forget's word, seeker, the better. How many As do this kind of work on themselves, to see what they do not want to see, to explore their shadow, to identify their darkness, and to challenge their demons? And how many have the intellectual honesty to process what they discover?

Cs, in my experience, make better silent witnesses than As. They prefer to observe than to grab the microphone, they enjoy the distance, they are able to suspend judgement, and they often have the courage to see in themselves what they might prefer not to. For As, self-reflection of this kind is either beyond them, an indulgence or, worse, a sign of self-doubt, and unlikely to serve them well. If so, they should appoint an Anchor with a remit to be their seeker, a silent witness invited to observe, understand and report back what Forget calls 'the rhythm and impact of your dysfunctions'.

Pop star Justin Bieber needs his manager Scooter Braun to have more impact as an Anchor. Braun describes himself as a 'camp counsellor for pop stars' and told the *New Yorker* that his job was, 'to make sure a client doesn't have any what ifs – to make sure, when you look back, you don't say, "What if I had done this? What if I had done that?"' Questions Braun should fear his young charge looking back and asking him include, 'What if I had *not* done this?' 'Could you *really* not have helped me more?' If Justin is not to disappoint his global fan base of Beliebers, he needs Braun to stop courting celebrity for himself on Twitter and TV and instead help his young client see the dysfunction of excess drink, prescription drugs, and drag racing. Scooter Braun needs to become Seeker Braun.

Spouses make great seekers so it was a surprise in my research among As to discover that not all seek the counsel of their partners at home. For my own part, there is not a right move I have made or a wrong one I have averted that has not, in some way, been first run past my wife. Much to my irritation in the moment, Rosie can distinguish a Merlot-induced moan from a legitimate complaint, and has acted as my not-always-silent witness throughout my career. For over a decade, 'to be fair to Kevin' has been her familiar refrain whenever I have offered up the merest squeak of displeasure about my A. When she has, on rare occasions, suggested that I may have a point, I have been able to act on her witness statement with the wind in my sails.

Those who rely on their spouses to keep them in check, to hold mirrors up to their excesses, to act as sane sounding boards, tend, in my research, to enjoy a more profound sense of well-being. Julie Ayliffe does it for husband Peter, recently retired president of Visa Europe; Sir Bradley Wiggins devotes pages in his autobiography, *In Pursuit Of Glory*, to the support and no-nonsense feedback of his spouse Cath; Denis Thatcher, the first male consort to a British prime minister, devoted a lifetime to supporting Margaret; just as many a first lady has done for the president, including Eleanor Roosevelt for FDR's four terms in office.

Amanda Blanc, AXA leader, uses her husband Ken as a sounding board every night before dinner. After she's heard what he has been up to with the children, Ken says:

> She'll start talking about her day from literally when she gets on the train in the morning to when she comes home at night, who she's met, who she's spoken to and in doing that, she downloads her day, replays it, works out where she made some bad decisions, where she made some good decisions, plays out what's going to happen tomorrow. We go through maybe 45 minutes to an hour playing out the day – 'Why did you do that?' As she's doing it you can see her thinking, 'Tomorrow I'm going to do something different' and she probably takes 10 per cent of my lines – 90 per cent is completely her own.

Hearing how important this pre-dinner ritual is to Amanda, one wonders why more As do not use their partners as Anchors. Perhaps they are worried they will show a lack of conviction. Some questions to seek yourself include: Can you see the rhythm and impact of the A's dysfunctions and are you prepared to share these with them? Is their rant a legitimate complaint or a chance to let off some steam? In addition to seeing to their supper, will you play seeker to their day?

## DELIVERER

The C can be a Lodestone who liberates, an Educator who enlightens or an Anchor who helps the A remain authentic, but they must also, in some way, help their A deliver successful outcomes. The C's reputation as someone who makes a difference rests more with what they make happen than what they say. Cs deliver in many different ways, some by keeping the peace, mediating and making sense of agendas; others by radiating energy, ideas and creating environments in which positive action thrives; others by fixing whatever needs to be fixed to get the job done; still others by seeing several moves ahead and playing the game with constructive cunning. All are legitimate leadership contributions.

### Sensemaker

Shortly after Jane Kendall graduated from the London School of Economics, Hurricane Katrina hit New Orleans, prompting Jane to work for FEMA, the Federal Emergency Management Agency, and its long-term community recovery unit. The state had one set of laws and ways of doing things, and FEMA had another. Kendall and her colleagues had to deliver a degree of cooperation previously unknown to both parties.

A high-ranking state official is unused to collaboration of this nature and FEMA was not skilled in getting across the benefits of collaboration. This is where Kendall came in. She describes the benefits to all parties of someone able, through mediation, to make sense of what appeared to be competing agendas:

> While organisations have an agenda, and people have their own personal agendas, there's something about how you make people feel that allows the many agendas to be shared in some way. I think the job is always to translate and mediate so that people feel not only that 'the outcome will help me' but also so that they can see how their agenda fits other people's agendas and vice versa. They're not all competing. There can be something shared.

One agenda that must be shared is that of the A, which too often gets lost in translation. Australian coach Shane Sutton became translator for Brailsford and his Team Sky riders, a conduit between the performance director and his performers; All Black captain Sean Fitzpatrick took responsibility for translating coach John Hart's intentions to the New Zealand rugby players, explaining to them why Hart wanted them to do what he did. Fitzpatrick would have to spell it out to them – 'the reason we're doing it is because of A, B, C, D, okay?' – or he would remind them of Hart's credentials, citing their first ever series win in South Africa, in 1996, and Tri-Nations victories in '96, '97 and '99. Translators and conduits make sense of agendas and mediate by drawing on their ability to see the world through the eyes of all parties, to immerse themselves in those worlds, soothing and smoothing the way for action.

You may need to make sense of these questions: How good are your translation skills? Have you immersed yourself in each party's point of view? How will you mediate to deliver collaboration in the face of conflicting agendas?

## Ambienceur

Those Cs with a natural ability for delivery create an environment in which their A and everyone else can thrive. They set the tone in which their As would like their affairs to be conducted and act as cheerleaders for the cause. They ensure the survival of the organisation's best ideas in a hostile environment. Rivalling the A's power shake and protein bar for energy provision, the C wards off the half empty glasses, the cynics and contrarians. Being the out-and-out leader is exhausting and the last thing As need are people who sap their limited energy resources.

Fernando Peire joined The Ivy restaurant in London as senior maître d' in 1990, shortly after the restaurant's refurbishment following years of neglect. The idea was for him to 'warm up' the service. Now on the board of Caprice Holdings, as well as front man for Channel 5's *The Restaurant Inspector*, Peire can create an atmosphere in which people see the best of what is on offer. He practises the art of the ambienceur in a world of constant conflict between the kitchen that has one agenda, the floor that has another, and the door that has one more: 'I have worked very hard at building harmony and completely breaking the "them and us situation" – management, non-management, floor, desk, kitchen. I make it clear that we are all in it together. I try to create the atmosphere of a happy family rather than a family in tension.'

In creating an atmosphere in which very strong egos can deliver, the ambienceur – or maître c' – role demands judgement, patience and empathy. The ambienceur must show sure-footedness in decision-making to those on the door, on the floor and in the kitchen, as well as humility in their position as the restaurant's focal point. According to Peire the temptation has been too great for some: 'Those who work in fine restaurants and become supremely arrogant very rarely end up doing well, very, very rarely, because they get sidetracked by glamour on the way, and they think that it is all about them, but it's not. It really is not about them.' Ambienceurs would do well to remember Edith Wharton's view on warmth and light: 'There are two ways of spreading light: to be the candle, or the mirror that reflects it.'

Look at yourself in the mirror and ask: Are you an energy sapper or an energy zapper, a drain on delivery or a radiator of it? Will you be one of them, one of us or the one to put a stop to them and us? Are you the candle or the mirror?

## Fixer

The fixer is less concerned with atmosphere and empathy. They are there to get the job done. Like the defender in football, they can anticipate danger, stop the opposition from attacking and prevent goals being scored. Like fixers, defenders do not always get the appropriate recognition or valuation. In football, one in five possession switches are attributable to full backs, yet these players rarely command the sums of their more spectacularly impressive teammates. As the defender is occasionally tasked by his manager to harry an opposition striker out of a game, the fixer can be tasked with carrying out unpleasant firings. In French, we know him as the sinister *porte flingue* (door gun), Deliverer of the A's dirty work without complaint and, one suspects, not without pleasure. Nicolas Sarkozy's appointment as president of the Republic was Lefebvre's declared life goal, and he was fast to fire his *porte flingue* at anything that threatened his man. Sir David

Brailsford praises his right-hand woman, Fran Millar, for her delivery: 'She's dynamic, intelligent, intuitive, but can be very bullish, very in your face and she's got a very fiery side to her, pisses people off, but she gets shit done.'

Harry Hopkins pissed people off, too. To some he was a latter-day Richelieu, with sinister designs on FDR, moving serenely and powerfully in the shadows. To others he simply set about dealing with whatever was uppermost in FDR's mind. The minute the most pressing problem before the administration had been fixed or superseded by another, Hopkins moved on to the next.

Lack of popularity in a right-hand man or woman can be a source of comfort to the A, a sign that people's resistance to action is being given short shrift, whatever pain that might give the fixer. In Aravind Adiga's *Last Man in Tower*, the unscrupulous real estate developer Dharmen Shah is a dangerous man to refuse. He has a fixer, a 'right hand that does what the A's left hand doesn't want to know about'. Some right-hand fixers do go to work without hatchets and with their left hand's explicit knowledge. Lord Deighton, as head of the London Organising Committee of the Olympic and Paralympic Games, oversaw a workforce of around 100,000 and procured £700 million's worth of contracts to deliver the hugely successful London 2012 Games. Deighton was a virtual unknown at the time, well outside the spotlight shining on Lord Sebastian Coe, politician and former track and field athlete. Seb Coe was the effective front man for the UK Olympic Games and was good enough to ensure Deighton got an elevation to the House of Lords. At least when Coe got the glory, Deighton got the gong.

If you want a gong for fixing, how often will you win the ball? Are you prepared to piss people off or do you care about your popularity? How fast to the draw are you when your A is threatened? Do you have it in you to occasionally do what your left hand doesn't want to know about? Can you do it quietly?

## Gamer

In pursuit of the desired outcome, fixers can be cunning. Like a chess grandmaster they have played out most of the game's moves in their head, before the first pawn leaves its square. Fixers are competitive gamers, with well-honed instincts that equip them to read the likely moves of their A's opponents. The accomplished A and C Lord Falconer, Labour politician, close friend and confidant of Tony Blair, had a unique window on the world of power during the Blair years. He describes the gaming qualities of Peter Mandelson and his influence on every leading player in the New Labour machine:

> Tony greatly admired Jonathan [Powell], but even he was not as critical as Mandelson, more the Robert Duvall character, Tom Hagan-esque. The pure consigliere. Mandelson was much cleverer than practically any other functioning politician at the time. His analysis and his advice were absolutely critical to everybody. He provided Neil Kinnock with all the advice he needed. He found and invented Tony Blair and Gordon Brown.

Even though Louis XIII once said he was 'freed from the tyranny' of Richelieu, when pardoning his brother Gaston he said, 'Monsieur, I pray for you to love Monsieur le Cardinal'. Tony Blair once said that his modernisation of the Labour Party would be complete when Labour learned to love Peter Mandelson. Thomas Cromwell, according to biographer David Loades, was 'a ways and means man' who understood the value of information and the value of friends. A master of cabinet committee politics and presiding over a vast ministerial machine, Mandelson, too, had access to unprecedented information which he used assiduously. Despite Mandelson's two damaging resignations, successive As – Blair and Brown – could not keep the architect of New Labour away from their cabinet rooms. For his realpolitik, Mandelson ranks alongside Richard Neville, better known as Warwick the Kingmaker, and more modern kingmakers like David Axelrod, credited with the ascendancy of Barack Obama, and Sonia Gandhi, named as a kingmaker on so many occasions that *Time* magazine called her India's leader in all but title.

The ultimate gamers get their thrills from knowing that a successful outcome can never be entirely guaranteed. Few can do what Svengali did in George du Maurier's novel *Trilby*, transforming a tone-deaf person into a singing sensation using hypnosis. Simon Cowell and other contemporary Svengalis use other means – the might of the media – to increase the chances of a Susan Boyle becoming an overnight till-ringer, but still cannot be sure. To be a successful gaming Svengali, the A has to listen to the C's ideas. According to Philip Norman, biographer of the Beatles, the Stones, Buddy Holly and Elton John, Brian Epstein cannot be called Svengali to the Beatles precisely because he did not change them. I asked Norman about Colonel Tom Parker, the man behind Elvis: 'He gave Elvis bad advice but he didn't essentially change the person, change the being.' The creator of The Monkees, on the other hand, was a true Svengali according to Norman:

> Don Kirshner decided what people should record, told them to record it, recorded it and it was a hit. He was the Monkees' man in the background. The Monkees were invented as a television series, they weren't even going to play their instru-

ments. Kirshner picked most of their numbers. 'If you record this song, 'Sugar, Sugar Honey Honey' it will be a hit' … 'no, Don, we want to do our own' … and of course in the end 'Sugar, Sugar' was recorded by cartoon figures, the Archies, and it was a massive hit.

Norman's favourite example of a Svengali was Andrew Loog Oldham:

Oldham was absolutely brilliant, truly perspicacious. He real-ised that if he created some anti-Beatles, some nasty Beatles, some Beatles whose hair wasn't just in a nice shampooey mop, but went down their backs and over their ears, then the kids would take them to their hearts because they could be their heroes, the ones their parents would really hate – that was the Rolling Stones.

So, how good is your chess? How many moves ahead do you see? How critical is your counsel to the A and their other Cs? Will others look to you to make the next king or queen? Could you survive a couple of sackings to get asked back into the A's inner sanctum? Do you have the patience and loyalty, like Mandelson and Richelieu, to bide your time in exile, waiting for your next call-up? Could you, Svengali-like, create the next overnight success? Will your A do as they are told and record the hit you have in mind for them?

We have examined a variety of C leadership roles. We have seen people to emulate and some to avoid. Whichever archetype or blend of archetypes most appeals to you, it is time to take up your position in the shadows, and let the A on centre stage receive some advice.

# PART THREE

# 6

# ADVICE FOR THE A

Even if you are an immodest kind of A leader you should pay more attention to this chapter than you do to your press cuttings. It is about choosing the best people to support you and keeping them in check and at peace – curbing excesses, sparking successes. Remember that Cs spend years perfecting the art of acting in your best interests. How much time have you devoted to thinking about how to make your C's job easier? Your answer can probably be measured in minutes because, when things are going well, you tend to let your Cs get on with it. It also explains why it is the As who are most in need of relationship coaching. Cs ought to read this chapter too, as a catalogue of demands for proper treatment from their As. Without being helped, you cannot help, and the A/C relationship is fundamentally about helpfulness. In the *Journal of Personality and Social Psychology*, Baron and Boudreau lay out the alternatives: 'Helpfulness requires a helper and a recipient, competition requires a rival, and dominance requires a subordinate.'

You probably don't need any more rivals than you already have and dominance and submission are best left off your agenda. Many a politician has been caught with his pants down getting that one wrong. This is a relationship of profound reciprocity, in pursuit of a cause that is greater than either of you, so it is worth taking the time to work out what both of you need from each other. We may not like some of Niccolò Machiavelli's reflections on the state of play in the early fifteenth century, but as Segretario of the Second Chancery of the Republic and Secretary of the Ten of Liberty and Peace, he had thirteen years to see close up some of the most important political leaders shaping the future of Italy and Europe. One observation in *The Prince*, which he wrote as former secretary, and with which it is unwise to disagree, is on the need for this reciprocity between prince and minister, A and C: 'When ministers and princes are related in this way, they can trust each other. When they are otherwise, the outcome will always be harmful either for one or the other.'

Bad As beget bad Cs, so take a look at yourself. Did Henry really *have* to have Anne Boleyn and another five wives? How much did his unfettered lust for marriages, money and monasteries grant master secretary Cromwell the opportunity to grab more and more power? How much did Louis XIII's youth (he was sixteen when he ended the regency of his mother) allow Richelieu to build his power base? How much did the weakness of the Tsar allow Rasputin to reel in the Romanovs? Cs have narcissistic tendencies, too, and will make unreasonable demands on you and the organisation if circumstances allow it. Dark and selfish streaks can be triggered or validated by A behaviour. Curb your excesses and you will curb those of your C.

The central message of *Consiglieri* is that the best leadership teams beat to a reciprocal drum. Find out what your C needs and they will show you what *you* need. Responding to A/C problems and successes in an emotionally intelligent way will service a relationship that could define your tenure. It will not always be easy to get your C to open up like a book and there are dangers in leaving them to their own, closed, devices.

We are fascinated with the limelight leader and their journey from hero to zero. Halls of Shame are devoted to leaders who fall from grace. No equivalently punitive mechanism for public humiliation exists for the advisers of these As. Perhaps it should. It is difficult to believe that there were no Cs complicit in the demise of Richard Fuld, former CEO of Lehman Brothers, Angelo Mozilo, former CEO of Country-wide Financial Group or John Corzine, former CEO of MF Global, and other leaders who top the league table of losers.

We may have to wait for history to play its part in ascribing responsibility to those behind the A bad boys. The *Twenty-Four Histories* that cover the period in China from 3000 BC to the Ming Dynasty in the 17th century describe eunuchs who basked in adulation, wealth and power, ostensibly in the service of the Emperor. Wei Zhongxian, born in the late 16th century near Beijing, is considered one of the most powerful and notorious eunuchs in Chinese history. The Confucian scholars of the 17th and 18th centuries tell us that his cunning equipped him, through fawning over and swindling his superiors, to become the managing grand eunuch in the Ceremonial Directorate of the Ming court. By 1623 he was made the director of a secret police establishment, known as the Eastern Depot. He used his position to harass or remove those he deemed undesirable and to unleash a reign of terror. Himself a former gambler, he exerted an unhealthy and improper influence over the young emperor, swaying him towards darker pleasures. He manipulated the emperor so effectively that he was eventually granted absolute power over the court.

Malevolence like Wei's was missing in the many interviews I conducted. In fact, I failed to probe or expose a single truly dark art C practitioner, hard though I tried. Happily, like rogue As, rogue Cs are rare. People want to get promoted, rather than fired, and they know behaving decently is their best chance. Perhaps there was a villain lurking among my interviewees who played me like a violin. Maybe they so eagerly volunteered the Machiavellian monsters they most 'reviled' in a spirit of confession by projection. Scar's murder of his brother Mufasa and his manipulation of nephew Simba to become King of Pride Rock gets its fair, if not the lion's, share of admirers; a few were enthralled by the eunuch in *Game of Thrones*, Lord Varys, member of the king's council and royal spymaster, officially known as 'Master of Whisperers' (is there anyone in your organisation who deserves such a delicious title on their business card?); and Darth Vader's relationship with the dark side, according to the American Film Institute, ranks him as the third greatest movie villain in cinema history, the ruthless cyborg denied the opportunity to have a light-sabre duel with either Hannibal Lecter or Norman Bates.

Where are today's real-life devious deputies? Sport is populated by unscrupulous agents who prey on their vulnerable stars. Once described by Steve McClaren as 'the new David Beckham', David Bentley was a hero when playing for Blackburn Rovers between 2006 and 2008. Bad advice and a sizeable financial incentive took him to Tottenham Hotspur where he spent five years on the payroll, and considerably less time on the pitch. Shaun Wright-Phillips got similarly lousy advice. For four seasons running he was Manchester City's young player of the year, before his head was turned by more money and the promise of fame at Chelsea. At City, he had the world at his feet. At Chelsea, he barely kicked a ball. His career never recovered.

Devious deputies feed their A's inappropriate appetite for power. Bob Haldeman, White House chief of staff and one of the seven indicted by a grand jury in 1974 for their role in the Watergate scandal, was considered the second most powerful man in the government during Nixon's first term and was 'loved like a brother' by the president. He could have shown some brotherly love and tempered Nixon's ambition. Instead he authorised criminal activity, the cover-up of which brought about his A's downfall.

Along with former CEO Kenneth Lay, Jeffrey Skilling transformed Enron from a pipeline company into the world's largest energy trading company. The two leaders were also responsible for arguably the largest accounting fraud in history, one that cost investors and employees billions of dollars. Was there no sinister second working in the shadows of Lay and Skilling? Step forward Andrew Fastow, Enron's chief financial officer and the key C behind the complex web of fraudulent funds in which he had a personal financial stake. Fastow proved more reliable as an accomplice than as an Anchor.

Cs rarely carry criminal intent but it is useful to be able to predict dark art deputyship and gauge its contribution to inappropriate outcomes. Larry Page and Sergey Brin set out to make the world's information universally accessible and useful, a noble cause which has led to people making five billion Google searches every day. Now they need to keep a very close eye on possibly wayward Cs who might treat our petabytes of user-generated data with impropriety, and make money at the expense of our privacy.

It was his C's casual disregard for privacy that embarrassed Gordon Brown when he was prime minister. Damien McBride, former Whitehall civil servant and former special adviser to Brown, has at least come clean about the rumours he fabricated concerning the private lives of some Conservative Party politicians and their spouses. His confessional memoirs, *Power Trip: A Decade of Policy, Plots and Spin*, would make good bedtime reading for those who mistake Machiavelli's *The Prince* as a primer for the practice of evil.

Some C magicians may wish to avert their eyes here, to avoid the pain of seeing their tricks revealed, but the reflective ones will enjoy this peek into their kitchen, because they know how similar the qualities of a successful dark arts practitioner can be to those of a legitimate operator. We have seen some of their cunning legitimised in Chapter 5. As an A you should occasionally allow your Cs some mild deception if it helps them deliver for you, accept when they strew your path with flowers rather than break bad news to you bluntly, and put up with their foolery as long as it remains professional.

When the boundaries of propriety are breached our unmasked ministers and cunning cardinals need to be reminded of the sanctions. You have enough demons to deal with, enough volatility and vulnerability to withstand, without some villainous Iago pouring pestilence into your ear. An A should know what to watch out for and how best to pre-empt malpractice. Some of Shakespeare's scheming No. 2s offer a chance to hone your manipulation radar. Have you had a turn served upon you, like Othello, by a seemingly honest deputy? 'In following him I follow but myself.'

Iago enjoys more lines than any other character in Shakespeare, but he is not the only subtle schemer worthy of study. Beware those who remind you of Angelo, Bolingbroke or Claudius too. Such devious deputies deserve a spell under the microscope because they personify traits that modern Cs continue to manifest. Who knows, you may be left breathless with admiration for Iago's persuasive cunning, and want a crack at a C role yourself. Can you imagine planting a seed of doubt in your A's mind quite as destructive as the handkerchief?

*Iago:*

Nay, but be wise: yet we see nothing done;
She may be honest yet. Tell me but this,
Have you not sometimes seen a handkerchief
Spotted with strawberries in your wife's hand?

*Othello:*

I gave her such a one; 'twas my first gift.

*Iago:*

I know not that; but such a handkerchief –
I am sure it was your wife's – did I today
See Cassio wipe his beard with.

(William Shakespeare, *Othello*, Act III, Scene iii)

Assuming you remain attached to the A role, how can you divert the C's darker inclinations? What extremes should you look out for? What motives? Try hard not to hire someone like Iago, whose behaviour was described by Samuel Taylor Coleridge as 'the motive-hunting of motiveless malignity'. For the rest, look out for revenge, thwarted ambition, envy and events to which your C might respond excitably. Would Iago still have brought ruin on Othello had he, and not Michael Cassio, been promoted? Probably. Would Bolingbroke have been so intent on grabbing Richard's crown had he not been disinherited and forced to 'eat the bitter bread of banishment'? Possibly. Possibly not. Would Frank Underwood, played by Kevin Spacey in the US series *House of Cards*, have hatched his plan to destroy his enemy 'the way you devour a whale, one bite at a time' unless he had been passed over for the Secretary of State role he had been promised?

While the odd bloke admires the banished Bolingbroke,

whom the soon-to-be deposed King Richard describes as the 'thief and traitor, who all this while hath revell'd in the night', more women than you might imagine hold a candle for Lady Macbeth. Historians and Hilary Mantel lovers cannot get enough of Thomas Cromwell, enthralled by his rise from lowly origins to become Henry's chief minister, with his extensive network of spies and informers and his pathological lust for power. It only adds to his allure that he ended up facing away from the city in disgrace, his head on a pike. The humiliation of Henry's man would have been more drawn out today – extradition to the United States to do the Perp Walk. Some lift their cocktails to Molotov, a Stalin protégé. Others bow to Beria, Stalin's most influential secret police chief, and another thoroughly nasty piece of work. The Nazis produced a roll call of nasties with Himmler and the man they called his brain, Heydrich, high up on the list. Heydrich is the current chart topper, courtesy of Laurent Binet's brilliant novel *HHhH*. Might this excerpt resonate with your C's baser instincts?

> Heydrich is well aware that everyone considers him the most dangerous man in the Reich, and it is a source of vanity for him, but he also knows that if all the Nazi dignitaries court him so insistently, it is above all to try to weaken Himmler, his boss. Heydrich is an instrument to these men, not yet a rival. It's true that in the devilish duo he forms with Himmler, he is thought to be the brains ('HHhH,' they say in the SS: Himmlers Hirn heist Heydrich – Himmler's brain is called Heydrich), but he is still only the right-hand man, the subordinate, the number two. Heydrich is so ambitious that he will not be satisfied with this situation forever. But when he studies how the balance of power within the party has evolved, he congratulates himself for having stayed faithful to Himmler, whose power continues

to grow while Göring mopes in his mansion, half in disgrace, since the Luftwaffe's failure in England.

Does your C think they are the brains? Contemporary historians coo about Kissinger's influence over Nixon; rave about Karl Rove's ruthless, at times obsessive, promotion of President George W. Bush; and either admire or abhor Peter Mandelson, New Labour's Prince of Darkness. These and other cunning foxes, schemers and confidants grip us precisely because of their complexity. They are riddled with paradox. That which makes them good makes them bad and vice versa. Richelieu himself wrote: 'The virtues of a man in favour are his vices in disgrace.' Carried away on a wave of success or under fire and scrutiny, your C's qualities can also translate into destructive behaviour that will leave you, their A, with a problem. So we should examine what kind of excessive behaviour to watch out for from what kind of C, note the feelings that that behaviour will prompt in you, and suggest some immediate countermeasures.

## EXCESSIVE BEHAVIOUR
### Lodestones

A very effective Lodestone can end up taking such command of your daily affairs that they become a control freak and you become dominated and dependent. Does any deviation from your routine – writing your own speech, going to a meeting without their briefing papers, dropping in on a colleague for an impromptu discussion – make you feel like a rebel and your C a little threatened? If you are a proud A you will begin to feel claustrophobic in the presence of a C intent on making life so easy for you. Whatever kind of A you are, your over-dependence could leave you vulnerable to the departure of the Lodestone or, more importantly, to manipulation that you won't be able to recognise.

*Countermeasures*
- When your Lodestone goes on holiday (which you may have to insist they do) use the opportunity to get a better grip on your affairs.
- When they return let them know that their stand-in showed promise.
- Keep increasing the load. Their control freakery may diminish when they feel a little out of control themselves.

## Educators

Perhaps one or two of your Educators have got carried away with their own brilliance, and are providing more smugness than sagacity. Aren't they the smarty pants? After a while, you tire of that whiff of intellectual superiority, the pause for the applause as they share their latest thinking, some of which you find underwhelming. You may be able to live with someone who wonders at their own wisdom. Or you may begin to feel stupid, concerned that you cannot come up with an original thought yourself – music to the ears of the crafty consultant.

*Countermeasures*
- Sit your Educator down and explain that you appreciate their input but want them to pick their moments more carefully and to drop the smug tone.
- Tease them with Touchstone, the fool in *As You Like It*: 'The fool doth think he is wise, but the wise man knows himself to be a fool.'
- Call your C's bluff. Peter Murray observed how business

minister Nigel Griffiths dealt with advice he had concluded was foolish. The minister was being urged by his civil servants to issue a press release that highlighted the considerable dangers that fizzy drinks bottle tops presented to consumers. 'Nigel said it would make him look ridiculous. The permanent secretary disagreed. Nigel said, "Good, I've had the press release retyped with your name on it, so now will you issue it?"'

If your C is not prepared to put his own name to a recommendation, it might not be as wise as he is suggesting.

- Never give up on your own learning. Ever. If you are too busy to figure out the best way to teach yourself, think about enrolling on a course. If you don't fancy the formality of the classroom, ask somebody to customise a programme for you. Bruno Demichelis was impressed by Carlo Ancelotti's appetite for learning: 'Carlo is a very intelligent, very smart guy. He was saying, "I don't want to study, I don't want to read, I don't like to do that, you do it for me." So I made it very practical for him, to learn by experience, to learn by active methods.' I asked Bruno who his best ever footballing student was. He had no hesitation in naming Dutch international Clarence Seedorf:

> He was a real student; I mean a student that had the real motivation. He was consistent, persistent and always so fascinated. He wanted to become an interpreter and I said, 'Clarence, if you really want to be an interpreter you need to study a little bit.' He said, 'I'm not an expert in that. How can I learn it?' He went to the University of Bocconi here, you know, to get a master's degree in that. And when we started to talk about this he was coming in every day, listening, listening, studying, reading and

giving feedback. A student is someone who has a purpose, follows it and is disciplined.

- Put your consultants in a room together to exhaust themselves in an ego-charged battle for intellectual supremacy.

## Anchors

You know how important it is to have your Anchors. So much so that you have surrounded yourself with a troupe of professional fools. They rain the hard truth down upon you like a tropical storm. 'Did you see how you left that person feeling, you hard-hearted son of a bitch?' 'You didn't thank the receptionist on the way out of that crisis meeting,' 'How are you going to live with that decision, now that it has unravelled?' All this friendly fire leaves you permanently on the back foot, feeling isolated, manipulated and robbed of self-esteem.

*Countermeasures*
- Ask your Cs to tone it down and keep their criticism constructive.
- See how they would feel if they turned their critical faculties inwards: 'Do unto others as you would have them do unto you.'
- Tell them that, unless you specifically request it, you have no interest in hearing their advice.
- Criticise their dress sense. Attack is the best form of defence.

Other Anchors are showing you bucket loads of empathy. They repeat each statement you make, inserting a question mark at the end. Is there an echo in here? Eventually you feel lonely and lacking a true compass.

*Countermeasures*

- Quote them some Confucius, referencing the philosopher's aphorism in the *Analects* that emphasises the need for loyal opposition. A country is at risk, he says, when a prince finds the only joy in being a prince is that no one opposes what he says: 'The gentleman is harmonious although he does not assent. The small man assents, but is not harmonious.' If Confucius confounds, be explicit: 'Please do not confuse harmony with conformity and subservience. A harmonious Anchor of mine will point out flaws in my thinking and present me with alternative courses of action.'
- Challenge them with the four best words in the leader's armoury: 'What do you propose?'
- Keep asking them until they understand that your office needs windows into other points of view, not well-polished mirrors.

Your C's points of view are false mirrors, reflecting a touched-up image of you, for the purpose of manipulation. The only person critical of your standpoints is you, and you are beginning to lose the knack.

*Countermeasures*

- Learn from Carlo Sant'Albano and fuel a fear of flattery: 'When you say something that you know is the wrong thing and no one says anything to you, you have to make it clear: "If you guys are going to let me say something like that and not react, I don't need any one of you in the room, right?" Next time that happens, I may clear the room altogether.'
- Read them 'Of How To Avoid Flatterers', your favourite bit in *The Prince*, Chapter XXII, and watch them blush.

- Ring a bell, like Stalin did, to let your acolytes know when their sycophancy has become embarrassing.

## Deliverers

Deliverers, too, can take that which you value most in them to an unwanted extreme. Nothing can happen without their say-so. Operations and logistics head every meeting agenda. Your C becomes the bottleneck in the organisation. You begin to hear, 'There's no such thing as strategy,' or 'It's not what the vision is, it's what the vision does.' Your C issues T-shirts emblazoned with the Nike swoosh and 'Just Did It!' Your right-hand man has chopped you off at the knees. You feel weak, ridiculous, redundant, ready for the scrap heap. Your kingmaker now holds all the cards to make (or be) the next king.

*Countermeasures*
- Issue a plan for a shiny new project and assign responsibility to a Turtle, special adviser or chief of staff, who will report directly to you. Tell your Deliverer that they will have no part to play on the new project because you cannot risk distracting them from their existing projects which you expect them to execute flawlessly.
- Send them on an assignment of unspecified duration to Turkmenistan, Uzbekistan or Kyrgyzstan where the odds of them succeeding are small. Tell them the promotion is for growth and personal development, that you see them as a possible future chairman (or chancellor) and want them to learn some new tricks. Ask your PA to book just the outbound flight. The equivalent countermeasure in the political world used to be a reshuffle from the Home Office to Northern Ireland.

Your Deliverer has radiated so much heat about your vision, values and leadership that you are left looking faintly ludicrous. They have become, as it were, a flatterer facing outwards. How on earth can you live up to the promise?

*Countermeasures*
- Haul them in and ask them to turn the volume right down. Explain that your grand vision requires people's contributions to be represented fairly. Say, in as humble a tone as you can muster, 'I am only one piece of this puzzle, please try not to forget that.'
- Get out in front of your people and reveal some vulnerability. They need to see the authentic leader, not some cult of your C's creation.

Over and above these immediate countermeasures, how can you keep your C on the straight and narrow? Get familiar with their excesses, not to punish, but to pre-empt. Is their limelight aversion an authentic allergic reaction or a sign of something sinister? You need to distinguish between operating from the shadows fruitfully and from the darkness deviously. Scope their ambition. The ambition of an A is usually worn for all to see, but the C's can be more difficult to detect.

There may be good reason to think of the C as your Prince of Darkness. You will sometimes need them to operate surreptitiously when, for example, you suspect that someone is lying to you. But the majority of activities are best carried out in the open. Is your C deliberately starving their colleagues – and you – of the facts? Secrets ignite ambiguity, drive insecurity, heighten fears and give their bearer too much power. Show zero tolerance on this. If you are worried that your C is operating too much in the dark, you might consider inviting them onto the board, where they will be more in the light.

*Snakes in Suits: When Psychopaths Go to Work,* a book by industrial psychologist Paul Babiak and psychopathy expert Robert Hare, studies characters that make their way into business organisations in spite of their psychopathic tendencies. They use the term 'psychopath' in its broadest sense – a manipulator of people, causing problems in psychological and emotionally abusive ways. Babiak and Hare's thesis is that psychopathic traits can be readily mistaken for critical business values.

We saw in Chapter 1 the importance of confidence as a shared quality of all leaders. Cs can misuse their A's confidence in a number of ways: letting their A into a secret implies trust that raises expectations of friendship and respect. Snakes in suits share snippets of their own 'personal' information, seemingly letting their guard down with false honesty, encouraging the same in return. They can then exploit what they discover. Emotional intelligence is another critical quality. If abused, it allows the C to calculate the inner workings of the A's personality, using their insight into the A's motives, needs and vulnerabilities as a springboard for manipulation. After getting to know the characteristics that As value in themselves, the psychopath can use flattery and ego stroking as powerful influencing techniques. Equally, after carefully assessing the A's Achilles heel, the C can weaken them further, preying on their anxieties. Cs should note that As, too, can be slithery snakes in expensive suits. There is one A I have observed at close quarters whose ability to encourage his Cs to let down their guard kept them perpetually in his service, fearful of their revelations to him.

Most relevant to the A/C relationship is Babiak and Hare's examination of 'pawns' and 'patrons'. The C with snake-like traits would view as pawns those who have the power, status, or access to desired resources, to be used until they have served their usefulness. They would also, according to Babiak and Hare, attract 'patrons', mentors or godfathers, who take talented employees under their wing and help them negotiate their way to the top of the organisation: 'Once this patronage is established, it is difficult to overcome. With a patron on their side, psychopaths could do almost no wrong,' say the authors. Powerful organisational A patrons (unwittingly) protect their Cs from the criticism of others and support their career advancement. While you should protect your C from doubts and accusations, you might find that his relentless promotion through the ranks has an unhappy ending: you are dumped, and your back is firmly stabbed.

So As need to distinguish between the serious snakes and the Severus Snapes. An excess expert will not need to read all seven Harry Potter novels to question whether Snape is in fact something other than the malicious antihero he appears at first to be. An early prediction that he would land the position he yearned for, teaching Defence Against the Dark Arts, is what you are after. If you sense you have a snake in a suit you can keep him close in order to qualify your suspicions, knowing that his immediate proximity and access to all that you say and do are not without risk. Or if you are feeling more confident in your position of authority, subscribe to the view that 'an open hand is the tightest grip' and encourage him to roam free, giving him plenty of rope. To reel in a large fish, release more wire and exhaust it. Whichever choice you make, make it a conscious one; learn all that you can about his nature so that you can recognise and interpret his motives and moves.

Be aware that the darker your own behaviour, the darker

the possibilities for your C. Complete failure to combat your weaknesses (see Chapter 7) will put even the purest Cs to the test. Having looked at ways to curb the excesses of Cs, we will now concentrate on how to release their potential, how to create and maintain the best possible A/C relationship. The 'Living with your Leader' guide that follows has six categories filled with the wisdom and practices of some particularly artful As. These are mirrored by C know-how in the next chapter and, together, should make for a constructive A/C conversation. Choosing and Cohabitation are the longest sections because you really must choose the right people and learn to live with your choices. The other sections are very important too, letting you know what to do when things go wrong – Conflict Resolution – when things go right – Celebration – and when you aren't certain how they are going – Checking. And finally, Changing.

## LIVING WITH YOUR DEPUTY
### Choosing

> The selection of ministers is of no little importance to a prince; and they are good or not, according to the prince's prudence. The first thing one does to evaluate a ruler's prudence is to look at the men he has around him.
>
> (Niccolò Machiavelli, *The Prince*)

*Casting your consiglieri*
Dreaming of better deputies? When you fantasise about a C, what do you see? A tub of ibuprofen for faster acting pain relief? A velvet glove to wrap around your iron fist? There are many variations on the supportive C theme and one of the A's most important responsibilities is to pick wisely.

Inconveniently, Cs do not tend to walk into casting sessions with 'No Axe To Grind' or 'Advice You Can Trust' tattooed on their foreheads. You have to figure out what kind of person you want, make your best call on each candidate's reliability, and then define your relationship with them. Whether to splash out on a CEO at the top of their game, and charm them with a chairmanship; to opt for an *éminence grise*, proven in the dispensation of wise counsel; to go strictly low budget, and bring in a BP Turtle, with an iPhone thrown in if they haggle hard; or something in between?

Do you, like Don Corleone, want one consigliere for war and another for peace, one for the crisis in which you have five minutes to make a decision, the other to challenge you when the heat is off? Or do you always want to rely on one confidant because you believe situations come and go but people you can trust are forever? If you are smart, you will do a deal with your headhunter and take one of each. You need them, and more besides, for diversity of experience, background, orientation and ambition. The best leaders surround themselves with a full cast of Cs. Maybe you can't do an *Ocean's Eleven* and have Clooney, Pitt, Damon, Garcia and Roberts, but hopefully you can hedge a little. Football managers indulge themselves with whole teams of assistants. Tony Blair's cabinet was chock-full. Smart As have multiple advisers, and know how to use them and when. A good way to find out what you need others to bring to the table is to ask yourself what you personally lack. All Black captain Sean Fitzpatrick learned as much from John Hart:

> He was a great man manager and good with the public …
> but when he came in as coach, he'd been out of rugby for five
> years, and he came to me and said, 'Look, I still want you to
> be an All Black, but I need you to help me coach this team.'

I thought, 'that is just unbelievable that you've actually held your hands up and said that to me.' He was big enough to say … 'Look, I'm actually not good with this, I will do everything off the field to help the team to be the best it can possibly be. You'll get the best of everything. I'll give you whatever you want. Sean, you just deliver on the training field.'

Once you have identified a leader's outlying strength, you can often identify corresponding weaknesses. So if you have a great intellect, congratulations. How wonderful. But what when your colleagues find your intellect intimidating? You are a stellar salesman and you cannot help winning orders? Ker-ching. But who exactly is going to fulfil the promises you have made and can they really live up to them? You are a master of execution who gets things done at warp speed? Impressive. But can somebody please tell me what the long game plan is around here?

Understanding what, uniquely, you bring to the relationship and what, if you are candid, you are incapable of bringing to it, is a good place to start. The collaboration between Richard Strauss and Hugo von Hofmannsthal was one of the greatest composer–librettist relationships of all time, spanning nearly three decades until the poet's untimely death in 1929. Such were their differences that their collaboration has been likened to a Siamese cat working out a *modus vivendi* with a Labrador retriever. Unless you have a Woody Allen knack for bringing together a bunch of oddballs and misfits, you should write a casting brief and run a thorough casting session. It's quite expensive to keep shooting alternative Cs. As you review the candidates as a collective, check for their distinctive features. Ask yourself whether each can march to your drum, what each will uniquely contribute to the whole. Have you got a group that includes a Lodestone, Educator, Anchor and Deliverer?

Vivienne Durham, headmistress at Francis Holland School in London, is clear that her senior team of five clearly reflects who she is and who she is not:

> They are the most important part of me doing the job, the people who work most closely to me. They've got to be as good as you can get and they've got to be complementary to you. Until she joined me, my academic deputy was head of Maths at North London Collegiate and she's really detailed, really methodical, loves graphs, loves charts, all the things I'm not. I have another person who is strong on providing the general, the overview, and who is calm, positive, not an anxious personality, different from me.

Durham actually has an extraordinary calm herself, particularly in a crisis, leading from the front when her school was subject to great uncertainty because of its proximity to the London bombings of 7 July 2005. Durham feels that reliance on the A alone in a crisis leaves operations unnecessarily vulnerable, so she places great emphasis on the need for the strongest possible C around her:

> My number two, my deputy, is very like me in lots of ways. I wouldn't think twice in a crisis. I would do what I had to do and she'd run the show. In that situation, your number two runs the show. You've got to have somebody in whom you've got absolute confidence ... like in any good business you need a great deputy, the co-pilot that flies the plane. You take the chief executive or the pilot for granted but what if a pilot has a cardiac arrest?

Cs are as important as you and they should be different from you. Phil Townsend, director of communications at Manchester United, says that Sir Alex Ferguson and David Gill were bound by common values, that 'they both always saw the club as a club', but that there were differences between them that led to a healthy balance in the relationship:

'One's obviously a socialist and the other is certainly not. I suspect if you're looking for opposites, you could start there ... They clearly have very different backgrounds and upbringings.'

Avoid a leadership matryoshka doll, containing a set of advisers functionally identical to their leader, only incrementally smaller. The A should never cast mini-me's. Take heed of the worse-case scenario of Dmitry Medvedev, who was not even the casting director of his leadership doll. Mick Brown, reviewing Masha Gessen's *The Man Without a Face: The Unlikely Rise of Vladimir Putin*, describes the peculiar case of an inverted A/C relationship: 'In the four years that Medvedev has served as president he has been not so much matryoshka doll as puppet, in the shadow of Putin, nominally his prime minister, but the man who by his iron rule has shaped Russia in his image over the past 12 years – the matryoshka doll in whom all Russia is contained.'

Better to create a leadership team that resembles a packet of Revels, each thickly daubed with the same sweet sense of purpose, but every one different in taste and texture. Tony Blair's packet was extra-large. You could have hours of fun trying to stack every one up in order of importance, but that would miss the point. Each offered something different, dealing with aspects of his job that Blair and others could not: Gordon Brown, Peter Mandelson, Andrew Adonis, Philip Gould, Jonathan Powell, Charlie Falconer, Ruth Turner, Anji

Hunter, Alastair Campbell. For Team Sky, Sir David Brails-ford hand-picked a great bunch of Revels, some hard, some soothing, some crisp, some, like the coffee-flavoured Revel, not to everybody's liking. Again the constant was their collective embrace of a cause – British cycling, fair play and excellence.

Some As harmonise particularly well with one deputy in particular – the C major; Dr Watson to Sherlock Holmes, Charlie Munger to Warren Buffett, medal-hungry hound Mutley to Wacky Races' villain Dick Dastardly. You must stand back-to-back with this C major, one of you whistling the belief that anything is possible, perhaps an entrepreneur oozing self-confidence and visions of a better future; the other, restlessly curious about what is bound to go wrong at any minute, a black hat pessimist checking and double-checking that everything is in tune. If you are numbers driven, factual, logical and operational, hire yourself a visionary, instinctive, empathetic Nicki Chapman, agent to the stars. If you are an out-and-out rock star who leads with their gut, like Amanda Blanc at AXA, bag yourself a make-things-happen man like Max Carruthers, her chief operating officer.

It is worth asking this difficult question, 'Who will be the defining C of my A tenure?' Ask this not to create a favourite, like a bad parent might, but rather to find out which role matters most in the situation you are in. Is your biggest issue strategy or execution? Or is it perhaps talent management or communications? In politics nowadays, for example, what matters more, policy or reputation management? Future historians will debate the answer, but you need to do your best to figure it out now. Fifty years from now who will be most closely associated with Blair's premiership? Mandelson, self-anointed Third Man, was on and off stage a little too much; on strategy, one would have to conclude that it was

Philip Gould; for policy, certainly in Blair's second term, Lord Adonis; on Northern Ireland, Jonathan Powell saw the resolution through to its conclusion. Re-watching British political satire *The Thick of It* and Rory Bremner's impersonations, my own view is that, retrospectively, the slightly bigger Revel in the packet will be Alastair Campbell, responsible for almost as much of the story as Blair himself.

## Defining the relationship

Once you have decided on a C it is important to do as the Americans do after a couple of dates, and Define the Relationship. Are they clear on the role you wish them to play? Have you chosen them because you saw them play a role in somebody else's movie and you want them to replicate it for you? Or would you like them to try something different? You should allow your C to preserve some mystery. Life on the second date would be dull if they had told you everything on the first. At the same time, you need to be explicit at the outset about any behaviour that might damage the chances of an enduring relationship.

When he became Sir Alex Ferguson's assistant manager, Mike Phelan was not told exactly what was expected of him in the role. Having been a player in Ferguson's European Cup Winners' Cup team, Phelan knew the behaviour that his boss most valued, and took comfort from the one piece of explicit direction given to him, that he should keep Ferguson informed at all times. 'He did once say to me, "look, you're my assistant. Whatever choice you make and whatever decision you make, I'll back you. Just as long as I know what you're doing, I'll back it."'

In my research, I was surprised how few As gave their new Cs an explicit brief. Some were, like Phelan, already known to their As, meaning the As knew how the Cs might approach their new role. In cases where the A/C relationship is new to both parties, briefings should leave little to chance. In the early days, you should spend more time consciously reviewing how you make each other feel and letting each other know the qualities you most value. You need to explore each other's boundaries. In which areas of your work do you value their counsel? And which do you want to be left alone? What is your appetite for, or intolerance of, overlap? Look out for skirmishes in the early days and welcome them for the learning they provide. What is really going on? Are you showing signs of insecurity because you are new to this A assignment? Are you up to it? Have you worked out how you are going to approach it? Are you wondering why the C is doing what they are doing? Is the C thinking wistfully that you never tell them what you're doing, that you're making them look silly because they are left in the dark not knowing what on earth is going on? If so, it is time for the first heart-to-heart, where you say 'Look, this is what I'm finding difficult and frustrating ...' and they reply, 'Well, I'm finding this is a bit tricky because ...'. Let them fill in the blanks.

You must have the courage to have the kind of conversation that many As and Cs do not have, at least not until sores are festering and resentments are running deep.

## Cohabiting

You think you have got your borders in order? Living together will be the ultimate test of that. There will be challenges on many fronts. You will have to find it within yourself to give your C some space, show some grace, let them find their voice, allow them time to roam, and give them your regular undivided attention.

*Give them some space*

Simply keeping out of the way of your C is not enough. You must work out what kind of space they need, by knowing the particular skills that they love to exercise freely. Gaytri Kachroo, lawyer and lead counsellor to the famous 'Fox Hound' whistleblowers in the Bernie Madoff affair, now leads her own firm:

> There has to be a willingness to bring into the firm each person as they are because they have to be able to impact the thing that they are creating ... Everybody's got individual talents and brilliance. What is it about their spirit that will really help to move mine? If you don't address this, then you're stifling something, an opportunity for progress, theirs or mine, or the larger vision.

Being gracious with the space you provide and the involvement you encourage will help the C find and use their unique voice. This applies to the PA as much as to the VP.

Depending on your attitude to space, the C may begin to feel like a space invader. There may be no malign intent, merely a passion for sharing ideas and a hunger for involvement. If this is unwelcome go back to your boundary definitions and, respectfully, tell your C to back off a little. Big Bruno Demichelis warned his As in advance that he might become an unintentional impostor:

> Before I even started with Fabio Capello, and then Carlo Ancelotti, I said 'I warn you because I am so passionate in what I do and I love so much my ideas and this vision, I may invade too much your space. It is because it is part of the passion that I have. If I am pressing you too much, or going too far, please stop me.'

Have the conversation as early as possible. If you have a grievance it is very likely that the C will have one too. Be clear about your no-fly zone, and beware of encroaching into the C's, especially when you are dealing with someone whose calibre deserves operational freedom of manoeuvre. Before taking on an equivalent supporting C role to David Gill, CEO of Manchester United, Michael Bolingbroke had been the right-hand man to John Stevenson, the A who ran animation company The Jim Henson Creature Shop and was then chief operating officer at Cirque du Soleil, working for Daniel Lamar, the A for the business of the circus. Bolingbroke described to me the complexities of running operations for both Manchester United and Cirque du Soleil.

For the football club, his operational leadership ensures that when 80,000 people, a quarter of the population of Iceland, come to Manchester United's stadium on match days, all they have to worry about is the performance on the pitch of their team. Bolingbroke's match day responsibilities are a fraction of his overall duties as a Deliverer. They also seem like a kick about in the park compared to delivering at Cirque du Soleil.

Cirque would arrive in a city, the tent was set up, the show was set up, safely and on time, the artistes arrived, the artistes trained, tickets were sold, the curtain went up every night on time, the artistes performed. Two thousand five hundred people saw the show ten times a week for six weeks then everything got packed away and moved on to the next city. There were twenty shows at Cirque being staged in different countries all around the world. So the show complexity is multiplied by twenty, as Bolingbroke describes:

There were many periods where at any time in the 24-hour clock Cirque du Soleil would be performing. On top of that, of your artistes in all of your twenty shows, 20 per cent are churning out every year, so you've got to have a constant funnel of artistes coming in which means they need to be scouted, hired, brought in, trained for a year and then ready to perform. That whole funnel has all got to be working smoothly so, at the end of the day, you as a paying punter go in and see a top-class show the like of which you've never seen before. Add to that all the administration, finance, legal, IT, HR; not forgetting the complexities of different languages. When you package all that up, throw into the mix all the sponsors, the international sponsors, the worldwide sponsors and the local sponsors, all expecting the same level of service, all expecting the personal touch ... That is what the COO sits on top of.

Imagine, then, micromanaging a Michael Bolingbroke.

If someone ever started telling me how to do it? Well, I don't need that, I mean, there's no point having someone of my firepower if you want to do the job yourself. That wouldn't work. Daniel Lamar and David Gill both understood what I could do, respected me for what I did and, quite frankly, enjoyed doing their jobs much more than they would have done mine. You need to have a CEO saying, 'Okay, we're here, we're going there, please can you tell me how we can do it.'

Another of Gill's direct reports at Manchester United, Phil Townsend, confirms his A's desire for the Cs around him to express themselves, 'not in an unquestioning way, but David values expertise and he allows you to do your job.' You cannot tell a Deliverer exactly how they should deliver. Getting involved in the nitty-gritty will close down your C's space, chip away at their autonomy, undermine their authority and, worst-case, render their job pointless. It also sends out a signal that you are no good at your own job, which is to employ the right people in the first place. Theodore Roosevelt knew this: 'The best executive is the one who has sense enough to pick good men to do what he wants done, and self-restraint to keep from meddling with them while they do it.'

*Let them find their voice*
Hog all the airtime and the oxygen, and your C will be unable to breathe. If you would rather hear yourself, buy a tape recorder. If you find it impossible to keep quiet, do not go to the C's meetings. You do not necessarily need to be at them to show complete support for what your C is doing, as Big Bruno explained to Carlo Ancelotti: 'I told him, "Listen, if you don't want to come, don't come, but I want you to listen to what I am saying. I want you to know what I am telling your players because if you don't follow what I'm doing then you destroy my job and you destroy what you do, too."'

Best of all, attend and keep quiet. Your rapt attention will mean a lot. To have Carlo Ancelotti, Fabio Capello and Arrigo Sacchi pay attention while Big Bruno was in full flow sent a message of endorsement to the players. They had their coach sitting there listening to a psychologist, educating them on his vision of what they could achieve mentally and physically. Many Cs may not crave centre stage, but there are times when they have to perform. As the A you should lend a generous ear to the C as they deliver their soliloquies, scraps that may be compared to yours.

*Let them roam*
Ambitious Cs are pioneers. They love unearthing new opportunities, new ways to approach old problems. Wherever

possible leave this process to their discretion. Michael Boling-broke was given the chance to experiment with something that David Gill did not believe in initially. In 2005 there was talk about Old Trafford, Manchester United's stadium, being used to host Olympic football matches in 2012.

'When I joined, David handed me this and said, "Well, this won't take you long, just read the file and then tell them "no".' That was his opinion. I said, "Well, leave it with me." My predecessor had basically toed David's line. I thought, "Let's just have a conversation with the Olympic organisers about it and we'll see." I figured that, come the time, we might be uncomfortable with the idea of anybody else being the hub for the football games. We are Manchester United, who else should take on that mantle and host the main games ahead of the final at Wembley? And over a period I said to David, in one-to-one conversations only, "I'm not sure you're right, I think there's something for us here, I think there's something for the club here for many reasons." He backed me. Three years on David was all keyed up and talking to the press about how we were going to be hosting the football Olympics.'

Once they have accepted the responsibility of satisfying you on the things that matter to you, give your C the space and support to do things that you would not. I can tell when Kevin Roberts thinks I have had an average idea. He gives me a clue: 'Ah, you've been taking your stupid pills.' Extraordinarily, this will nearly always be followed by encouragement to give the idea a go. I get fired up with excitement at an experiment with no certainty of outcome, and suitably keen to prove him wrong. The only certainty is his full support. An inspirational A encourages his C to keep pushing what psychologist Herbert Simon calls a 'network of possible wanderings.' Remember that Cs are lifelong learners, so give them licence to roam.

*Give them time*

When living under one roof it can be tempting to ask your flatmate to take on all the tasks that you don't fancy. Washing your dirty laundry, emptying the dishwasher, paying the bills, cleaning out the rabbit hutch, the list can get long and exhausting. Once proven to be an effective problem solver, Cs can soon find themselves being given more problems to resolve than just for their A. For Ira Dubinsky, the thrill of being the man by Jack Layton's side wore off as more and more business cards were thrust into his hand, with requests to resolve an increasing mountain of problems. Lodestone or not, every C benefits from having some time to think, to feel contentment through contemplation. The technology-inspired idea that we should be Always On is iniquitous. If you want your C to be any good, they must be Often Off. It is in off mode that they will do their deep, complex thinking, the benefit of which the leader gets when their C is back on. In his TED talk, Russell Foster shows that Often Off should include good long sleeps because while we slumber our brains keep solving problems, and a well-slept brain performs better in cognitive tests.

You want your C for their mind, their spirit, yet you seem to have no interest in their body. Mistake. After a while your rabbit will become morose in their filthy hutch, fatigued by their lengthening To Do list. If you say enough times 'Here's another thing I'd like to get done. Can you get it done?' the C will begin to curse you. Do not make your C pick up the tab for your ill-discipline. Tying your C to their desk will diminish more than their productivity. It is no use muttering, 'You really must rest, you know' as you hand them another foolscap folder. To be sure, Tony Blair squeezed the best out of Alastair Campbell, but sometimes he squashed him too. Campbell describes the workload:

It was relentless and whenever I stopped I had a crash. Holidays were a disaster for us because the first week, crash – ill.
Tony had – maybe this is just a quality you need as the leader –
Tony had the ability to recharge his batteries in half a day – go
for a swim, go and play tennis, watch a film. He felt better. If
I sit and watch a film I fall asleep and wake up fucked for the
next three hours. I remember Peter Mandelson saying, 'What I
love about Tony is his absolute total selfishness.'

When Campbell had a stomach illness and ended up in
hospital, he remembers how: 'Anji Hunter totally lost it with
Tony because he felt my illness was a real inconvenience to
him. She said, "Do you realise what we do for you? You may
be working long hours, we're working either end of that to
get your day sorted, to get everything in shape, to pick up the
pieces."' That Campbell and Hunter got ill occasionally must
have felt to Blair like proof that they were giving it their all
and evidence of their effectiveness as Cs. It is still not a good
idea to work your support acts into the ground, however.
Given your own propensity to sacrifice life for work, be sure
to have someone you trust on hand who has a better balance.
And don't resent them for it.

### Allow them access
You must make time for your C. Being busy at the office
every day will not make for a robust relationship. Nor will
hiding what you are up to when your C is not around. The
less you share, the less directly you will feel a C's, especially
an Anchor's, benefit and the more you will open yourself up
to criticism: 'he's making it up as he goes along.' Giving only
partially of yourself will starve the Anchor of insight. For the
Lodestone, access means entry to your diary and your emails.

For Turtles and assistants it means time spent with you off the ball or on the train. You must give your Cs your ear, the whole story and your full trust.

Being an open book can be uncomfortable. One of your HR team has hired a Turtle for you. You say to yourself 'Most people won't give their partner their email password … am I really going to let this upstart play with my Blackberry?' Fair question. You can mitigate the risk by getting to know the Turtle first. Jean-Pierre Farandou, chief executive of SNCF subsidiary Keolis, saw Karim Chaiblaine in action before asking him to become his assistant. Jack Layton, Canadian opposition leader, and Ira Dubinsky had a previous relationship before Layton tapped him on the shoulder. Says Dubinsky:

> He already knew me and trusted me, and he gave full access and full honesty all the time: 'I'm tired. I don't want to go to this meeting, I don't know who these people are, I don't know their names.' I think that it's helpful to show your adviser your vulnerability, because people respond well to that. Jack did that well and people loved him for that reason. Certainly with your closest adviser, you have to be honest. If you're not, your adviser will soon know about that.

Access also means carving out dedicated time for your C. You may find that regular calendar commitments make you claustrophobic or bored, but unless your C has some certainty that they will get access to you, how can they be on your wavelength?

*Focus properly*
That time you give them is likely to be the most important part of their day. Even if it feels like your least, you must give them

your unconditional focus. They are busy because of you, and devoting attention to them is a form of appreciation. If you look like you have other things and people on your mind, then they know where they stand. If the time you have to give is limited, make sure it is of the highest quality. Of Ian Powell, PwC's chairman and senior partner, Louise Scott, at the time Powell's executive assistant, says: 'He can really focus, that's the thing. So he really focuses on you when you've got a meeting with him, makes you feel important.'

If you find sustained focus difficult, you will never make it as a truly top A. If you are good at focusing, perhaps you have the ability to focus on several people at once. This is useful, but not the kind of focus that your C needs. Sir Alex Ferguson, friend and mentor to Alastair Campbell, taught him a trick about focusing. He shared it just before Blair was anointed leader of the Labour party, when people were starting to seek out Campbell incessantly: 'That's when Fergie said what he does in those situations: "I just put the blinkers on. I imagine I have blinkers on and I don't let anyone into my space unless I want them there." And I've done that ever since.'

According to David Gill, in his regular Friday morning meetings with him, Sir Alex was consistently an outstanding listener. To know how not to listen, look no further than mercurial football manager Brian Clough. 'What do you do when someone disagrees with you?' he was once asked. 'Oh, we have a conversation about that for twenty minutes and then we agree I was right.' The ability to listen is the difference between the good and the great. The limitations to Clough's listening lessened the greatness within his reach. Lead with your ears rather than your mouth. The very best do not simply ask open questions, nor listen intently to the answers, they listen to what is not said, to the yell of silence and what that signifies.

The support of many a changing room in sport has been lost by the coach's inability – or unwillingness – to listen to his players. Of course an A must always judge opinion on its merits and if a C gives consistently bad advice then they are not in the right place. Yet for the sake of the leadership team there can never be a time to stop listening. Had he not listened to Lady Macbeth's bad advice in the first place Macbeth might not have got himself into a pickle at all. When we think of Macbeth as corrupted by Lady Macbeth's darker desires we tend to forget that Macbeth begins to unravel only when he removes himself from his wife's counsel. While he has her to step in between his desires and his actions, to deputise, discuss, argue and encourage, he maintains, with and through her, some level of control over himself and the world around him. It is when he steps outside of the relationship – with the murder of Banquo and attempted murder of his sons – that he loses control, loses himself in the darkness of his desires, and begins to fail.

Listen to your C – their eyes are your eyes, and their ears your ears when yours fail or when you aren't around. Even with transparency, predictability of access, and your undivided attention the A/C relationship will not be without strain or occasional failure. Let us assume that your C has messed up. Your first instinct has to be to stand in front of them and forgive them. (There will be time later to offer a little coaching on the matter.) Campbell told me that Blair knew how to forgive him his mistakes:

> I can remember once I did a briefing – it was about the Genome Project. I didn't know what I was talking about. I sort of had a vague idea but I hadn't expected it to come up, hadn't really prepared it, which was rare because I used to

take those briefings seriously. I used to think through every question because I knew they wanted to catch me out every day. After this briefing on the Genome Project, suddenly left, right and centre, share values were being wiped off these big science companies. I just went to Tony and said, 'I'm really sorry about that.' Another time I was with Gordon – something with Gordon – I can't remember what the story was, but it was just a bit of a disaster – and I went to both of them and said, 'I'm very sorry about this.' And both of them said, 'Let's be honest, it's amazing you don't fuck up more than you do.'

Instant forgiveness in the face of failure buys the A large doses of loyalty. The good C is perfectly capable of chastising himself, learning from the episode and getting it right next time. Peter Murray, special adviser to Blair's former business minister, Nigel Griffiths, distinguishes between ministers who do and don't stand up for their Cs:

> I've worked for three ministers now. Nigel told me on day one, 'If you fuck up I'll back you up.' I needed to know that and I believed him because he knew that that was the only way that it worked. With others you know it won't work like that. Look at what happened with Jeremy Hunt's guy: 'I'll look after you in due course but, right now, you're going to have to take the bullet.' And he did. And I would still take a bullet for Nigel, even though I've moved on and so has he.

Vivienne Durham is supportive of her senior team:

> I say to them, 'you may make a mistake but, conceptually, if there's a mistake made, it's not you because I trust you always to have done your absolute best. If I've appointed you at senior

level, I know or I believe, arrogantly, that you'll have wanted to do your absolute best for the place. So, if it's gone wrong, we're in it together, just come in and tell me.'

If you make your Cs live in fear of failure, you will hold them back and inhibit their boldest moves. By crippling their adventurous wanderings, you may close the door on your next best move. Oliver Hardy never discovered his C's true potential. By chastising Stan Laurel with the catchphrase admonishment, 'Well, here's another nice mess you've gotten me into!', Hardy left his hapless, confused C crying like a baby.

## Conflict resolution

Most relationships will at some stage come under strain, resulting in their not functioning optimally, and both partners will in some way be responsible. Partners will produce what Alissa Goodman and Ellen Greaves call 'negative interaction cycles'. The A and the C together can resolve conflict in their relationship by first of all acknowledging that a problem exists and getting it out in the open. Might you have a relationship problem? How might you know?

If you have a robust constitution, you could adopt the system used by David Brailsford, introduced by Dr Steve Peters, a clinical psychiatrist with experience working with mass murderers and psychopaths. Brailsford describes Peters' quality as an Anchor:

He wouldn't hold back, he was just blunt in terms of 'Right, okay Dave, listen, I've seen three or four people today, very upset with you. You've really dropped the bomb here, and these are the issues, and you said, this, this and this and it's been taken like this and they are furious.' And, I'd be like,

'Bloody hell, that's not what I meant,' and he'd go, 'No, I know that's not what you meant, but that's what you've got to deal with.'

If you do not have a Peters to hand but still want to understand if you have a relationship issue with your C, you could adopt his 'toilet test'. Brailsford explains:

We used to do these sessions, which were tough to do, where we'd sit together and Steve would say, 'Right Dave, we're going to do this kind of scenario. You're sitting on the loo minding your own business and these guys walk in not knowing you're there behind the door on the loo. They are now going to tell me again what they just told me. Dave, you just have to sit there and listen. You have to listen to what they honestly think, about you, about what you say and how you say it, because they have no inhibition whatsoever.'

What would you do in this scenario? Shout out, 'I'm in here, be careful what you say.' Or would you put your fingers in your ears? Or would you sit there and listen? To start with, Brailsford found it very uncomfortable to take the criticism of himself, without a right of reply. Over time, he appreciated knowing what the issues were, hearing first-hand how he was making his Cs feel, knowing there was nothing malicious or personal in the directness of the feedback.

Nick Booth is CEO of the Royal Foundation, working with the Duke and Duchess of Cambridge and Prince Harry to initiate lasting, positive change through their convening power and philanthropy. Before that he was campaign director of the largest social service organisation in Great Britain, the NSPCC, raising over $540 million for its Full Stop Appeal, and vice president of philanthropy at Big Brothers, Big Sisters in the US:

> You have to be completely honest with people. So if I'm doing terrible things my advisers have absolute permission to sit down and tell me I'm doing terrible things. You can't be doing with ego in this job at all. We all have that, of course, but you've got to park it at the door. And certainly with Kath Abrahams, whom I had for a long period [now director of fundraising at Breast Cancer], we had a very honest relationship. The same with Rebecca Hunter, who was my No. 2 in America and who stayed with me the whole time I was there. Sometimes it was quite edgy. I remember once Kath stormed out of the room in tears about something. I thought, 'Oh, God, I've just upset the person closest to me now.' I sent her text messages and stuff. Luckily she said, 'That's all right, we'll still love each other.'

David Gill stresses that the open relationship he enjoyed with Ferguson was rooted in being, 'honest with each other: either of us could say, "you've been a bloody idiot there", or, "that's wrong"; it comes from having complete trust in each other and a common sense of purpose.'

Why do close relationships break down?

Judith Leavitt, in her book *Common Dilemmas in Couple Therapy,* identifies forces that contribute to relationship stress. They include breakdown of trust; lack of respect for each other; contempt for each other; too many irresolvable issues; lack of intimacy or attachment, often associated with increased time pressures and time spent apart; incompatibility of beliefs, needs, lifestyles; lack of communication and negotiation skills; significant unmet needs; power struggles. Dr John Gottman, co-founder of the Gottman Institute with his wife, Dr Julie Schwartz Gottman, has conducted forty years' worth of breakthrough research with more than eight thousand couples, providing marital therapists with the most comprehensive understanding of marital interactions that exists today. Gottman suggests that there are a number of predictors of divorce, including 'the four horsemen of the Apocalypse' – criticism, defensiveness, contempt and listener withdrawal.

How many times in the last hundred days, as an A, might you have criticised your C? How often have you, in the face of their counsel, attempted to justify your position? Might you have shown even just a smidgeon of contempt for your C, directly or indirectly? Might you have stopped listening? Engaging with conflict is tense and uncomfortable. We spend more time avoiding it than resolving it. In couple therapy, there are two notable types of 'stonewalling'/conflict avoidance. The first is the refusal of both parties to engage in conflict; the second is called the 'demand-withdraw' pattern, where one party is committed to airing problems, but the other isn't.

Do you and your C claim rarely to disagree? How often do you say to your C, 'Well, let's agree to disagree,' to avoid potentially hurting each other? Both As and Cs often repress or deny problems in this way, refusing to confess to the existence of a conflict. They may genuinely be under the illusion that communication has taken place. They are, subconsciously, conjoined in a contract to avoid talking about their relationship issues.

The A needs to break these bland denials of difficulty and put a stop to the stonewalling, the skirting around confrontation, the stubborn avoidance of responsibility. Withdrawal from interaction appears to be a particularly male phenomenon, as shown by two longitudinal studies on the relationship between marital interaction and marital satisfaction (again, Gottman). This male attitude can be especially attributed to As – any discussions about relationships are for softies: 'Let's get on with it, shall we, and leave emotions for the playground?'

Conflict avoidance may leave issues unresolved and cause feelings of resentment and anger whereas conflict engagement (disagreement) may have negative implications for a relationship in the short term but will drive up satisfaction in the long term. You need to draw out your C, show them some warmth and empathy, and a willingness to resolve the disagreement.

Is your C showing you a lack of respect? This may be because of poor communication. Are you listening actively, demonstrating that your C's views have been heard and understood, their opinions valued? Sprinkle your conversations with what the therapists call 'response tokens' or 'continuers' (mm, uh huh, mm hm, yeah), essential components of conversation that indicate your ears are engaged. Use language that hints at how receptive you are: 'Can you expand?' 'I don't quite see it that way but I'd love to think about it some more.' You can afford to use your sense of humour, too, to cajole your partner into confronting serious issues.

Of course, it takes two to tango. However tempting it may be to blame your C for the failure of the whole, you are part of a system in which each plays a role. You are stuck in this circle together so you both need to examine the cause and effect of your conflict and its reciprocal patterns.

If your relationship problems seem insurmountable, it's important not to overwhelm your C with a list of all the issues you have identified. Fred Hanna, in *Therapy with Difficult Clients*, provides a good solution to help you pick your battles wisely. Before you even raise an issue, judge its intensity, its immediacy, you and your C's history with the issue, and what you are both ready to make happen to resolve it. It might be wise to start with a safe issue, something low key that can be resolved easily, one in which the couple is not highly invested.

Jacobson and Christensen also give some good ground rules for picking your battles:

- In stating the problem, **try to begin with something positive**. The way a problem is first stated sets the tone for the entire discussion: 'I have to tell you, C, that the bulk of the analysis in the paper you prepared for me last week was top drawer ...' is preferable to, 'What on earth were you smoking when you put together this recommendation?'
- **Specificity beats generalisation**. Go with 'I disagree with your indicated action in paragraph 6 on page 41 and have a different suggestion that I would like you to consider' rather than, 'Your indicated actions are the stuff of wild fantasy.'
- **Discuss one problem at a time**.

To this list we can add the A's need to apologise when he concludes he is in the wrong. David Gill and Sir Alex Ferguson would row from time to time, 'particularly when it was a testy time of the season or there was a big game coming up', but Gill appreciated Ferguson's willingness to apologise:

The good thing about Alex was ... he was better than me, actually ... he would get over our disagreements pretty quickly. I remember one Friday morning meeting when he was just ranting and ranting and I walked out, and I said, 'you just can't speak to me like that. I'm leaving.' I went back to the office. And by the time training had finished at 12.30 he had rung me to apologise.

Now that you have read about snakes in suits, maybe you have cause to doubt your C. What if the relationship feels as if it lacks trust? The British judicial system is not the envy of the world without reason. 'Innocent until proven guilty' should guide your thinking. Roald Dahl has a story about a vindictive couple who devote all their time to making each other's lives hell. Of the nasty tricks the Twits play on each other, my favourite is Mr Twit's addition of a thin piece of wood onto Mrs Twit's cane and chair legs every night, so that she begins to believe that she is shrinking. This and her retaliatory tricks are rooted in mutual suspicion: 'Whenever you go all quiet like that I know very well you're plotting something … You'd better be careful,' Mrs Twit said, 'because when I see you starting to plot, I watch you like a wombat.'

Watch each other, but not like wombats.

## Celebrating

Relationships deserve recognition and positive contributions demand celebration. Not many enjoy living with a mean-spirited boss who counts the cost of every transaction, rather than appreciating their value. Usually the C's contributions are a bit of a secret, recognised properly by the A only in private. Occasionally a triumphant celebration of C input will warm everyone's heart. Chris Froome told teammate and roommate Richie Porte to lead Team Sky past the finish line at the Champs-Élysées so as to honour his sacrificial role in Froome's overall victory, where he rode shot gun to Froome throughout. Porte acknowledged that he may not (yet) be the guy to win the Tour de France, opting instead to be Froome's best support rider, but he could also by now have left to win other big races. Plenty have told Porte to leave Sky to give himself the chance of winning a Grand Tour. One day he might. While helping Froome, the 28-year-old Tasmanian has finished second to him in the Critérium International and second in the Critérium du Dauphiné. When Sky let him loose on his own, he won Paris-Nice. Team Sky will give Porte his chance to lead a Grand Tour team. Until then, he continues to feel content as Froome's Lodestone: 'I know he's the leader,' Porte explains, 'I know him well enough in training and all of that, to see that he's stronger. The goal is to win the Tour and for me to support him.' While gaining experience to win the Tour de France for himself in the future, helping Froome, particularly when he is so liberal with his recognition, remains Porte's preferred option.

Here's the advice, then, A: just say thank you! You know perfectly well how much your C is contributing. The private pleasure they feel in seeing you succeed is not always quite enough. You cannot rely forever on their sense of duty and devotion to your cause. There has to be sincere recognition one-on-one from you, the boss. Few can maintain and deepen their sense of duty unless its beneficiary every now and then says, 'Thanks very much, I really couldn't do this without you.' We most appreciate recognition when it arrives out of the blue, as with any gift. Turn to your C occasionally and say, 'You know what, thank you, that was very well done.' In some cases that may be all that the C needs. Sara Rajeswaran was a researcher for home secretary Theresa May when she was shadow leader of the house, and special adviser to Theresa Villiers providing her shadow transport secretary with advice and political support. Rajeswaran feels lucky to have worked for As who were as quick to hand out praise as to take it:

When one of the Theresas [May or Villiers] was praised for a great policy, they would often say, 'Sara did all the groundwork for it, so if you have any questions, ask her.' In public it was, of course, their policy, as it should be, but I honestly didn't care as long as somebody knew that I had worked on it. You only get that when you are not seeking it.

Jazz musician, composer and band leader Wynton Marsalis praises his band members without saying a word. When one of them does something remarkable he turns to the audience and, by raising an eyebrow, begs the question, 'How on earth did he do that?' The gesture invariably triggers an outbreak of applause. We owe our Cs these occasional admiring gestures. Rather pathetically, I still tell my wife when I receive a smiley face drawn by Kevin Roberts on his response to an email or a document I have sent him. He uses them sparingly, along with other inventive drawings that are less easy on the eye.

The As should not become modern helicopter parents hovering over their Cs, indulging them with praise where none is warranted. I made that mistake, telling one of my Cs so often that he had done a great job that he soon believed he was owed a 'great job' for any task swiftly completed, regardless of its quality. I have learned that there is a distinction to be drawn between a 'thank you', a common courtesy to be used when a courtesy is extended to you, and a 'well done', which should be used to set and recognise a standard of excellence achieved. Matthew Reed, in charge now of AXA's commercial branches in the UK, working for Amanda Blanc, still remembers the thrill of getting a 'well done' from the commander of *HMS Boxer* when he had successfully completed a complex piece of navigation. Mike Phelan says that in the six years he served as Sir Alex Ferguson's C he got a 'well done' five times. That he can count them suggests that they were memorable. The As will have to judge for themselves how often a celebration or small recognition is required. Less secure Cs need more recognition than others. And some may let the subtlest suggestion of a job well done go to their heads.

Use your head and use the words (or emoticons) that many simply do not. I have heard stories of As having conversations with their best and most potent advisers along the lines of 'You should be very grateful to have this opportunity.' Clipping the wings of your C may make you feel all-powerful in the moment but, when dealing with a C of talent, it will lead to corrosive resentment that could destroy the relationship.

## Checking

However well it feels to be in the A/C house together, regular check-ups are essential. Every six months, you should sit down with your C and carry out a check of the A/C relationship. Any more than that will feel like an extra burden to you, any less and your C will feel that the relationship is one you take for granted. If Othello had had the appraisal form below, Iago would have been putty in his hands.

This form is for illustration only and does not substitute regular reflection about each other's contribution. It is designed to start a conversation. The exact nature of the questions and the words you choose should be tailored to the kind of A/C relationship you have defined. If yours is the kind of C who needs time to formulate their thoughts, ask them to fill in the form ahead of the check-in. If they are likely to accuse you of taking up their time to roam and contemplate, with yet ANOTHER form to fill out, then work through the questions on your next flight or train journey together – assuming you will make an exception to your general rule of travelling alone.

Dear C

To quote your pin-up counsellor, Cardinal Richelieu: 'A capable prince represents a great treasure in state. A skilful counsel is no less a treasure, but the acting of both in concert is invaluable, because from it derives the true happiness of states.' I would like us to think about our acting in concert. While I am the A and you are the C, we are jointly responsible for this relationship. If one of us takes 100 per cent responsibility and the other takes zero, that would be no kind of relationship. We could say it's 50/50 but we might take responsibility for the same 50. I want us to consider the possibility of both taking 100 per cent responsibility, so that nothing falls through the cracks. It may sound Herculean but it means that if you see something going wrong you will do something about it rather than just say, 'Oh look, A, that's going wrong, isn't that interesting?' and then keep going. Not for us, C.

In particular, I welcome your thoughts on my own contribution to your performance as my C, how I hinder and how I help. My sincere intention is to reflect on your feedback and to act on it appropriately. You should feel free to tell it as it is, knowing that it will not be used as evidence against you.

## Opening questions

How would you define our relationship? Are we in a marriage of convenience, having a secret affair, or have we become trapped together like two business-class travellers on a long-haul flight? If you were the casting director charged with finding your successor, what qualities would you look for? How do these qualities complement my own?

When historians write about our partnership, how will they describe our differences in character and qualities? What are the distinct flavours we represent? Which of my other Cs do you most admire and why? (This question serves a double purpose: it will help you plot together the relative importance of your C circle and remind this particular C that he is not the only C in town.)

Are you clear about the role I wish you, uniquely, to play? Lodestone, Educator, Anchor or Deliverer? Or a special blend of two or more of these? Of these C archetypes, which would you like to play more, and which less? Do I encourage you to be open to more possibilities and how can I help you pursue those that excite you?

## Cohabitation
### Space
How often do you feel I am interfering? When was the most recent example of this? Describe what that felt like exactly as you described it to your partner when you got home. How can I give you more space when you need it most? Do you ever feel I give you too much space? When, if at all, would you want my deeper involvement?

### Voice
Am I listening to what you are telling me and am I showing others that I am listening to you? I realise it's easier to be candid with people who are good at receiving candour. Have you found me to be more jujitsu master, deflecting what you say, and trying to put you off balance as I receive your feedback, than sponge, soaking up all that you have to offer? Or would you describe me as an avoider?

Do you feel you have enough oxygen? When you last saw me leading from the limelight, how much of you thought that you might need a stint in the sun yourself? In what situation, and purely for your own development as a leader, might I persuade you to step out of my shadow?

### Roaming
Are there projects that you have a burning desire to instigate? When did I last unwittingly put the brakes on an initiative of yours? How can I help you increase your 'network of possible wanderings'?

## Time

Do you have enough Off Time? How often have you felt overwhelmed by my requests for further help? When did you last squeak to your PA that I was an ungrateful bastard who wouldn't notice if you were doubled up in pain, but would notice if you were two minutes overdue on something I'd asked for? Have you taken your full complement of holidays? How are you ensuring that your well-being is not being compromised by me or others?

## Access

Am I making enough time for you? Would you like more or less attention? What is it you think you need to know about me that I have held back from you? You know from my aversion to Twitter that I will not give you a minute-by-minute update of my every movement, nor will I accept you as a friend on Facebook. But, if I appear to be keeping you in the dark on something material to your ability to support me, please list these for discussion.

## Focus

What is my listening really like? When you need me to focus, have I managed to put my blinkers on or am I prone to distraction? Tell me about some of these distractions. Was I looking at my Blackberry, iPhone, PC, or all three? Was I looking over your shoulder to see how long the queue was of those waiting to see me next? If so, forgive me.

Do I forgive you? Give me an example of the last time you messed up and how I responded? You're still here, so it cannot have been too bad. But could my response have been better? If so, how?

## Conflict resolution

How well have we acknowledged that we have problems and disagreements? When you review the last six months, help me identify those times when we have aired a disagreement and dealt with it maturely and effectively? Would I pass the Steve Peters 'toilet test' (see page 202)?

Taking a look at Gottman's 'four horsemen of the Apocalypse':

1. How well do I take your criticism?
2. Am I defensive?
3. Do I ever treat you with contempt (when you don't deserve it)?
4. Do I ever stop listening?

Are there any conflicts that you feel I have tried to sweep under the carpet that you would now like us to engage in and resolve? What pain have I left unmanaged?

I subscribe to Don Quixote's prescription on pain:

'When the head aches, all the other members ache, too; since I am your lord and master, I am your head, and you my part, for you are my servant; for this reason, the evil that touches or may touch me will cause you pain, and yours will do the same to me.'

How much more do I feel your pain than Don Quixote felt his squire Sancho's pain? How could I offer you faster-acting relief from it?

**Celebration**

Have I congratulated you on a job well done in the last six months? If the answer is 'no' and you have been waiting for some recognition, now is the time to end the wait. Just remind me what it was that deserved my praise. If I disagree, I will do you the kindness of telling you why it merely met my expectation.

Do I say thank you?

Thank you.

# Changing

This 'Living with your Leader' appraisal, taken with the C's corresponding appraisal of you in the next chapter, forms an agenda for change. If not a love-in, the experience for the C should feel positive. They have been given every opportunity to appraise your behaviour in the relationship, to codify what they find most helpful in you and to air what they do not. If you are a great A, they will feel valued for their candour and ready to embrace your guidance on enhancing their own contribution to your leadership.

Rather than attempt wholesale change, choose the one or two things that you would most like to see done differently by your C and agree these explicitly with them. Any book on managing change will tell you that attitudes only ever follow behaviour, so you must be as willing actively to change as they are. 'Having discussed your hesitancy in giving me your undiluted advice, we have agreed that you will show more courage and tell it to me straight' must be followed by an equally meaningful change of your own. Once you have agreed a new way of doing things, give your C time to implement it then review their behaviour in action. The very next time they offer you some tough love, show them that you know the extra steps they have taken to adapt and congratulate them effusively. What happens if the C consistently fails to implement the behavioural changes you have agreed on? Either give them an outing as a different kind of C, or invite them to consider their options. If your C is simply unwilling to change you will need to change them and choose afresh.

# 7

# COUNSEL FOR THE C

Unless you are a sports-pages-first kind of reader, you will know by now what motivates a C, what qualities you need to be one, and the four archetypal roles you can play. The last chapter will have shown you how the A can counter excessive behaviour that you – the C – might display under stress (or temptation), as well as create the best conditions for you to thrive. Now the flipside. How to counteract the A's inherent hazards. Your A may be the final decision-maker, but this does not entitle them to ride roughshod over the relationship. If you can combat their weaknesses, you will make them a better A. Of the two of you – A or C – who do you think is best qualified to keep the relationship under surveillance? Perhaps the one with the greater EQ? Ideally, both of you. Before we think about creating excellent A/C living arrangements, we should – simply to be equitable – take a swift tour of the excesses to which the A is vulnerable, as they fall prey to pressure or their own publicity.

Just like those of the C, the A's extremes are usually brought to light by the situation. Through his successes an A can seem to be making his and the organisation's situation better and better, but his very success can sabotage him as it feeds the insatiable ambition in him, his colleagues, the organisation and its ecosystem of stakeholders. That, at least, is the learning from Lehman Brothers and the pernicious sub-prime fiasco. Having a larger-than-life chief carried away with his own fame is one of Marianne Jennings' *Seven Signs of Ethical Collapse*. Intentionally or not, the A begins to embody and envelop the organisation and everything it stands for. He and his people believe that they would be snookered without him. The A outstays his welcome, his ideas become familiar, and finally, wholly uninspiring. We stop listening to him. He stops listening to us, more and more convinced that his way is the right way. We argue. He ignores us. We argue some more. He fires us or promotes us out of danger, a trick we taught him.

What's to pity about the A? Very little when he cannot be trusted, when he reveals his basest ambition, when his interpersonal skills are lousy, or when he simply proves to be managerially incompetent. We owe him little sympathy, too, when he chooses to forget where the breakthrough idea came from, hoovering up all the credit for the victory, soaking up every ray of sunshine. Nor does he deserve much sympathy when he neglects privately to thank us for saving his bacon. So, of course, we'd all like to let the air out of his inflated tyres – and we will. I concede I wrote this book in part to remind the more grandiose As that theirs is but one job on the team. We may need them but we do not need the nonsense they bring with them.

Yet how much of the nonsense is of our own making? We look for leaders who provide solidity in our uncertain world. We may protest otherwise, but most of us are spooked by change, both the nature and the speed of it. We are thankful for strong parental role models who are willing to step forward and provide a semblance of certainty and protection. Randall Peterson, professor of organisational behaviour, and deputy dean, London Business School, describes the hazards that we create by choosing the leaders that we do: 'More and more we select CEOs who will rise above the din and attract attention. We want our leaders to stand out so we choose ones that are more and more extreme, and we insist they are visible.' We adore them when they live up to Napoleon's vision of leaders as 'dealers in hope'. We celebrate them as charismatic iconoclasts. We crave them in times of turnaround or crisis. We conspire in their inexorable rise and inevitable fall. We thrust them centre stage, demand the spotlight follows them, and then accuse them of stealing the oxygen, grabbing the credit, hogging that limelight, casting that shadow.

The cycle of hero to zero is no less painful for its predictability. It occurs at the meeting point between the A's personality and the expectations we put on them. Personality-driven dangers include the qualities that made the A so suitable for handling the accountability of their out-and-out leadership in the first place. They are charismatic. They are decisive. They have stamina. They have conviction. They are visionary. They can stand up to multiple incoming attacks, whether from regulators, shareholders, opposition parties, commentators or competitors.

Intensely competitive, rampantly driven, operating on four hours' sleep a night or less, life as an A is eventually exhausting. We can hardly be surprised when the hinges come off. At some point, fuelled by success or failure, we begin to detect enduring patterns of extreme behaviour. Professor Robert Bor, in his work as a consultant psychologist and counsellor to leadership teams, has seen As who have become overly self-assured, dogmatic and increasingly isolated. They refuse to listen and instead assert themselves to the point of bullying. The effect on the organisation and those in their immediate circle is profound. Voices are hushed in the corridors of power; the leadership team's disagreements with the A's decisions are raised only in whispers among themselves, for fear of reprisal. The rest of the organisation goes about its business with heads – and volume – down. Initially some of the more bold – or reckless – take on the A. But over time, however ridiculous the A's ranting gets, it becomes easier to agree with them or walk away. Better to bury one's head than let it roll, goes the thinking.

The characteristics that made our A so good – their competitive streak, fastidiousness, drive – under conditions of considerable pressure have delivered a disagreeable and destructive force. Where once we loved the rush of excitement that came with our fizzy pop leader, they have now left us feeling distinctly flat. At the extremes, these As become overconfident, neurotic and even psychopathic. It is easy to forget that we had a hand in their creation: despots, bullies and dictators.

Eventually, perhaps many years later, we can sometimes separate the self-deprecating wheat from the self-publicising chaff. In his talk to the Open University in 2005, Robert Lyman quoted Mountbatten's assessment of the great British generals of the Second World War. He sympathises with Slim not Montgomery of Alamein: 'Slim's failing was to deprecate any form of self-publicity believing, perhaps naïvely, that the sound of victory had a music all of its own. The "spin doctors" of our own political generation have sadly taught us something Monty knew instinctively and exploited to his own advantage, namely that if you don't blow your own trumpet no one else will.' Mohan Mohan, peerless professional in many roles at Procter & Gamble, sums up the metamorphosis that the most driven As are at risk of undergoing: 'If you want to win the rat race, don't forget, you end up a rat.'

Contemporary leadership counsel tries to hold a mirror to our As, keeping them on the rails, keeping them human, with encouragement to be more inward focused, more Zen-like, and more comfortable with that part of themselves which is introverted. I am not convinced. Rather than take the shine off the A's rougher edges, the very edges that make them worthy of the A's armband, I think we have to give permission to these crazies at the top, to accept their appetite for power, to embrace their drive with its inherent dangers.

What we do need are more accompanying Cs, achievement motivated rather than power motivated, acting as buffers to the As. To do the job properly requires the acknowledgement that these As are creatures made occasionally volatile by their willingness to do a job so volatile it would explode many others. After all, we cannot have it all. Too many of us want to be on the winning team, be rewarded, have fun and at the same time sit on our backsides and wait for someone, a leader, perhaps a parent, to make it happen for us. Slip into our employee outfits and we start behaving like children. We can hardly complain that being an A occasionally leads to autocratic behaviour. We needed them to come to our rescue, cut staff, eliminate a team or two, close a factory, buy a business, but their success in these activities has bred a ruthless bully, out for themselves, using our organisation merely as a stepping stone to their next, bigger, shinier, doubtless more lucrative, opportunity.

Until that offer has been made, the A's life as head of our organisation, in effect their ongoing job application, continues. It is a life of unremitting pressure: the daily increase of expectations; the performance targets, ramped up year on year, realistic or not; the need to justify their pay, their position and decisions; the constant exposure and scrutiny. Such physically and emotionally stressful conditions are not ideal for making critical decisions, thus the A is tempted more and more to look at the nearest thing to stillness they can find: himself. We saw in Chapter 1 how important it is for leaders periodically to look inwards, to contemplate how they could be better. This useful self-seeing becomes destructive when the A perceives a perfect version of themselves, the one that the flatterers have created, itself born from their desire to be led perfectly. The A's tendency to love themselves is their weakest link, and ours too.

Whether in politics, business, sport or culture, our history is littered with vainglorious leaders who lost the plot in their longing for more land, more victories, more trophies, more adulation; who had to be thrown out because they could not bow out; who surrounded themselves with yes men, only to rant when nobody would say no. Might you have an A capable of this kind of impulsive autocracy? Does he, like Julius Caesar, keep ignoring his counsellors' advice until they get fed up of giving it to him, opting instead to give him something altogether less pleasant to think about? Having defied three separate warnings that his life would be in danger were he to go to the Senate this very day (the ides of March), Caesar sits amid noblemen and denies their request to repeal the banishment of Publius Cimber. With fantastic conceit, he lets them know he will not change his mind:

> I am constant as the northern star,
> Of whose true-fix'd and resting quality
> There is no fellow in the firmament.
>
> (William Shakespeare, *Julius Caesar*, Act III, Scene i)

With this speech, Caesar seals his fate. His ego and self-importance grow stronger by the word. When he compares himself to an Olympian god – enough already – he is stabbed to death by men who, until that point, were on their knees asking him to repeal Cimber's banishment.

'Et tu, C?' may not quite have the same ring to it, but with whom do you more closely identify as the dagger is plunged, Brutus or Caesar? How do you react when confronted by such self-assurance, the A's image of self so overblown, and his blindness to ideas so obdurate? 'Pass me that dagger, will you, Brutus old chap?' Is Caesar's stabbing an example of the C's dark art, or did he have it coming?

One sure sign that the A's self-importance is becoming more of a hindrance than a help is the addition of new responsibilities to their title trophy cabinet. Rather than assign the job to a colleague, the A announces that they are now chairman as well as chief executive or handling Human Resources as well as Finance. Should you be concerned when their patch becomes Asia Pacific as well as Europe, Middle East & Africa (oh, and the next eleven emerging economies)? Can you still count on one hand into how many government departments his tentacles now reach? Perhaps he has become the *Mikado*'s modern-day Grand Poobah, 'First Lord of the Treasury, Lord Chief Justice, Commander-in-Chief, Lord High Admiral, Archbishop of Titipu, Lord Mayor, Lord High Everything Else' and Chief Inspiration Officer?

You will somehow have to persuade them to tone it down a bit. If not, they will lay the groundwork for your own worst excesses to thrive. You will have your work cut out trying to stop them engaging in the least helpful kind of self-reflection, where they ask themselves 'who is the fairest of them all?' The A's temptation to look – and like what they see – can be great. In *Surviving the Destructive Narcissistic Leader*, Joseph H. Boyett argues that some of the world's most famous leaders suffered from the condition 'narcissistic deprivation'. Not made to feel glorious enough by their parents, they retained an infantile need to be at the brilliant centre of the universe. For the A, leadership has obvious attractions: 'Narcissistic deprivation leads to "mirror hungry" leaders, with an insatiable desire for admiration, for exhibiting himself to the world, and for securing power. Charismatic leadership is a natural outlet because it comes with a clutch of followers who can feed his need for devotion.'

Boyett quotes David Aberbach's *Charisma in Politics, Religion and the Media* on the immense excitement aroused by John F. Kennedy: 'This at times bordered on worship, mainly among his female "jumpers", "leapers", "clutchers", "touchers", "squeezers", "screamers" and "runners".' Your A may like the sound of that. If so, he should keep that unwholesome thought to himself. How much weakness would it reveal to a lesser C than you, one with ignoble ambition? There is some excellent academic work on how best to avoid these and other perils for the A, most notably the article 'Narcissistic Leaders: The Incredible Pros, the Inevitable Cons' in the January–February 2000 issue of the *Harvard Business Review*. Give them a copy. Its author, Michael Maccoby, understands the value of leaders whose narcissistic tendencies can be forces for good but asserts that narcissism's darker effects are not likely to be controlled by the leader, chiefly because relatively few narcissistic leaders are interested in looking inwards to make sincere self-appraisals.

The A needs his trusty sidekick. What can the C do to halt the A's descent into darkness, triggered by situation, personality or stupidity? One solution is to assign a slave to them. In ancient Roman triumphal processions, a slave would follow the leader's chariot and chant, *'Respice post te! Hominem te memento!'* ('You are only mortal! Do not forget!') The A needs this kind of reminder from time to time. If no slaves are forth-coming, you can become a momentary Ultra-Anchor and say the words yourself. Another way is to make it clear to the A that their performance is sub-par, unacceptable according to your standards. We saw in Chapter 5 that this can be done succinctly, as Angelo Dundee told Sugar Ray Leonard, 'You're blowing it son, you're blowing it!'

The practices that follow are about keeping the A out of the darkness so that they can legitimately enjoy the limelight. Whether fool or friend, seeker or reasoner, the Anchor's role is as much about helping the A see a real depiction of them-selves as it is about helping them see situations. Anchors are forever, patiently, playing the unadulterated mirror. But that of course is not enough. If the reflected image is wrong in any way, the C must be sure to notice and to offer counsel on how to make it right. At times like these the C may convince the A of something it behoves them to believe. In this context, the C leads the leader.

Self-aware As will sometimes ask their Cs to lead them in this way. In Racine's play about the Trojan Queen Andromache, a young woman called Hermione is betrothed to King Pyrrhus of Epirus. Hermione is then spurned by Pyrrhus, who is instead infatuated by the prisoner-of-war, Andromache. Hermione, humiliated that her royal match is at an end, nevertheless knows that another man, Orestes, is madly in love with her. She knows that her best course of action is to leave Epirus with Orestes, and move on from the whole messy, painful and embarrassing affair. Her confidante, Cleone, corroborates all this, but, as Hermione confides in frustration, only if her C actually leads her can Hermione feel what she ought to – contempt for Pyrrhus and love for Orestes:

Why must you stir the embers of my anguish?
I fear to face my heart in my sad state.
Try and forget all that you may have seen;
Believe I love no more and praise my will;
Believe my heart is hardened in its hate;
Ah! if you can, make me believe it too.

*(Andromache*, Act II, Scene I)*

Create a relationship with your A in which you have an open invitation to tell them how they feel, when and if they need to know. Remember that the A/C relationship is a balancing act. What started with the best of intentions from both parties can deteriorate if one or other weakens. It can happen that just when the A most needs their Anchor they cut that Anchor loose. Prevention can be better than cure, so the 'Living with your Leader' framework (mirrored in the previous chapter) is full of practices used by some of the most content, catalytic, constant and courageous Cs.

## LIVING WITH YOUR LEADER
### Choosing

This may be easier for the C, who only has to choose one partner, than for the A who has to select many. True, the A can hedge their bets but the C only gets one roll of the dice, one chance to get it right. Reputationally, you will be bound together. Even now, as Tony Blair continues to attract negative press in the UK, it hurts those who were closest to him. They feel the injustice for him and they, as people who supported him, feel the blows personally. Distancing themselves now would be disingenuous and of little use. When you choose to subordinate your own ego to another leader, the stakes are high. You need to choose your A carefully.

*Casting your fantasy A*

What is your brief? Right now in your career, what kind of A would be best for you? One to give you the chance, as a Lodestone, to become a better Deliverer? Or one who needs an Educator, who will help you on your way to Anchorhood? Are you after an easy ride, looking for an A you can trust, one who is emotionally rock solid, still adored by his parents, with no trace of self-doubt? You may be looking for a while. In any event, how dull a life would that be for an ambitious C? What kind of a test of your own abilities? Wouldn't you prefer an A with some edge, one who can develop you into an A if you choose to go in that direction? Was it by chance or foresight that on her way to becoming a headmistress, Vivienne Durham worked for four headmistresses that served as president of The Girls' Schools Association, which represents independent girls' schools in the UK? Only one out of 250 every year becomes, in effect, the head of heads. Durham worked for four of them. If you want to be an A, find yourself an A of As.

The A may be the one running the casting session, but that doesn't stop you doing your research. The discipline of due diligence, developed to serve companies wishing to buy other companies, is rarely exacted by those about to make significant career decisions. An exhaustive search of the press cuttings may not reveal much more than the creation of the corporate affairs function. Off-the-record phone calls to your A's previous Cs, in an attempt to probe their strengths and weaknesses, should get to some of the truth, but the exes will probably hold back on you. Moreover, whatever you have read or heard, vanity will override most of your misgivings about working for the tyrant, because you believe yourself that much more skilful than your predecessors. You have been warned that when it comes to their Cs, the A is a fickle old dog, so you determine to be the first to make them faithful.

You need to start the job before you start the job. Do not let fifty-five minutes of your sixty-minute interview elapse before you politely interrupt them with some searching questions: 'What most upset you about your previous C?' (Pause, they may have a lot to say.) 'What upset your previous C about you?' (You are looking for deviation from the answer you were given when you posed the same question to their previous Cs); 'Just how badly can you behave and what drives you to it?' Tell them that you know full well they are a narcissist because all great leaders are. Ask for specific examples of their excessive behaviour. Make them laugh at themselves. Then ask why they would want to enlist you as the mirror to their worst excesses. Finally, the killer question: 'When your money man asks what your new C will be doing to justify his annual salary, what will you say to him?' (Note, if they have to justify anything to their money man, proceed with caution. Money men, despite the fact that many are fine Cs themselves, tend not to see the value in other Cs.)

You may be satisfied by their answers, but have they asked enough questions of you? Ask them if they would like you to run through your personal purpose. Are they keen to know about your dreams, your vision of what you would like to achieve in the next three years, what beliefs you hold dear, what you will never do, what kind of character you are? Ask them: 'Do these things align with where you are taking the organisation, and can you see how you can help me live by this purpose?' If they show no interest in this part of the conversation, then working as their C should be of no interest to you.

If they sail successfully through your subtle due diligence procedure, you may still find that you have made an error of judgement. Choosing the perfect A is about as guaranteed as predicting the next blockbuster movie. You thought the personal chemistry was good in the courtship, you seemed to like each other, the two of you made each other laugh and yet, a few days into the new relationship, the nightmare scenario unfolds: you have lent your work life to a truly lousy boss. All is not lost. This is probably your best chance to learn how to be a much better A yourself. Watch how they alienate everyone beneath them, alongside them, even above them. See how they take a well-functioning department and subject it to misery and turmoil. An ineffectual leader presents you with the opportunity to learn how to deliver in adversity, to navigate the carnage they leave in their wake, and prevent it going any further down the organisation.

Being high in EQ, you should not be quick to blow your own trumpet. Humility and self-deprecation will serve you well, particularly early on in the relationship. At the same time, because we have allowed stereotypical images of As to build in our minds, we admire our bosses a little too much, thinking we could never achieve what they have. We treat the advice 'never underestimate your boss' as licence to overestimate them. Making a realistic appraisal of your A will inform the kind of contribution you think you should make. Does their tyranny need tempering or does their confidence need a boost?

*Boundary exploration*
Define the boundaries and understand that your incentives may be different. What are the A's incentives and how is their performance assessed? For football managers, this is

increasingly simple. If you're at the top of the table, you are the best, you are a genius. If you're at the bottom, you get kicked out. Aside from Arsène Wenger, for whom securing the long-term financial health of Arsenal was more important than securing trophies (for more seasons than Arsenal fans care to remember), the A will do everything he can to stay at the right end of the table, sometimes taking dangerous shortcuts. The same is true in Formula One. Does the driver really care about the damage he does to a particular engine? Milliseconds are his obsession. His incentive is to win. The Cs behind him also want to win, but may have incentives that involve, say, engine protection. A transparent conversation about incentives can help you work out the rules of engagement before you start. Work out and agree what kind of involvement is being sought by your A. What is it that you wish me to do? And what is it that you wish me *not* to do?

On what kind of decisions do I have the final say? In which areas of my decision-making do you expect, and wish, to be involved? Tell me where previous advisers have gone horribly wrong. Over what have you fallen out? An A who is any good will find these questions unsurprising and helpful. Be suspicious of the A who ducks any of them. Find out about their attitude to friendship. We have seen in Chapter 5 that there is a clear role for friends to the A. Are you to be one of them? Do you have enough empathy to know whether they will be able to live with the decision they are making or whether, having made it, they will struggle to come to terms with its consequences? Some As will say that they have no regrets about decisions they have made but the best of them admit to being troubled by them years later.

Simon Fuller, A at XIX Entertainment, feels that his lifelong C, Nicki Chapman, is a lifelong friend too:

I have a very special relationship with Nicki. It is a friendship that has lasted for almost two decades and that will continue forever. I would trust Nicki with my life. We have been good for each other over the years and we know exactly how each of us functions very well. It is a very relaxed and special friendship, powerful and effective in work and easy and fun socially. We enjoy the same things in life, travel, good food, relaxing and being with our friends and family.

Does your boss want you to be their friend? Olympic cyclist Victoria Pendleton valued friendship with her former coach, Scott Gardner, so much that she married him. Constancy does not demand quite this level of affection. Most As I interviewed recognised that there is a limit to how close they can get to their Cs because, at the end of the day, they are in charge. Vivienne Durham distinguishes between being friendly and having friends:

The only time staff members can *really* become friends is when they leave the school or I leave the school. I've definitely had employees who've turned into friends. We've been hugely friendly when we've been here but I never quite let myself believe they're friends because, actually, first and foremost I'm their employer. I'm paid to be their employer on behalf of the governors.

As a C you owe the A enough social distance to ensure that in a disagreement their view does not prevail simply because you like them. Being an occasional thorn in their side, rather than a constant echo in their head, will make you a better friend anyway. 'What kind of friendship?' is a question worth exploring. Cs should not expect the depth of friendship that

Elizabeth I extended to William Cecil, the driving force behind her reign for four decades. Much as I have affection for my A, I cannot see him coming to nurse me personally on my death bed, nor would I wish him to. And I would not expect him to say, as Elizabeth did to her trusted counsellor, that he would not wish to live any longer than he had with me. But the C should try to get a sense of desired intimacy from their A.

Ask them in what areas of their work will your counsel be most valued. In what exact circumstances will they want to be left alone? What is their appetite for, or intolerance of, overlap? You can explore more mundane boundaries too: How often are you likely to want to see me? How shall we best communicate with each other? Do you prefer email, text or voice? How would you like me to collaborate with others who are important to you?

You may get the sense that the A really is as balanced and self-assured as they claim to be, that they do in fact need you for little more than gentle suggestion. But if they are more of a front man for the enterprise's needs, like Simon Cowell at Syco, there will be less suggestion and more instigation. You must listen to the A's description of the type of person they *want* you to be, and at the same time begin to gauge the type of person they *need* you to be. One thing they don't need you to be is jealous. You must accept that while the A/C relationship is of primary importance to you, the A has other dance partners. Of course you value the proximity and the feeling that they crave your company, but the leadership team will always be bigger than your relationship. Alastair Campbell admired Jonathan Powell for understanding this:

People kind of knew that Tony really liked having me in the back of the car. Go by the organogram and technically, as chief of staff, it should have been Jonathan [Powell]. It just never bothered Jonathan. He didn't have that sort of ego that said, 'I'm the chief of staff I should be in the car' and it never bothered me if Tony said 'Sally, can you come in the car?' – wouldn't bother me at all, I'd just jump in the car behind.

Whether we believe that Campbell was as relaxed as he suggests about being bumped into the car behind the boss's, the truth remains that you can only sensibly define your boundaries when you acknowledge that you are just one member of the A's C circle. As a demonstration of your confidence, take a piece of paper and map with the A their circle of advisers. Discuss who sits in the circle and what your A specifically values from each player. Offer to ensure that each gets the access and support they need. Drive mutual appreciation in that circle:

> Jonathan and I were very different sorts of people. A lot of people basically saw me as doing his type of a job and that didn't bother Jonathan at all and it didn't bother me. Jonathan never wanted to do my job and I never wanted to do his job and I never wanted to do Sally Morgan's job and she never wanted to do my job. Obviously with something as intense and as important as that, we had our moments, but they were moments, they weren't running sores.

Being paranoid about controlling access is a fool's game. Robert Tansey, as chairman of Team Sky, has more regular contact with Sir Dave Brailsford than anyone else on the team. He is not, though, the most senior person at Sky, which is chief executive Jeremy Darroch. How relaxed is Robert about Sir Dave having access to Darroch, his boss at Sky?

Dave has a very good relationship with Jeremy, and I wouldn't feel at all bypassed if he needed to pick up the phone to Jeremy. Actually, Dave would probably ask me before he did it, but even if he didn't we have a good enough relationship that I know he wouldn't be trying to go round behind my back to get something done.

Being relaxed about not being the circle's exclusive member, and appreciating the unique contributions of the other Cs, should influence the shaping of the boundaries you put in place with your A. To be both contented and effective, Cs must honour the boundaries. Once you think that you belong even a millimetre over the line, you can start counting the days. Cardinal Richelieu never forgot that he was the servant of the king and of France, not the master. Even at the peak of his influence he 'took care always to act on the authority of the king and never to usurp it for himself'. You will hopefully not need the threat of execution for high treason to keep you in check.

Alastair Campbell got a kick out of his leadership role when he was lifting the load off Blair's shoulders, along with others like Jonathan Powell. He cites Kosovo and Northern Ireland as among the highlights for him of that era. In his foreword to Campbell's *The Irish Diaries*, former Taoiseach, Bertie Ahern credits the unelected PR supremo with having 'played a huge role in stopping the murder and mayhem that had defined Northern Ireland'. But Campbell never forgot who was the overall A. Successful boundaries should not only be defined in relation to your A, but to other Cs in the A's circle. Remember, too, to define realistic borders around your own contribution. There are some simple practices to help you do this:

- **Call the A something that signals that you know they are the A**. Gianluigi Gabetti never called Gianni Agnelli by name, only 'Avvocato' or 'Mr Chairman'. Without being obsequious a name can demonstrate continuing respect for the A's position. The Gaffer is what players use in football. We may earn more millions than you, but we still know you select the team, Gaffer. Calling them 'A' would work just as well, unless their first name is Alex, in which case it might sound too familiar.

- **Check your distance**. Keep an image in your head of the chevrons on a motorway and ask yourself, could I stop in time? As Peter Drucker says in *Managing the Nonprofit Organization*, know your own degenerative tendencies so that you can counteract them.

- **Turn down invitations** to join the boss in situations better served by, or enjoyed more by, other members of the circle. Do not wait to be told to jump into the car behind.

- **Remember who is calling the shots**: The A can have an adviser for almost every aspect of their accountable activity. (Sometimes they can have too many.) The football coach is surrounded by tacticians, medics, statisticians, but who actually runs onto the pitch or comes on as a substitute is down to the A. His adviser may say he doesn't like the way a player is running, he looks tired, but this, to the A, is just another piece of information. Having heard all the opinions he has invited, the deliberations and the final decision are the A's to make.

- **Remember you are not the only C show in town**. There may be others with credentials and expertise that you do not have, with C qualities that differ from your own. So, even if you have most of the grey cells in the meeting, be clever enough to conceal your cleverness, if only to diffuse the insecurity of the A and his other Cs. One of Charles

Garland's fellow Cs at Syco is Philip Green, a close friend of Simon Cowell. Garland listens to Green, not just because he has a valuable point of view:

> Well, with Philip, it's his way or the highway. 'I'm a billionaire. What have you got to say? What bit of you is cleverer than me?' So with Philip, it's actually much more about being a very good listener. As my father used to tell me, 'You've got two ears and one mouth for a reason.' So with certain people, you've just got to listen to them. You've got to read it and even with Philip, occasionally, he'll come round to a different point of view.

- **Remind yourself** of the extremely valuable C qualities that have brought you to where you are, and be a little proud. But do not expect to be awarded the grand title that Tord Grip had with his coach – 'one half of Sven Goran Eriksson's brain'. Carlo Sant'Albano always has a tight grip on his own boundaries:

> I was on the board not because of me but because Exor owned the biggest stake in a bank. It needed a representative and I was a representative of John Elkann. But it's not because I am a genius of the revenues that I was on the board. Ultimate power was nothing to do with me, it had all to do with John Elkann. And as long as you can keep that straight in your mind, you're fine. If you start thinking it's all about you then you're dead.

- **Choose your title carefully**. In his latest promotion, Robert Tansey became development director for Sky Sports. Any idea what that signifies?

It doesn't scare anybody. I could have pushed for something like deputy MD, or something important sounding like chief operating officer, but actually that would have just ended up pissing off a whole load of other people internally. A lot of people are looking forward to the next few years, and they've spent a bit of time under the hammer. The last thing they need is to feel they've been pushed down.

I've become fond of 'deputy chairman' at Saatchi & Saatchi. It implies that I am deputy to the chairman but there isn't even a forum in which the chairman chairs the board, so I can never deputise for him. It gives me zero executive authority to upset anybody. All it does is hint at enough seniority to help me make things happen.

- **Ask for less money**. Not less money than you are already being paid, but insist that your boss never pays you as much as they get paid. Not that they would, but the gesture will relax them – and maybe even put your pay on their radar.

Colonel Tom Parker, the man behind Elvis Presley and ostensibly one of the most successful managers the entertainment business has ever seen, would not have cut such a divisive figure if his personal cut hadn't clearly signalled – at 50 per cent – that he thought he had as much to do with Elvis's success as Elvis himself. Had Parker not been incentivised to extract every ounce of value from his only client, history might have been more forgiving of his hand in the King of Rock's descent into third-rate Hollywood movies. Scooter Braun has been compared to the Colonel. He may not earn 50 per cent of Justin Bieber's takings, but his fiscal health has not been harmed by the highest-grossing concert film in US history, which he produced in 2011 about

Bieber's nineteen-year-old life; nor by a range of merchandise that boasts singing toothbrushes and dental floss; nor by an endorsement deal with acne remedy Proactiv. Will Bieber's adoring Beliebers forgive Braun if their young idol goes the way of Elvis? As Elizabeth's chief minister and trusted counsellor for nearly forty years, William Cecil amassed an estate of immense wealth while all the while pretending to be poorly paid for his extensive work. These days, of those who feed off high office, we demand greater transparency about the takings.

- **Grit your teeth**. If you find it extremely painful to have to know your place you should learn as much as you can as quickly as you can, so that you are ready to grab the A role with both hands when the time comes.

## Cohabiting

*Focus on their feelings*

While living with your leader there will be times when they become unbearably pleased with themselves, when they use 'I' and 'me' as much as teenagers use 'like'. There will also be times when you detect a dash of self-doubt. The C's art in the cohabitation game is to know when to deflate the A's tyres and when to fill their tank. Estimates vary, but a safe rule of the road is that 80 per cent of the job is to fill the tank. The US presidential system fosters reverence and appropriate respect, which produces presidents with a developed sense of their own importance. By comparison there is something grounded and grounding about the British system. Certainly Blair's circle of advisers took it upon themselves to act as tyre deflaters whenever they felt it necessary. Alastair Campbell has an anecdote to illustrate this point:

I think it is hard to keep your feet on the ground. We felt, Jonathan, myself, Andy [Lord Adonis], Sally, we felt it was partly our job to stop Tony being too self-important. You've got to have a sense of humour about yourself. Some of the coppers couldn't believe quite how we took the piss out of him. I used to do this thing where, in the back of the car, I used to do this Northern accent radio commentary like, 'Tony Blair is driving in the back of his car and would you believe it, he's the prime minister – he's got no qualifications for the job, whatsoever.' He'd laugh – we could have a laugh. I think some people, right at the top – maybe particularly in presidential systems, I don't know – actually Bush and Clinton were both very human, Chirac sometimes up in the stratosphere – find it difficult to keep their feet on the ground.

It may be that your leader is not suffering from too much confidence, but too little. Cricketer Michael Atherton's approach to confidence-building involves reminding people of what it felt like to get out there and lead in their youth, when they were more carefree. Atherton counselled an out-of-form Nick Compton, 'to remember what it was like hitting the ball on a beach in Durban, when you were growing up. Find your inner Compton.' Throughout his career, says Atherton, he knew deep down that what he was doing was trivial and unimportant: 'I never found trouble laughing at myself or the absurdities of the game. For the most part, that knowledge helped me to succeed in international cricket. I never felt much different walking out to bat for England than I did for my school team or my village club side.'

Luiz Felipe Scolari, Brazil's World-cup winning coach in 2002 shares this philosophy: 'My priority is to ensure that the players feel more amateur than professional ... We have to urge players to like the game, to love it, to do it with joy.' Jürgen Klopp, the Borussia Dortmund coach, shows his team videos not of the scarily good opposition, but of their own goal celebrations.

What will you do to help your A discover their inner Compton? What should their goal celebration look like? Some As may resent the suggestion that what they are doing compares to playing cricket or football. Being a CEO is neither trivial nor unimportant. Take a grander approach with the A who lingers on the serious nature of what he does: 'Humankind represents a flash in the pan of evolutionary history, itself a flash in the pan of cosmological history. So relax, A, and enjoy your tiny moment in the sun.'

Depending on your tone of voice, that could be a tyre deflater or a tank-filler.

## Giving counsel

Telling people what to do, ordering, directing, instructing, is all too easy. Doing so removes a sense of responsibility and ownership of the outcome, thereby taking the fun away. 'You have to do this,' however well intentioned, however passionately felt, is a lousy phrase for a C to use with an A. How irritating, too, to be congratulated for being correct, as if your moves are being marked. Giving good counsel is a more subtle art than that. Practices include:

- **Know when to give counsel**. We saw in Chapter 4 how good David Gill was at timing his counsel to Sir Alex Ferguson. Choosing the moment requires thought. One should be careful, but not eggshell careful. If the counsel needs to be given, give it.
- **Put the idea in their head**. Lead with questions like,

'What do you think about doing…?' or 'Have you thought about…?' My all-time favourite is Sergeant Wilson to Captain Mainwaring in *Dad's Army*: 'Do you think that's wise, sir?' Here is Sant'Albano on Gianluigi Gabetti:

> What I find fascinating about Gianluigi Gabetti is that if you sit down with him he will already know what you're dealing with. You don't even have to explain it to him. He may not say, 'I know exactly what you're talking about', but you know in his eyes, he knows exactly what you're going to throw at him. Nor does he tell you exactly what you have to do or even how you want to hear it. He tells you something, you walk about 500 feet down the street and you go, 'Oh, shit, he's right!' He has this ability to put it in your head, not as 'this is what you should do'. What is quite extraordinary is that you end up discovering it for yourself.

Master the Gabetti skill so that your A can make their own discovery 500 feet down the street.

- **Know how to deliver bad news well**. There are two things worse than delivering bad news: the first is dressing it up as good news. The French call this, 'perfuming the pig'. The second is delivering bad news without a plan. One of Steve McClaren's roles as Sir Alex Ferguson's C was bad news breaker. McClaren tells the story of Dwight Yorke opening the door of his hotel room to McClaren on the eve of the FA Cup Final. Before a word had been spoken, Yorke, knowing what was coming, pleaded: 'Oh no, please let me play, I've never played in a final.'

'Well you're not going to today either,' said McClaren.

'But you are playing on Wednesday,' said Ferguson,

who was just behind him. The immediate follow up helped Yorke deal with the bad news.

Because As feed off positive energy, bad news can be hard to handle. When she was executive assistant to Ian Powell at PwC, Louise Scott told me that: 'I don't like to give him bad news, but sometimes he has to have a bit. In which case, at the very least, let's not put him in a bad mood.'

Avoid the temptation to drip-feed bad news. Many As may not like to hear it, but it's best to get it over with in one sitting.

Don't get so skilled at delivering bad news, however, that you forget to deliver what the A most values: good news.

- **Know when to stop**. Some Cs misjudge their A's appetite for opinion, over-enthusiastically drowning them in counsel. It is called feedback, not confrontation: 'I know when to stop pushing her [Wintour],' says Grace Coddington. 'She [Wintour] doesn't know when to stop pushing me.'

- **Keep a record of your counsel**. You may think that your advice was unambiguous and unforgettable, that your spoken word spoke for itself. Yet important conversation is often best followed up with a note: 'Just to be clear, this is the plan we discussed, this is what we agreed, this is what you're doing, and this is what I'm doing.' It will give the A reassurance – or a chance to shape the indicated action – and it will give you the confidence to act on the agreements.

- **Keep your own counsellor**. The most feedback Cs get (if they get any) is from their direct report. How many of us actively seek feedback from elsewhere? For the psychotherapist or the counsellor, clinical supervision is a prerequisite of their right to practice. It should be a pillar of personal and professional development, too. Who is giving the C their counsel? Alastair Campbell conferred often and deeply with Philip Gould. Sometimes it is not obvious to whom to turn. Benedict Nightingale described the responsibilities of a theatre critic at an event for Mousetrap Theatre Projects: critics may be paid by their newspaper but their greater responsibility is to their readers, which is why they get precious little feedback from their editors. The best Nightingale ever got, he said, was in 1957 from his then A, the editor of *Kent and Sussex Courier*. Nightingale had seen and reviewed a terrible local amateur dramatic production. 'It was,' he wrote, 'like a pudding.' His editor called him in: 'A pudding? What kind of pudding? What did the pudding taste like?' Nightingale welcomed the feedback and from then on knew always to expand his analogies and back up his opinion. You cannot give advice unless you have learned how to receive it.

When you sit in the chair of power little by little it can make you arrogant. Managers, executives, coaches, interpreters, all manner of successful people can succumb to the seduction of power. Cs are no exception. Retain your own counsellor to help you deal with problems, to challenge you, and to keep you anchored.

## Conflict resolution

A simple way to deal with conflict is to prevent it occurring in the first place, particularly if, like Charles Garland, your A doesn't value it:

I have no confrontation with Simon Cowell whatsoever, never had an argument about anything, because actually people like him and like Simon Fuller, they don't like confrontation. They really don't. The best forum is discussion because sometimes it takes days or weeks to get to the right answer. It's not like, 'I thought about your idea and you're wrong, because one, two, three, four, five.' The people that I've worked with, their brain doesn't operate that way. More often than not what Simon would do, for example, is he would go, 'I hear that, I hear what you're saying. I'll think about it and then we should talk about it some more.'

There is little value in putting the A in a corner, insisting they accept your irreversible position on an issue. Better to offer them a way out: 'Okay, I hear what you're saying. You really want to make this happen. I don't necessarily agree with it, but if that's what you really want to do, we'll try it.' If you are strongly against your A's view, you might say, 'Okay, leave it with me. I will go away and investigate it.' Instead you leave it for a while, do nothing, knowing that by next week there may be a shift in the A's perspective or priorities.

Avoidance will not always be enough. The ability to give and receive feedback, to facilitate it, to structure it and to share it is critically important to resolving the spats that will lend some spice to living with your leader. How you disagree is a key determinant of a healthy relationship. You can only say 'that's brilliant' so often before even the vainest A will get suspicious. Practices include:

- **Put in place arrangements for signalling discord**. Agree at the outset that when either of you feels strongly enough about a disagreement, you will make the need for a robust discussion obvious – perhaps by pulling an imaginary cord to stop production as Toyota line workers do when they anticipate a fault. Being playful can take the heat out of potentially heated situations.

If the A is willing, it might also make sense for a disagreement to be shared with another trusted counsellor who can act as mediator. Ultimately, A and C know that the A's view will prevail if the A chooses, but a smart A, when challenged constructively and with passion by their C, will welcome other voices before plumping for a binding resolution.

- **Separate the critical from the merely important**. Take disagreements on the flight deck between captain and senior first officer (and second-in-command). There may be differences of opinion about, for example, what altitude the plane should be flying given the weather conditions. Such issues may influence the comfort of the journey or the flight's profitability but they are not safety issues, critical to the survival of the organisation, which deserve different treatment.

- **Decide your laundry policy**. Agree what laundry, if any, you will take to your meetings and what will be aired in the privacy of your own launderette. It can be helpful to both A and C for others participating in a debate to see that the A and C do not always agree – that the C is not the A's lapdog. As Michael Bolingbroke says: 'if you want to be a CEO and surround yourself with nodding dogs I would say two things. One, I'm not interested in working for you, and two, your business won't succeed.'

  So when the A says something stupid, as their trusted adviser you should feel free to pipe up: 'I hear you but can I play devil's advocate here?' 'Have we thought about this?' 'Are we forgetting something?' It should feel comfortable disagreeing with the A and having the A disagree with you. As long as you have given your opinion, it has been persuasively argued and it has been heard, you cannot be upset when the A's final call does not go 'your way'.

But, for those strategically important issues and seriously heated debate, you should head for the confines of closed doors. Keep the significant disagreements between the two of you, if for no other reason than to preserve the A's face. Gary Neville, the shop steward of the Manchester United team and adored by Sir Alex Ferguson, once felt the full force of his manager's wrath when he swore at him from the touchline in a Champions League game. David Beckham got the infamous boot (accidentally) kicked in his face when he answered back in the dressing room. Peter Schmeichel, the Danish goalkeeper, who could do no wrong in the eyes of Ferguson, got lambasted when he replied to Ferguson's half-time accusation that 'You're slipping!' with 'So are you.' Gary Neville recalls:

'Everyone looked up, thinking: "Oh my God, here he comes." And sure enough, the boss ripped Peter's head off.'

'Face' is of more importance in some parts of the world than in others. In Indonesia face is about avoiding the cause of shame ('malu'). Wherever your A hails from, imperfections that you might wish to draw to their attention should only ever be addressed privately.

- **Pay attention to your tone**. Conflict can be aired in ways that will both placate and provoke. George du Maurier's character Svengali 'would either fawn or bully and could be grossly impertinent. He had a kind of cynical humour that was more offensive than amusing and always laughed at the wrong thing, at the wrong time, in the wrong place. And his laughter was always derisive and full of malice.' You need to strike a different tone, respectful, thoughtful, full of good intention.

Nick Booth, CEO of the Royal Foundation, and the Royals on whose behalf he is acting do not always agree. In airing conflicts, Booth has to be sensitive to thousands of years of constitutional history. He has concluded that, despite their passion for philanthropy, emotional arguments are less likely to convince his As than those rooted in reason – 'Here is why we should do this in the context of both the project and the wider Royal organisation.' Crisp and unemotional briefings leave the As the room to respond with their own emotions.

Booth also had the benefit of some feedback from Jamie Lowther-Pinkerton, private secretary to The Duke and Duchess of Cambridge and Prince Harry, when he was feeling his way into the job:

> The private secretary took me for a coffee one day and said, 'How's your relationship with the household?' And I looked at him, and said, 'You're only asking me that question because it's clearly not very good; you didn't ask me that question to say, well done.' He said, 'Well, you just need to understand that, you know, The Royal Foundation is an incredibly interesting project, but it lives alongside all the normal and somewhat opaque processes of the royal household, and how things are decided.'

- **Look to members of the wider family**. Booth was given reassurance and confidence as well as feedback from the private secretary. When A and C encounter differences that go beyond the routine, the C should look far and wide for wisdom and additional perspective. It is no accident that a vast amount of money is spent on executive coaches, mediators, facilitators and mentors. Consulting others is not without danger either because those consulted may have their own agenda. The C cannot guarantee the neutrality of these people and may legitimately fear that the A has agreed to enlist help to do a more effective silencing of the C than the A has been able to do. It still has to be better than reaching an impasse and, in the knowledge that the A's word is final, what's to lose?

- **Take it slowly**. There will be times when you need the A to act decisively and fast. The A may encourage you to speed up, because they love to test their agility in the fast lane, best of all in foul conditions. Sometimes, though, you will need to steer the A into a cruise in the slow lane, to give an idea of yours enough time to have its impact.
- **Avoid seeming like a victim**. Carlson, Melton, and Snow (2004) describe some of the symptoms of passive aggressive personality disorder, which include feeling misunderstood and underappreciated, and lacking appreciation for the role that your behaviour played in the problems of the relationship. A basic principle of marriage counselling is that each party's perceptions of and assumptions about a relationship will be different. Pause in the heat of the moment and ask yourself whether your feelings of contempt and anger are linked to your own assumptions more than to the reality. Become aware of the causes of your strongest emotions and raise your A's awareness too.
- **Learn from the therapist**. What might that involve? A lot, according to Leavitt in *Common Dilemmas in Couple Therapy*: 'As the therapist, you need to play many roles in working with dilemmas: supporter, confronter, witness, navigator, referee, container, leader, guide, director. You need to give your clients limits, direction, warnings, meaning, deep wisdom, and reassurance. Thus, you need to be versatile and flexible, often changing roles a number of times in a session.'

## Celebrating

*Generosity*

'You get a shitty salary. You work your ass off for a few years, and if you have, you know, a nice boss, maybe they'll remember you when they leave, but quite often they won't and the next person won't know what you did or who you worked for and you almost have to, you know, look out for yourself.'

In Jack Layton, Ira Dubinsky had a really nice boss. However nice your boss is you are likely to be disappointed if you bank on gratitude from them. The advice is there for the A in Chapter 6. Expect it to be ignored.

This does not mean you should show the A little gratitude yourself. In order to thank the A without sounding like a sycophant you must be sincere. If you really feel like the A has made your life easier, helped you to perform better, taught you something important, or secured you a new opportunity, fear of flattery should not get in the way of your manners. Say thank you and do it in a way that does not create awkwardness between you or that inhibits them from bringing you down a peg or two soon after.

There is one thing you can do to offset the A's miserly record on recognition. If your A doesn't lavish gratitude on their grunts, do it on their behalf without them knowing: 'By the way, the A thinks you're doing a magnificent job' will not have the same impact as hearing it from the A himself, but will be well received all the same. As for you, give yourself a pat on the back. Give the A one, too. For as much as you crave a thank you, so do they. Generosity should flow both ways. There are no prizes – and probably a shortish future – for being an uncivil servant.

# Checking

Before sitting down to adapt the 'Living with your Leader' appraisal questions for you to ask your A, you should check yourself in three areas.

*Anger*

First, are you firmly on top of any anger, resentment or defensiveness? In most jobs in an organisation you are set a target or an objective, and there are metrics attached to it that are easy to define and monitor. In a lot of the C roles you get people, not just CFOs, asking loudly, 'I can't see the value, I just don't know what he's doing.' There will be constant carping about your perceived lack of delivery. This might make you rather cross. You are working ridiculously hard, you know the impact you are having directly on the A and indirectly on the organisation and you feel, strongly, that your contribution is significant. You have selflessly kept very quiet about your achievements. Now there are question marks in the air. I have faced this many times in the seven years I have played deputy to the A and my irritation, as well as sometimes my anger has, too often, got the better of me. This is neither dignified nor helpful. A six-monthly appraisal may be the time to reflect on one's feelings of resentment and to confront the two other areas that most require candour, anonymity and authenticity.

*Anonymity*

Am I happy for my relative contribution to remain largely anonymous, even as my A appears to the world to be conquering great heights without effort?

As Nick Paumgarten wrote in *The New Yorker* in June 2013:

Steck and Moro, by climbing alpine style, may appear to be

self-sufficient, but they use the fixed ropes and ladders in the icefall, and they rely on porters to help establish their comfortable, well-appointed camps on the lower parts of the mountain. While they make videos for their sponsors of themselves hiking up to base camp in trail shoes and carrying only day packs, somewhere outside the frame Sherpas are lugging their batteries and cheese. This occasionally irks the Sherpas.

If you have had enough of the A's 'Just Done It!' T-shirt, you may be tempted to design your own, perhaps a photo of Edmund Hillary and Tenzing Norgay climbing Everest, with the words 'Occasionally Irked Sherpa' printed above Norgay's half-out-of-shot head. Even some of the world's largest Cs remain in the shadows, as Big Bruno Demichelis demonstrates:

> I was always behind … I know that, it was always clear in my mind, don't try to be under the spotlight. They are all prima donnas around here. They want to be under the spotlight. In fact I never was mentioned, I never had my picture taken and no one ever knew that I was working with AC Milan for 23 years. I was never in the pictures, always behind there, you know.

David Gill did occasional turns in the spotlight when the business of Manchester United demanded it, but he is emphatic that, 'you can't have everyone in there. You've got to have one spokesperson, which in the case of a football club, to my mind, is the manager.'

The ultimate role out of shot has to be the ghost-writer. Live with your study for four months, take the pain, and enjoy not a jot of recognition. There is a pragmatic reason to stay out of frame. Was Alastair Campbell's becoming part of the Labour leadership story predictable? He himself thinks that the changing media world made it pretty much impossible to stay out of shot and that in his own case he was part of the story from the minute his new job with Blair was announced. He's astute enough to hint at the responsibility he may have for that:

> The profile that attached itself to me, I never quite worked out whether that was accidental or whether part of me was creating that, or a combination. Or whether it was the fact that the media was changing so fast. I remember the day it was announced that I was doing the job, I was presenting a radio show at the time and I got outed on the radio show because one of the papers had written it before we'd announced it. So I was presenting my own radio show and I think it was Julie Kirkbride who said, 'What about this story in the morning newspapers?' I couldn't deny it. Then I remember the next morning in the *Daily Telegraph*, Robert Schrimsley, now at the *FT*, had this piece with a big picture of me which just said 'Is this the man to put Labour in power?' something like that 'Is this the man to turn Blair into a prime minister?' something like that. I became the story, I kind of was the story straight away.

If you wish to be more central to the published story, or even the story itself, own up and search for an A position.

## Authenticity

Are you sure you don't want to be the A? If you do, you will be found out fast. Are you actually in it for yourself? Just playing politics? As soon as people perceive you're cannily in it for yourself, your ability to make things happen diminishes – people will not collaborate with you, other than with deep suspicion and, quite possibly, a desire to help you fail. As a supportive C there cannot be a sliver of inauthenticity about the absence of your desire to upstage the A. We send signals all the time that others pick up on. If you are a C who says, 'You know, actually I don't want to be an A, I am really happy leading from behind, I'm just the support act,' while everything in your behaviour signals to people that this is not true, you will be quickly unmasked.

Maybe you are a C on the way to reaching your preferred role as an A? Surely wanting to be an A discounts you from being a C, so better to keep that ambition to yourself? How can the A trust you if your eyes are trained on their office view, and your ambition so naked? Psychologist Robert Bor describes the conundrum that faces the A when the C is inauthentic:

> So for now they're your friend, but one day, you know, they will do something that will jeopardise your position as the overall leader. So there is a fundamental issue of trust. If that is the case you will do all you can to support, cement and augment your own No. 1 position by not talking about the other people's contributions. You make yourself even more important so that if your No. 2 acts against you in some kind of way, that level of insurrection can be seen in the negative light that you would like it to be perceived in. Better that than people get to know who the No. 2 is, and how good he is.

Actually, being a C with this agenda is a legitimate place to be as long as you and your A share it. If the A has agreed that you are destined for greatness and takes an active role in your journey from C to A, they will get fine, trustworthy advice until your own A time comes. If you harbour your ambition in secret, beware. Your A will be the first to realise what's lurking in your mind and, even if you have bamboozled them, advisers they can trust will alert them. I have worked for an A whose favourite sport was arm-to-arm combat with those who, secretly and venally, coveted his crown. If they had told him, it would have ruined his playtime, though it might have increased their chances of succeeding him.

One final check on your authentic dreams: do you really want the A's life? Check once more. Sit and observe how many people are trying to get a piece of the A, how many of their questions the A has to answer every day. Record the number of decisions the No. 1 makes in a day and ask yourself how many you would have liked to have made and at what speed. Of course, we can all see ourselves doing a better job of parts of the A's job. But can we do as good a job at *all* of it? Can we cope with the volume, the intensity, the sheer pace of it? Bosses are often less busy than we are, so we think we are the ones who are good at dealing with the long hours and volume of work. We can kid ourselves that we are making all the decisions when, in truth, we are dealing merely with the implications and the fall-out from the A's decisions. Go through their diary and ask yourself how many of their meetings you'd like to have been in, knowing in each one that you would have been at the head of the table. The A is always 'Always On' – on show, on duty, and on their very best behaviour. Off days are off-piste, verboten. Even holidays, if they get any, are on days.

With these pre-checks completed, you are now free to attend to the 'Living with your Leader' appraisal. Again, this form is a prompt to your own script, which should be in your own language. Give the A plenty of time to gather their thoughts, sending them your questions well in advance of your get-together. They may wish to ask their partner at home for their view. This is to be applauded, if you are known by that partner.

Dear A

Thank you for the appraisal form and for Richelieu's opening remarks. I thought I might reciprocate with a snippet from your own pin-up Prince:

> When you see that the minister thinks more about himself than about you [*as if!*] … such a man as this will never be a good minister, and you'll never be able to trust him … On the other hand, the prince should be mindful of the minister so as to keep him acting well, honouring him, making him rich, putting him in his debt, giving him a share of honours and responsibilities; so that the minister recognises that he cannot exist without his prince.

Don't worry about the riches and honours. I am just delighted that you have encouraged us to think about our relationship. I have valued the chance to answer your own searching questions and have attached my own for you to consider. In particular, I would love to know how I can make your life easier, your performance (even) better and how I most hinder and help you. You should feel free to give me your undiluted responses knowing that I will neither call home and cry, nor call out for a new job. I simply intend to reapply myself to whatever new directions we agree with even greater enthusiasm and urgency.

**Opening questions**
Many of my warm-up questions mirror those that you asked me: How would you define our relationship in human terms? If you were the casting director charged with finding your own successor, what qualities would top the list? How do these qualities complement my own?
When historians write about our partnership, how will they describe

the differences in our characters and qualities? What are the distinct flavours we represent? Which of my fellow Cs do you most admire and why? I know you need more than one. What would it take for me to become your C Major and, once there, to avoid the change from Major to Minor?

Which of the C archetypes most accurately represent my contribution to date: Lodestone, Educator, Anchor or Deliverer? Or a special blend of two or more of these? Of these C archetypes, which role would you like me to play more often, and which less? How could I liberate you more? What, if anything, would you like me to do to enlighten you further? Do you feel the benefit of my truth-telling? What truths do you wish to impart to me? What more might I deliver in order that you can be seen to be (even) more decisive?

Overriding all these questions, I would like to know: How useful am I to you? Please illuminate. How well am I protecting and nurturing the organisation's greatest asset?

## Cohabitation

### Feelings

How do I make you feel when I am at my best and at my worst?

When did you most recently feel that I had overstepped the mark? Describe what that felt like exactly as you described it to your partner when you got home. I'm not sure *'irritating sonofabitch'* is allowed in Scrabble, but feel free to use it here.

Do I deflate your tyres or put air into them? Have I helped you find your inner Compton (or inner Cantona, if you prefer)? Do you feel that I listen to what you are telling me? Do you ever feel that I deflect the limelight from you? Or take the credit for your achievements?

Do you feel that I respect the space you need? Would you prefer to travel together to converse, or apart so you can have more 'off time'?

When was the last time you found my request for clarification or firmer direction unnecessary and just wished I'd sort it out without you?

What is it that you squeak to your PA about when I am the subject of your squeaking? What would I have to do to remain unsqueaked about?

### Giving counsel

When I give counsel, is it generally well timed? Please tell me when I missed the moment, chose the wrong moment and when the timing felt just right.

Can you recall the last time I gave you bad news? How might you prefer me to serve it to you in the future? Have I always given you bad news with a plan? Am I delivering candour in a way that doesn't leave you feeling affronted? Is the truth I tell unimpassioned? Have I helped you challenge your beliefs or, as you have become more powerful, do I only serve to reinforce your opinions?

## Conflict resolution

How well have I pre-empted and minimised conflict? Have I been willing to test your ideas? Have I listened to others in your C circle?

For those times where conflict avoidance was neither desirable nor possible, I have plundered your own questions on conflict resolution. Comparing our answers to the same questions will make for a good discussion.

How well have we acknowledged that we have problems and disagreements? Are you happy with the frequency in which we raise disagreements? What different arrangements might we put in place to enable us to disagree with each other more easily? When in the last six months have we aired a disagreement and dealt with it maturely and effectively? Taking a look at Gottman's 'four horsemen of the Apocalypse':

a) How well do I take your criticism?
b) Am I defensive?
c) Do I ever treat you with contempt?
d) Do I ever stop listening?

Are there any conflicts that you feel I have tried to sweep under the carpet that you would now like us to engage in and resolve?

## Celebration

Have I congratulated you on a job well done in the last six months? If the answer is 'no' and you have been waiting for some recognition, now is the time to end the wait. Just remind me what it was that deserved my praise. If I disagree, I will do you the kindness of telling you why it merely met my expectation.

Do I say thank you?

Thank you.

# Changing

Once the A has had time to absorb your appraisal of them from the previous chapter, you must reflect on their suggestions for C change. They should value your candour and be ready to embrace your guidance on contributing to the leadership. There may be other changes to consider. Is it time for the A to call time on their current A role? Will that mean another A assignment elsewhere or a C change? Is it time for the C to try a different C role, to learn under a new A, or to become an A themselves? Personal growth for both A and C demands a willingness to change, to park the familiar, to cede comfort and to endure some pain.

A and C can make each other aware of, and help each other deal with, this need for change. Put a ten-year egg timer on your A's desk on arrival. Even if they are still riding high as the sand completes its descent, challenge them to deepen their contribution, by trying a different leadership position. Encourage them to make an active choice, as we all should regardless of where the leadership and its shared activity takes place within the organisation. Introduce the

A to the joys of C leadership and put forward the idea of bi-leadership.

What the A does, of course, will be for the A to decide. You have your own decisions to make: what is it I still wish to learn and which A can best unlock that learning in me? It may not be a natural conclusion for someone thrusting to get to the top, but there is no hurry to end your apprenticeship. The more time you have to learn from great As the better a C (and eventual A) you will become. Which C roles have I mastered, which remain left to master? Is there more joy to be had using my C qualities in a different leadership context?

It is natural to aspire to be the A. One assumes that the next one up, the next level up, the job just gets bigger and better. You can be any number you like in the organisation, number one, two, five or six, and still get promoted beyond your area of greatest competence or passion. It is a mistake to think, 'Well, I've done a great job. It must be time to step up, manage more people.' You may be a mediocre manager but a brilliant doer. This will be brought sharply into focus at the very top: 'I used to love being a team player, having a laugh. Now I'm lonely as hell.'

Can you see yourself in an A role, if only to help you become a more complete leader? Now is the time to dream of revolution.

The *Consiglieri* revolution is less violent and bloody than that of the critic Moon in *The Real Inspector Hound*. I propose that we turn the spotlight periodically away from A leaders and reflect instead on what makes their concealed C leaders magnificent. Leadership needs a circle of diverse Cs as much as it needs a lionised A. We need to celebrate the dynamic collaboration between A and C (and C and C). Throwing occasional light on C leaders is intended not to bring them out of

the shadows from which they lead, but to make their contribution more visible and their impact more valued. In leadership, if not in the playground, one can argue whether first is
the worst and second is the best. What is unarguable, in my
view, is that to be a complete leader one needs to have a long
stint leading from the shadows.

# FURTHER READING

David Aberbach, *Charisma in Politics, Religion and the Media*, Basingstoke: Macmillan, 1996.

Aravind Adiga, *Last Man in Tower*, London: Atlantic, 2011.

Reuben M. Baron and Louis A. Boudreau, 'An Ecological Perspective on Integrating Personality and Social Psychology', *Journal of Personality and Social Psychology*, vol. 53, issue 6, December 1987, pp. 1222–1228.

Roland Barthes, *On Racine*, New York: Hill and Wang,1964.

Laurent Binet, *HHhH*, London: Vintage, 2013.

Julian Birkinshaw, *Reinventing Management*, Hoboken, NJ: Wiley, 2010.

Jean-Vincent Blanchard, *Eminence: Cardinal Richelieu and the Rise of France*, London: Walker & Company, 2013.

Sue Erikson Bloland, 'In the Shadow of Fame: A Memoir by the Daughter of Erik H. Erikson', *Contemporary Psychoanalysis*, vol. 42, no. 3, 2006, pp. 488–495.

Joseph H. Boyett, *Surviving the Destructive Narcissistic Leader*, Atlanta, GA: Boyett & Associates, 2006.

Alastair Campbell, *The Alastair Campbell Diaries* (4 vols), London: Hutchinson, 2010–12.

Alastair Campbell, *The Irish Diaries (1994–2003)*, Dublin: Lilliput Press, 2013.

J. Carlson, K. Melton and K. Snow, *Family Treatment for the Passive-Aggressive Couple*, in M. McFarlane, *Family*

*Treatment of Personality Disorders*, New York: Haworth Press, 2004.

Miguel De Cervantes, *Don Quixote* (translated by Edith Grossman and Harold Bloom), London: Vintage, 2005.

Cicero, *On Duty*, Cambridge: Cambridge University Press, 1991.

J. Collins and J. Porras, *Built to Last: Successful Habits of Visionary Companies*, New York: HarperBusiness, 1994.

Roald Dahl, *The Twits*, London: Cape, 1980.

Edward De Bono, *Six Thinking Hats*, London: Penguin, 1987.

Peter Drucker, *Managing the Nonprofit Organization*, London: HarperCollins, 1990.

George Du Maurier, *Trilby*, London: J. M. Dent, 1992.

Alex Ferguson, *My Autobiography*, London: Hodder & Stoughton, 2013.

Alain Forget, *How to Get Out of this World Alive*, Raleigh, NC: Lulu Publishing, 2012.

Ronald Fried, *Corner Men: The Great Boxing Trainers*, New York: Four Walls Eight Windows, 1991.

Masha Gessen, *The Man Without a Face: The Unlikely Rise of Vladimir Putin*, London: Granta, 2013.

Gilbert and Sullivan, *The Mikado*, Mineola, NY: Dover Publications, 1999.

A. Goodman and E. Greaves, *Cohabitation, Marriage and Relationship Stability*, London: Institute for Fiscal Studies, 2010.

John D. Gottman, *The Seven Principles for Making Marriage Work*, London: Orion Books, 2003.

Tyler Hamilton and Daniel Coyle, *The Secret Race*, London: Bantam Press, 2012.

Mohammed Hanif, *A Case of Exploding Mangoes*, London: Vintage, 2009.

Fred Hanna, *Therapy With Difficult Clients*, Washington, D.C.: American Psychological Association, 2001.

Robert Hare and Paul Babiak, *Snakes in Suits*, New York: Harper Collins US, 2007.

Horace, *The Satires*, Book I, Satire I, Cambridge: Cambridge University Press, 2012.

David Hume, *The History of England*, London: Frederick Warne, 1884.

Neil S. Jacobson and Andrew Christensen, *Integrative Couple Therapy: Promoting Acceptance and Change*, New York: W. W. Norton & Co., 1996.

Marianne Jennings, *The Seven Signs of Ethical Collapse: How to Spot Moral Meltdowns in Companies… Before It's Too Late*, London: St. Martin's Press, 2006.

Daniel Kahneman, *Thinking, Fast and Slow*, London: Penguin, 2012.

J. F. Kennedy, *Profiles in Courage*, New York: Harper & Bros, 1955.

Richard Layard, *Happiness*, London: Penguin Books, 2005.

Judith Leavitt, *Common Dilemmas in Couple Therapy*, London: Routledge, 2009.

Anthony Levi, *Cardinal Richelieu and the Making of France*, New York: Carroll & Graf, 2002.

Michael Lewis, *Moneyball: The Art of Winning an Unfair Game*, London: Norton, 2004.

Niccolò Machiavelli, *The Prince*, London: Penguin, 2009.

Damian McBride, *Power Trip: A Decade of Policy, Plots and Spin*, London: Biteback Publishing, 2013.

David McCelland, *Power: The Inner Experience*, New York: Irvington Publishers, 1975.

A. A. Milne, *Winnie-the-Pooh: The Complete Collection of Stories and Poems*, London: Egmont, 2001.

Richard Miniter, *Leading from Behind: The Reluctant President and the Advisers who Decide for Him*, New York: St. Martin's Press, 2012.

Molière, *Five Plays*, London: Methuen Drama, 1982, esp. *The School for Wives*, *The Misanthrope* and *Tartuffe*.

Nigel Nicolson, *The I of Leadership*, Chichester: Jossey-Bass, 2013.

Friedrich Nietzsche, *Twilight of the Idols, with the Antichrist and Ecce Homo*, Ware: Wordsworth Editions, 2007.

Alexander Pope, *Essay on Criticism*, Oxford: Clarendon Press, 1910.

Jonathan Powell, *The New Machiavelli: How to Wield Power in the Modern World*, London: Vintage Books, 2011.

Mario Puzo, *The Godfather,* London: Arrow, 2009.

Racine, *The Complete Plays of Jean Racine*, vol. I, translated into English verse by Samuel Solomon, New York: Random House, 1967.

David Roll, *The Hopkins Touch*, Oxford: Oxford University Press, 2013.

Bertrand Russell, childhood diary, quoted in Herrick, Jim, *Against the Faith*, London: Glover & Blair, 1985.

Christopher Seaman, *Inside Conducting*, Rochester, NY: University of Rochester Press, 2013.

Bob Seelert, *Start with the Answer*, Chichester: John Wiley, 2009.

Anthony Seldon, *Blair: The Biography*, London: Free Press, 2004.

Seneca, *Moral and Political Essays*, Cambridge: Cambridge University Press, 1995.

William Shakespeare, *The Norton Shakespeare* 2nd ed., London, New York: Norton, 2008. Plays cited: *King Lear,*

*Hamlet, Macbeth, Julius Caesar, As You Like It, Othello, Richard II.*

Henry Tsai Shih-shan, *The Eunuchs in the Ming Dynasty*, New York: University of New York Press, 1996.

Walter Stahr, *Seward: Lincoln's Indispensable Man*, New York: Simon & Schuster, 2012.

Tom Stoppard, *The Real Inspector Hound and other Entertainments*, London: Faber, 1993.

Leo Tolstoy, *War and Peace*, London: Penguin, 2006.

Evelyn Waugh, *Scoop*, London: Penguin, 2003.

Bradley Wiggins, *In Pursuit Of Glory*, London: Orion, 2008.

# INDEX

# Consiglieri

Phelan, Mike 114, 126, 147, 188, 209
Philip, Prince, HRH the Duke of Edinburgh 152
philosophers 137–9
Pierce, Mary 141
Pinter, Harold 58
Piper, Billie 19
Pitt, Brad 18, 183
Plato 25, 27
Plouffe, David 149
Politburo (Soviet Union) 115
Ponzi schemes 26
*Pop Idol* (television show) 56
Pope, Alexander: 'Essay on Criticism' 27
popularity 40
Porras, Jerry I. 41
Porte, Richie 207–208
Powell, Ian 198, 241
Powell, Jonathan 68–9, 84, 96, 107, 115, 160, 186, 188, 231–2, 233, 238
power 7
  all-powerful leader 5
  apportioning 5
  of a deputy stage manager 59
  and ego-development 79
  of the eldest child in a family 38
  of emotional intelligence 27
  of eunuchs 50
  hard 63
  informal 111
  leaders doing things because they have the power 22
  motivating and corrupting 150
  over policy 112
  power struggles 203
  scheduling 111–12
  selfish 63, 66
  selfless 62–73
  smart 63
  soft 63, 66
  thirst for 40, 220
  vicarious 67–8
Prescott, John 36, 60–61, 147
Presley, Elvis 161, 236

privacy 56, 169
Proactiv 237
problem-solving 22, 61, 107, 108, 131
Procter & Gamble 29, 45, 219
Publicis 33, 67, 78, 100
Puzo, Mario: *The Godfather* 7–8, 81
PwC 198, 241

Queiroz, Carlos 126

Racine, Jean 145–7
  *Andromache* 146, 224–5
Railtrack (UK) 87
*raisonneur* characters 86, 143, 145, 147
Rajeswaran, Sara 208–209
RASCI project management tool
  addition of an O 8
  aim of 8
  assignment of letters 8
  conflation into just A and C 8–9
Rasputin, Grigory 63, 111, 138, 166
Real Madrid Football Club 21, 31, 114, 139
reasoners 143–5
reasoning 22
reciprocity 165, 166
Reed, Matthew 209
relationship coaching 165
Remnick, David 131
Renaissance 21
Republic of Ireland under 21s football team 139
'response tokens' 205
responsibility 6, 8, 30, 33, 42, 44, 49, 56, 59, 75, 93, 94, 100, 102, 156, 167, 178, 194, 204, 211, 239, 242, 251
*Restaurant Inspector, The* (Channel 5 programme) 157
Revels (sweets) 186, 187, 188
'Richard II, King' 171, 172
Richelieu, Cardinal 63, 120, 159, 160, 162, 166, 173, 211, 233, 254
risk-taking 40, 43, 44, 73, 137

Rive, Jean-Pierre 41
roadies 130–32
Roberts, Julia 183
Roberts, Kevin 29–30, 82, 103, 118–19, 194, 209
Roddick, Andy 141
Roll, David: *The Hopkins Touch* 150
Rolling Stones 161, 162
Romanov family 166
Romantics 21
Ronaldo, Cristiano 139
Roosevelt, Eleanor 15, 154
Roosevelt, Franklin D. 77, 150, 151, 154, 159
Roosevelt, James 150
Roosevelt, Theodore 193
Rose Theatre Kingston 97
Rove, Karl 173
Rowling, J. K.: Harry Potter books 17, 181
Royal family 245
Royal Foundation 202, 245, 246
Royal Navy 18
rugby football 41, 116–17, 156, 183–4
Russell, Bertrand 86
ruthlessness 20, 40, 41, 111, 151, 173, 220

Saatchi, Charles 29
Saatchi, Maurice 29
Saatchi & Saatchi 8, 29, 64, 89, 100, 118, 138, 236
  EMEA (Europe, Middle East & Africa) 1, 28–9, 59, 78, 82, 87
  Switzerland 78
Saavedra Fajardo, Diego de 120
Sacchi, Arrigo 62, 193
Salovey, Peter 22
'Sancho Panza' 116, 138, 139, 214
Sant'Albano, Carlo Barel di 31, 38, 81–2, 177, 235, 240
Santander, Grupo 38, 57
Santander UK 75
  Corporate and Commercial Banking Division 128
Sarkozy, Nicolas 70, 158
Sartre, Jean-Paul 35